T0171532

The Great Bahamian Hurricanes of 1926

Wayne Neely

iUniverse, Inc.
New York   Bloomington

The Great Bahamian Hurricanes of 1926
The Story of Three of the Greatest Hurricanes
to Ever Affect the Bahamas

iUniverse books may be ordered through booksellers or by contacting:

iUniverse
1663 Liberty Drive
Bloomington, IN 47403
www.iuniverse.com
1-800-Authors (1-800-288-4677)

ISBN: 978-1-4401-5174-3 (pbk)
ISBN: 978-1-4401-5175-0 (cloth)
ISBN: 978-1-4401-5176-7 (ebook)

Printed in the United States of America

iUniverse rev. date:11/10/09

Front cover photo shows the totally destroyed warehouse and roof of Mr. James Alvin
Haugh in Nassau, after the Great Nassau Hurricane of 1926. This warehouse
was used to store sponges, whiskey and gin for the Rum-Runners to smuggle into
the United States during the Prohibition era. The Nassau Hurricane of 1926
virtually destroyed this warehouse and many similar warehouses of this nature.
(Courtesy of Charles.J. Whelbell Collection-The Department of Archives)

DEDICATION

This book is dedicated first and foremost to all of the victims of the Great Hurricanes of 1926 which affected the Bahamas-By telling of their stories of heroism and tragedy in the midst of such adversity in this book; it is my hope and desire that their stories will forever be told in the annals of Bahamian History and will live on for future generations of Bahamians to read about and to appreciate why these storms were regarded as 'Great' Bahamian storms.

To my Mom and Dad-Francita and Lofton Neely, who over the years have been my rock and my source of inspiration with their unconditional love and support towards me in the good and bad times of my life-I will love both of you until the good Lord takes His last breath away from my body.

To Carole-without you none of my books would have been possible and thanks for taking me on a wild rollercoaster ride called LIFE which was filled with many ups and downs-I will cherish the 'ups' and never forget the 'downs'.

To Joshua and Darlene Taylor thanks for being such great true friends of mine through the good and bad times of my life I will never forget what you did for me and I will always value and cherish each of your friendship.

To Mr. Les Brown who at a conference held here in the Bahamas through his own unique way and method reminded me to 1) "Pass it on" 2)"It is important how you use your down time" and 3)"Someone's opinion of you doesn't have to become a reality and in the time of adversity EXPAND!!" and to Dr. Myles Munroe who always reminds me to 1)"Die Empty!" and 2)"To Pursue My Purpose!" and 3) "Maximize My Potential" I listened to them and this book is the end result... THANK YOU MR. LES BROWN AND DR. MYLES MUNROE FOR YOUR INVALUABLE CONTRIBUTION TO MY LIFE BECAUSE I AM A BETTER PERSON BECAUSE OF YOUR WORDS OF WISDOM!!!

Mahatma Gandhi once said "Be the change you want to see in the world!" and "There are 2 types of people in this world, those that take the credit and those that actually do the work. Take my advice and follow the latter, as there is a lot less competition there."

Dr. Martin Luther King Jr. once said "Faith is taking the first step even when you don't see the whole staircase."

Contents

PREFACE

Charles Dudley Warner, an associate of Mark Twain, said, *"Everybody talks about the weather, but nobody does anything about it."* Everyone, at times, feels as susceptible as Warner did at one point in time in our lives about the weather. The spoiled family picnic, the withered crops, the coastal flooding, or even a heavy tropical downpour, all reminds us how dependent we are on the weather. That is why weather is our most common topic of conversation, a factor in much of our agricultural, industrial, and civic planning, and an ever present concern of everyone. Weather affects our business, government, and our lives whether we like it or not. Warner was wrong to put it mildly, because something is being done. Today, the science of weather which is called meteorology is used to make our lives safer and better. Meteorology is the science that considers and tries to do something about the atmosphere and its elements. It is a physical science that looks at the past and present conditions of the atmosphere to predict or 'forecast' the weather of the future. We can eliminate the adverse effects of weather and even profit from them-with a simple knowledge of knowing what the weather is, what it does, and how to forecast and use it to our advantage. Some types of forecasts are up to 95 percent accurate with the help of modern technology.

Hurricanes are tracked and warnings are given, which results in mass evacuations resulting in many lives being saved in the process. A network of weather stations both on land and at sea enables planes to fly safely and boats to sail unscathed into port. Satellites and Radars constantly monitor and track dangerous weather conditions such as hurricanes, tornadoes and frontal systems allowing us to be well prepared for the approaching weather system. A continued program of research reveals more and more about the weather. Some of the greatest challenges humans' faces are environmental disasters caused by the weather-from droughts and famines to hurricanes and tornadoes. Dealing with these conditions is an inevitable part of life on our planet. Sometimes the weather only affects our lives in a small way, such as in choosing what clothes to wear, or where to go on holiday. At other times, its consequences can be far more serious, as those who have seen the power of a destructive hurricane can testify. Since the weather influences our lives in so many ways, scientists called meteorologists study patterns in the weather and try to forecast, or predict, what it is going to be like in the future. As research and technology advance, these predictions have become increasingly more accurate.

The word "Meteorology" comes from the Greek words: μετέωρον, *metéōron*, meaning "high in the sky"; and λόγος, *lógos*, meaning "knowledge." Meteorology is the interdisciplinary scientific study of the atmosphere that focuses on weather processes and forecasting it for the benefit of mankind. Meteorologists do two main jobs. They collect data and process the information about the weather from day to day. Then they use this information to help them forecast future weather patterns and trends. Meteorologists collect information from weather stations scattered all over the world to assist them with forecasting the weather on a daily basis. Weather is the day-to-day condition of the atmosphere in terms of temperature, pressure, precipitation, wind, and moisture at a particular time over a particular place. These are the elements of which the weather is made and occurs because the atmosphere is constantly changing. Where the atmosphere thins to near vacuum, high above the earth's surface, there is no weather. But near the surface of the Earth, where the atmosphere is dense and heavy, you see the ever-changing, dramatic, and often violent weather show with spectacular extreme weather events such as hurricanes. But it takes more than air to make the weather function. If the earth's atmosphere was never heated, mixed, or moved about, there would be no weather or more appropriately, there would be no changes in the weather.

There would be no winds, no changes in air pressure or temperature, no storms, rain, or snow. Because of this constant motion within the Earth's atmosphere and the Earth's rotation around the sun, makes the weather patterns on Earth very unpredictable.

Heat is the catalyst that mixes the atmosphere together to make the weather work on a daily basis. All weather changes are brought about by temperature and pressure changes in different parts of the atmosphere. Different parts of the world receive different amounts of heat from the sun. As a result, they have different weather patterns throughout the year. These ever-changing weather patterns within the Earth's atmosphere over a long period of time is called climate and it is the historical record and description of average daily and seasonal weather events that help describe a region. Statistics are generally drawn over several decades. The word climate is derived from the Greek word 'Klima' meaning inclination, and reflects the importance early scholars attributed to the sun's influence on the Earth. The planet's climate is therefore ultimately determined by the behavior of the weather systems of the various geographic regions around the world. In this region near the Equator, the climate is hot all year round providing the perfect conditions for hurricanes to form. These constantly changing, ever moving bodies of powerful whirlwinds called hurricanes are all natural phenomena that have swept the Earth for eons, bringing destruction and anguish to mankind whenever they encounter man's ever expanding society.

I have had the pleasure and the good fortune to have spent well over 7 years travelling throughout the Bahamas, being introduced and welcomed into the lives and homes of many Bahamians and learning about their experiences with these storms. Many of them are now dead but before they died some of them made me promise them that future Bahamians of all walks of life will get to know about and appreciate these deadly storms and how even at their lowest points in their lives they were able to rise and triumph over great adversity. During this journey, I spoke to a wide array of individuals and came to understand from them that these storms were more that just simply a day of widespread devastation, but a vital and forgotten part of our Bahamian history that was for many years left untold. To tell their stories required me to be open-minded and to simply be a good listener and an amateur historian. So this introduction to hurricanes in this book, in particular, these hurricanes of 1926 will help you better understand them and explain why they were such great storms in the annals of Bahamian history. The major objective of this book is to demystify their causes and to explain in layman's terms not only their origins but also the vast devastation they created on the Bahamian Society in 1926.

I must admit that when I first heard about these great hurricanes of 1926 from my parents and grand parents growing up on the island of Andros, I was a young boy with no appreciation for the scope and character of these storms. Many years ago in 1979, when I was nine, within a few hours I lived through a very powerful hurricane called Hurricane David. It was definitely a frightening and eye opening experience for me, because I had always heard my parents, grandparents and older persons within the community talk about these historic hurricanes but never had I experienced one. It was to become my first experience living through a hurricane and unfortunately it would not be my last. Since then most of my friends living in other parts of the world who fortunately doesn't experience hurricanes, have asked me, 'How did it feel? Were the winds as powerful as they say? Were you afraid? What did you do?' All briefly unanswerable questions, because the experience of a hurricane is so unreal that it is hard to describe: we expect anything to move but not everything around you with such violent force. Ever since my early childhood experiences with hurricanes, I have been fascinated by hurricanes. Where do they come from and what makes them work? How often do hurricanes occur? How do they survive or die out? Will we ever be able to find out precisely when and where they will occur? Am I in any danger of getting hurt or even killed, by a hurricane? How do I prepare for them? Since then I have learned the answers to many of these questions and will seek to provide you with the answers to these simple but thought provoking questions in this book. It made me decide to write this book on hurricanes in the hope of making you the reader less fearful of these scourges of nature.

When I first got the idea to write my first book 'The Great Bahamas Hurricane of 1929' I wrote that book to keep myself occupied during my spare time or to 'kill time' as we Bahamians often say, thinking it would be my first and only book published. As I started to write that book it took on more importance to me as I started to conduct the interviews of persons who had experienced that powerful and devastating hurricane. Many of them are now dead and the only thing I have now is the book and the riveting stories they related to me about that hurricane. I took my book manuscript to my mentor and former College of the Bahamas Geography lecturer Neil Sealey because I had heard that he was out of teaching and now into the book publishing business. I recalled sitting down with him very much excited about this book project and explaining to him what the book was about. To be quite frank, he was not too enthused about it. He asked me why I didn't write a book about the more recent hurricanes like Hurricane Andrew or Floyd, two hurricanes which were also very memorable and devastating here in the Bahamas and to which he said he had a lot of information and pictures which I could freely use. He said that this book would not sell because it was such an old storm and not many persons really know about this storm. Well I told him perhaps I will write about them later (hey I am not a fool, I did take his advice but just not then because I did write about them two years later in a book called *"The Major Hurricanes to Affect The Bahamas"*) but this book was important to me. In fairness to him, he did not grow up in the Bahamas so he didn't have the value of having family members and older persons within the community who related their experiences with this powerful and deadly storm to me. Well many hundreds of copies later of that book being sold locally and internationally were enough to convince him to change his mind. Infact, it was not just him but many of the persons throughout the country who I interviewed about *The Great Bahamas Hurricane of 1929*. They also encouraged me to write not just about this hurricane but also the hurricanes which occurred in 1926. These three storms were just as powerful and some can argue even more devastating as compared to the one in 1929. Infact, they affected more islands so it would mean that I would have a lot more persons to interview and a greater variety of sources to assist me with my book. Well I listened and this book is the end result, so I hope you enjoy reading about these storms as I have enjoyed researching and presenting them to you.

A question that has often been asked of me while doing research on these historic Bahamian hurricanes is; "Why write on historic hurricanes in the Bahamas, when hardly any one knows anything about them?"

My answer to this question is often twofold; first to inform or remind people that hurricanes can and do happen here in the Bahamas, and that many of these storms have and will continue to cause extensive damage and death. Second, to allow the people of the Bahamas to see what damage has been done in the past, and to show how to prepare for these storms in the future. Before I decided to write these series of books dealing with the impact of these historic hurricanes on the Bahamas, there was very little in the mainstream Bahamian historical books dealing with these hurricanes even though they were quite powerful, devastating, record breaking and deadly storms. If there were any mention of them, chances are they would often be summed up in perhaps just one or two sentences. I felt the many victims of these powerful hurricanes deserved more than that, so I sought to document these storms so that future generations of Bahamians can learn about these storms and the great impact that they had on our Bahamian Society in 1926.

With tourism the driving force that sustains the Bahamian Economy today, and more than five million visitors a year from every continent on this Earth descending on a population of approximately over 330,549 (2007 estimate) persons, the welcome mat is always spread out openly year-round to those who flock to Nassau, Grand Bahama and the rest of the Family Islands within this archipelago. That is simply because, all around the world, the Bahamas conjures up images of an island paradise of beautiful scenery, great sunshine and pristine white sandy beaches, but in 1926 these islands became known for country wide devastation. This was due in part to three powerful hurricanes which brought the Bahamas to its' knees and it took many years for this country to recover from them. The year 1926 has long been known in the Bahamas as the year of '*the Great Hurricane of 1926.*' However, there were at least three large Caribbean hurricanes which occurred within this same season to affect the Bahamas and they have been confused together and in most cases they are often considered as one, but were infact, three distinct powerful and unique hurricanes. These hurricanes struck at a peculiar time in Bahamian history. The nation was in the height of the sponging industry and tourism the number one industry today was still at its infancy. The average Bahamian family lived on less than $300 a year. These hurricanes crushed the economy because they devastated the sponge beds, sponging schooners and destroyed the large sponge warehouses used to store the sponges. Inaddition, these hurricanes practically wiped out the majority of the houses on most of the Family Islands. As a result, these hurricanes exacerbated the country's hardships, especially for those low on the economic totem pole.

FOREWORD

When scientists examine the hurricanes of the past, the Great Miami Hurricane of 1926 stands out. The damage and suffering that the same storm would inflict on South Florida if it happened again would exceed any other historical storm by a large margin. It was a massive storm that did tremendous damage in Miami and Ft. Lauderdale, but it was only the middle of three-hurricane pounding suffered by the Bahamas that year. In July, September, and October, the Islands of the Bahamas were lashed from one end to the other by major hurricanes.

Wayne Neely has done a great service in documenting the great historical storms that have had a tremendous impact on the Islands of the Bahamas. Many residents, no doubt, have heard incredible storm stories from their parents and grandparents. Wayne has pieced together those stories, along with the latest research, to document the greatest Bahamian hurricanes and bring them to life.

We all know that the Bahamas has been dramatically affected by hurricanes in the last decade. Floyd, Frances, and Jeanne left their marks, but Wayne Neely reminds us that, not that long ago, hurricanes were more frequent and even more vicious. Wayne's books are vivid reminders that living in the Bahamas means living with hurricanes, and that there is nothing to do but to be prepared for the day that another "Great" Bahamian hurricane comes along.

BRYAN NORCROSS

Bryan Norcross is the President and CEO of America's Emergency Network, a new National Emergency Communications System he founded with former-National Hurricane Center Director, Max Mayfield, previously, Bryan was the nationally-known CBS News hurricane analyst, appearing often on the CBS Evening News with Katie Couric during severe weather events. He is also the author of the book "Hurricane Almanac" published by St. Martin's Press.

INTRODUCTION

From the earliest antiquity, mankind has searched for a way to explain the mysterious and terrifying natural phenomenon we call hurricanes. Hurricanes are the most dramatic, most dangerous, and most feared of all weather phenomena that exists within the restless atmosphere called Earth. Yet these hurricanes are an integral part of the life and dynamics of our planet by inducing exchanges of heat and cold on a vast global scale from the Equator to the Poles, from the upper to lower atmosphere, and by the continual releasing of energy, hurricanes act as safety valves and essential balancers of the Earth's climate. They bring both life-giving rain and destruction, and in one form or another, these storms frequent nearly every section of the globe. The atmosphere has persistently protected all living creatures on Earth by forming a gaseous shield against destructive radiation and waves of solar and cosmic energy. With powerful winds, raging storm surges and torrential rains, more than 80 of these hurricanes rise from the tropical seas each year and rotate in large curved paths across oceans and lands. Towering up to 50,000 feet high and covering several ten thousands of square miles, these hurricanes rotate around its relatively calm central eye like a giant top, bringing death and destruction whenever it encounters segments of man's ever expanding civilization.

The first five chapters of this book will explain what is a hurricane, its origin, history and what makes them work from a meteorological perspective. The remaining chapters will go in-depth into the meteorological aspects of these three storms and their impact on the sponging industry and damages inflicted on an island by island basis here in the Bahamas. Also included are rare and vintage historical photos of these storms and the actual track maps of each particular storm as they made their way through the Bahamas. As scientists work to unravel the mysteries of global climate change, it is becoming increasingly important to establish a good base of historical data for comparison with contemporary climate conditions. That is why documenting of these storms in 1926 are so vital to this cause. During this time, details of newsworthy weather events of this magnitude in the Bahamas were routinely well documented in Bahamian and foreign newspapers, Family Island Commissioner's Reports, ship reports, House of Assembly Reports and through other means as well. If they were severe storms, they would often be given front page or prominent coverage by the editors of the two major local newspapers, *The Nassau Guardian* and *The Tribune* at that time. During the late 1920's the Bahamas experienced at least four major hurricanes and three of them occurred in the 1926 hurricane season and as you will see later they were quite powerful and very damaging to the islands of the Bahamas.

Communities and nations and especially their ships, have been ravaged by hurricanes from time immemorial. The ancient Mayan Indians of Central America, who named their storm god 'Huracán' wisely, built their cities inland from the hurricane prone coasts out of respect for which they had for hurricanes. In 1502, during his fourth and final voyage to the New World, the fleet of Christopher Columbus weathered a hurricane while docked at the island of Hispaniola in the Caribbean Sea, forcing him to declare in his journal that *'Nothing but the service of God and the extension of the monarchy would induce him to expose himself to such dangers from hurricanes ever again.'* Yet beyond scattered accounts from early colonists and mariners who lived through these storms they described as whirlwinds-and ancient images from the Caribbean and Central American civilizations whose iconic depictions of these storm gods featured anti-clockwise spiral-hurricanes remained almost entirely mysterious and rarely understood up through the eighteenth century. However, by the early nineteenth century some colonists began to gradually realize that hurricanes were seasonal and were likely to strike during summer months when temperatures were at their maximum.

Hurricanes are seasonal threats in the Caribbean and the rest of the North Atlantic region. Most storms develop in the eastern Atlantic Ocean off the African Coast, although some arise within the Caribbean Basin itself. In both cases, these storms originate in the region where the northeasterly and southeasterly trade winds converge, generally between 5 and 20 degrees north of the Equator. They form during the summer and early autumn months, when the ocean water temperature is highest, and are carried eastward by the trade winds and where the dynamics of the upper atmosphere is more conducive to the development of these storms. The wind speed of hurricanes ranges from 74 miles per hour, the minimum speed separating hurricanes from tropical storms, to in excess of 155 miles per hour, the base for today's definition of a Category-Five storm on the Saffir-Simpson Scale. In addition to pounding winds and driving rains, the most dangerous element of hurricanes is often the storm surge, floodwaters that can exceed twenty feet in height. Although loss of lives from tropical cyclones has significantly decreased over the recent years, especially in developed countries, the loss of property has increased substantially. Reductions in fatalities are usually attributed to improvement in the tropical cyclone forecasting and warning systems, while increases in property losses are attributed to accelerated property development in coastal zones.

Hurricanes originate in warm sunny seas in approximately seven general areas north and south of the Equator. These storms start out innocently enough as mere disturbances of gently whirling winds and slightly lowering pressures. Given a spin from the rotating Earth, young hurricanes travel leisurely at first, somewhat parallel to the Equator. Then, fed by immense amounts of energy from warm moist air and nurtured by certain conditions of wind, temperature and pressure within the Earth's atmosphere, these storms deepen in intensity and develop into full-fledged hurricanes which sweep towards the North and South Poles in great curves before losing their energy in colder regions of the Earth and dying out. Hurricanes in the North Atlantic occur mainly between June through November and although meteorologists have the basic knowledge and understanding of where and when hurricanes can occur, they are unable to predict the exact location of a hurricane before it develops. Hence, a hurricane's path can be forecast only after it is formed. These storms have killed thousands of people, flattened buildings, destroyed towns, flooded vast regions of land, sunk armadas, and even changed the course of history. But they have also brought much needed rainfall to parched regions of the Earth and may prove to be an essential balancing factor of the earth's meteorological system. These storms act as safety valves by transferring heat and energy between the Equator and the cooler temperate regions toward the poles, and even bringing torrents of fresh water to replenish crops and ground water. With weather instruments and equipment rapidly becoming more precise and advanced, meteorologists are exploring every dimension of these mighty storms, testing their vast reserves of energy and probing the complex mysteries of how they are created, develop, and dissipate. As yet, man cannot control their powerful forces or changes in their direction-and he may not wish to, for far more harm than good may come from tampering with such vast, complex and dynamic storms.

Hurricanes have the ability to profoundly affect the planet's entire dynamic and complex climatic and weather patterns. Episodes of violent weather events such as hurricanes remind us that much of the natural world is still outside human control. Meteorologists call the global climate a non-linear system, which is just another fancy way of saying that gradual changes are not all gradual. Some of them can, and have in the past, come suddenly, in huge and sudden movements with severe weather events such as hurricanes. Meteorologists say that the world's weather is best understood as a kind of heat engine for redistributing heat from the Equator to the poles. Much more solar energy is absorbed by the Earth between the Tropic of Cancer and the Tropic of Capricorn because the sun is directly overhead everyday all year long. By contrast, the sun's rays strike only glancing blows at the North and South Poles. Each receives the sunlight for only half of the year, during which time the other is completely in darkness. In the simplistic term, this is perhaps the main reason why the tropics are constantly hot and the poles are constantly cold. Hurricanes play one of the most important roles in this process of redistributing this heat from the Equator to the poles. In addition, this redistribution of heat from the Equator to the poles drives the wind and ocean currents-like the Jet Stream and the Gulf Stream. These driving forces of nature have allowed much of the same weather patterns to exist here on Earth since the beginning of time and disrupting them will perhaps wreak havoc to life here on Earth.

Less than 60 miles just off Florida's southeast coast is situated the islands of the Commonwealth of the Bahamas, comprising of over 700 islands and cays scattered over 100,000 square miles of breathtaking crystal clear turquoise and cobalt seas. Most of the 23 inhabited islands are sparsely populated. New Providence, on which the capital Nassau is located, is home to nearly two-thirds of the nation's population of about 330,549 persons. Over 80% of the population is of African descent. Though frequently associated with the Caribbean, the Bahamas is separate, situated north of the Caribbean Sea in the Atlantic Ocean and more closely aligned with its neighbour, the United States. The Bahamas has easy recognizable appeal to visitors, ranking among the world's greatest holiday destinations. That is the Bahamas of today, but this book will explore the Bahamas of yesterday, when the Bahamas was not a major tourist destination except for a few occasional winter guests.

Every once in a long while, the Bahamas is hit by what we meteorologists call a 'Great' hurricane that leaves an embedded set of footprints in the sands of Bahamian history for generations to follow. The 1926 Hurricane season was quite distinct and unique in the sense that three of these 'Great' hurricanes made their presence felt here on this island nation of the Bahamas in a significant way. This book will showcase these three powerful storms which caused widespread devastation on all of the islands here on the Bahamas and its then number one industry of sponging. Even to this day, these storms remain three of the most deadly and powerful storms to ever hit the Bahamas. These storms in 1926 killed more people than all of the storms that struck the Bahamas from 1927 to 2008 combined. These storms struck suddenly with little or no warnings especially on the Family Islands where communications were limited in scope. By the time these storms were over, hundreds of persons were dead and thousands more were left homeless. Many of them wandered the streets for hours in search of loved ones who were missing and those on the Family Islands wandered aimlessly throughout the settlements standing in awe of the significant damage and destruction brought on by these three storms. Throughout the Bahamas, there was widespread devastation because these hurricanes crippled the economy of the Bahamas and almost brought it to a virtual standstill. These hurricanes struck before satellites tracked storms or forecasters gave them official names, but from Grand Bahama in the north to Inagua in the south, they experienced the full fury of these hurricanes as no island was left untouched. Weather and climate extremes such as devastating hurricanes can significantly impact the economics of the Bahamas. Interdisciplinary in scope, this book will explore the meteorological, physical, cultural, economic, psychological, and statistical aspects of these three hurricanes and how they affected life here in the Bahamas. Inaddition, it will present a no holds barred look at hurricanes in general and then at these great hurricanes which occurred in 1926.

In 1921 a newspaper ad inviting tourists and investors to the Bahamas read: "Great investment opportunity, great shipping and sheltered port of the Bahamas...practically no dangers from summer storms and a great escape from the frigid Winter of North America." If this claim wasn't reasonable, it was at least understandable. The last major hurricane to hit the Bahamas was in 1899, and the last catastrophic storm occurred in 1866 where well over 387 persons died, "when the population of the Bahamas could be counted on one, maybe two hands." Today the population stands at a staggering 330,549 persons. However, in 1921, the population of the Bahamas had swelled to nearly 53,735 and by 1931 it was 59,828. This population explosion continued throughout the 1920's and into the 1930's. Infact, in 1926 the population of New Providence alone stood at well over 13,000 persons. On July 24, 1926, the National Weather Bureau in the United States issued storm warnings indicating that a large tropical storm was building in the Caribbean. For the majority of the Bahamian population, these warnings fell on deaf and uncomprehending ears. Most Nassau residents seemed to have received the warnings from the United States National Weather Bureau but very few had paid any attention to any of them. However, because of the lack of communications with some of the Family Islands, many residents on these islands and those at sea simply never got the message that a powerful storm was churning in the Atlantic and heading directly for the Bahamas.

In July 1926, a small but powerful hurricane known as *The Nassau Hurricane of 1926* produced torrential rainfall, massive flooding, many causalities and widespread wind damage. Then the "Big Blow" or *The Great Miami Hurricane* was the second powerful hurricane to hit the Bahamas that season. A longtime resident of Sans Souci in Nassau, Mrs. Macushla Hazelwood, schooled in hurricanes potential danger considered July's storm a good practice for inexperienced Bahamians. *"Before 1926, we have had a beautiful time with hurricanes apparently made to order for us, because we never had any major storms in the early 1900's prior to these storms in 1926, so no one really knew what to expect from a powerful storm of this magnitude, infact, no one knew what to expect when they eye of the hurricane passed over the Bahamas because many persons would go outside during this time thinking the storm was over"* she said, *"blowing with just enough energy to put the fear of the good Lord into the people, and very possibly make them see the light of what these hurricanes are capable of doing to our Bahamas."* Instead, the hurricane which many considered a minimal storm engendered complacency among residents.

On July 25, Nassauvians reluctantly heeded the Weather Bureau's hurricane warnings. The wireless telegram from Washington read: *"A hurricane of increasing intensity was heading towards Haiti and was following the usual track of storms originating in that location and was very unlikely that the Bahamas would be affected."* However, some people still barricaded and battened up their houses and made preparations for this underestimated but impending storm just in case it changed its course. However, by Sunday afternoon just before the hurricane struck, there were a series of additional Weather Bureau telegrams advising these residents that the storm will not only hit the Bahamas dead-on but will perhaps travel straight up the island chain affecting every single island in the archipelago. However, things were quite different on the Family Islands and they had to fend for themselves because many of them never got these messages because of the lack of communications with the capital of Nassau. The city of Nassau did not fare so well nor did any other island in the chain of islands. The storm crashed into Nassau at about 2:00am on July 26 and after the hurricane, Nassau became a hurricane ravaged 'war-zone.' The Governor of these islands in 1926, Sir Harry Cordeaux would later be compelled to write in his report:

"Nassau was isolated in a sea of raving white water, toppled trees, utility poles and hurricane ravaged houses throughout the island."

Finally, the first storm ceased and Bahamians who had boarded up their windows and doors unboarded them and stepped outside to assess the damage. Misinterpreting the calm, they didn't realize they were stepping into the eye of the storm. Some casualties succumbed after the lull. During the hurricane's second half, winds reached a terrifying 135 miles per hour, and rain drowned many persons who didn't reach shelter in time. Structural damages were astonishing, as utility poles were hurtled through the air, fields were destroyed and roofs were completely torn from buildings. Electricity, telephone and running water were cut off to the select few residents who were lucky enough to have those amenities. Even the beach seemed to shift; Long Wharf was covered in sand, boulders and water, as were the lobbies of prestigious oceanfront hotels of the Fort Montague, and British Colonial. At the time, this hurricane was considered the country's greatest natural disaster since *The Great Hurricane of 1866*. Today these three Category 4 storms ranks among the top ten most powerful and deadliest storms to ever hit the Bahamas. This book tells the story of three of the worst natural catastrophes in the history of the Bahamas and the people who had to endure them.

CHAPTER ONE

The History behind the word 'Hurricane' and other Tropical Cyclone Names

A Hurricane is a tropical cyclone with winds that exceed 64 knots (74mph) and blow anti-clockwise about the center in the Northern Hemisphere. A tropical cyclone is a powerful storm system characterized by a low pressure center and numerous severe thunderstorms that produce strong winds and flooding rainfall. A tropical cyclone feeds on the heat released (latent heat) when moist air rises and the water vapour it contains condenses. They are fueled by a different heat mechanism than other cyclonic windstorms such as nor'easters, European windstorms, and polar lows, leading to their classification as "warm core" storm systems. The term 'tropical' simply refers to both the geographic origin of these systems, which forms almost exclusively in tropical regions of the Earth, and their formation in Maritime Tropical air masses. The term "cyclone" refers to a family of such storms' cyclonic nature, with anti-clockwise rotation in the Northern Hemisphere and clockwise rotation in the Southern Hemisphere. Depending on their location and strength, tropical cyclones are referred to by other names, such as hurricanes, typhoons, tropical storms, cyclonic storms, tropical depressions and simply cyclones which all have low atmospheric pressure at their center. A hurricane consists of a mass of organized thunderstorms that spiral in towards the extreme low pressure of the storm's eye or center. The most intense thunderstorms, the heaviest rainfall, and the highest winds occur outside the eye, in the region known as the Eyewall. In the eye itself, the air is warm, winds are light, and skies are generally clear and rain free but can also be cloudy to overcast.

The actual origin of the word 'hurricane' and other tropical cyclone names were based on many cultures, races and people and were actually, based on the myths of these many races of people. In modern cultures, 'myth' has come to mean a story or an idea that is not true. The word 'myth' comes directly from the Greek word 'mythos'(μύθος), whose many meanings include, 'word', 'saying' 'story' and 'fiction.' Today, it is often used any and everywhere and people speak of myths about how to catch or cure the common cold. But the age-old myths about hurricanes in this book were an important part of these people's religion, cultures, and everyday lives. Often they were both deeply spiritual and culturally entertaining and significant. For many of these ancient races, their mythology was their history and there was often little, if any distinction between the two. Some myths were actually based on historical events, such as, devastating hurricanes or even wars but myths often offer us a treasure trove of dramatic tales. The active beings in myths are generally gods and goddesses, heroes and heroines, or animals. Most myths are set in a timeless past before recorded and critical history begins. A myth is a sacred narrative in the sense that it holds religious or spiritual significance for those who tell it, and it contributes to and expresses systems of thought and values. It is a traditional story, typically involving supernatural beings or forces or creatures, which embodies and provides an explanation, aetiology (*origin myths*), or justification for something such as the early history of a society, a religious belief or ritual, or a natural phenomenon.

The United Nation's sub-body, the World Meteorological Organization estimates that in an average year, about 80 of these tropical cyclones kills up to 15,000 people worldwide and cause an estimate of several billion dollars worth of property damage alone. Meteorologists have estimated that between 1600 and 2008, hurricanes have caused well over 100,000 deaths in this region alone and over 8 million deaths worldwide. Hurricanes, Typhoons and Cyclones are all the same kind of violent storms originating over warm tropical ocean waters and are called by different names all over the world. This same type of storm is given different names in various regions of the world. In Australia they are called Cyclones or by the Australian colloquial term of 'Willy-Willies' from an old Aboriginal word (derived from whirlwind) and in the Bay of Bengal and the Indian Ocean, they are simply called Cyclones (an English name based on a Greek word meaning "coil" as in "coil of a snake" because the winds that spiral within them resembles the coil of a snake) and are not named even to this day.

They are called Hurricanes (derived from a Carib or Arawak Indian word) in the Gulf of Mexico, Central and North America, the Caribbean and Eastern North Pacific Oceans (east of the International Dateline). A Hurricane is the name given to these intense storms of tropical origin, with sustained winds exceeding 64 knots (74 miles per hour). From the Timor Sea to as far as northwestern Australia they are referred to as 'Willy-Willies.' In the Indian Ocean all the way to Mauritius and along the Arabian Coasts they are known as 'Asifa-t.' In Mexico and Central America hurricanes are also known as El Cordonazo and in Haiti, they are known as Tainos. While they are called Typhoons[originating from the Chinese word 'Ty-Fung' (going back to as far as the Song (960-1278) and Yuan (1260-1341) dynasties) translated to mean 'Big or Great Wind'...] in the Western North Pacific and in the Philippines and the South China Sea (west of the International Dateline) they are known as 'Baguios' or 'Chubasco'(or simply a Typhoon) and in Japan they are also known as 'Repus,' or the more revered name of a Typhoon but whatever name they are known by in different regions of the world, they refer to the same weather phenomena a 'Tropical Cyclone.' They are all the same severe tropical storms that share the same fundamental characteristics aside from the fact that they rotate clockwise in the southern hemisphere and counterclockwise in the northern hemisphere. However, by World Meteorological Organization International Agreement, the term 'Tropical Cyclone' is the general term given to all hurricane-type storms that originate over tropical waters. The term cyclone, used by meteorologists, refers to an area of low pressure in which winds move counterclockwise in the northern hemisphere around the low pressure center and are usually associated with bad weather, heavy rainfall and strong wind speeds. Whereas, a tropical cyclone was the name first given to these intense circular storms by Englishman Captain Henry Piddington (1797-1848) who was keenly interested in storms affecting India and spent many years collecting information on ships caught in severe storms in the Indian Ocean. He would later become the President of the Marine Courts of Inquiry in Calcutta, India and used the term tropical cyclone to refer to a tropical storm which blew the freighter *'Charles Heddles'* in circles for nearly a week in Mauritius in February of 1845. In his book *'Sailor's Hornbook for the Laws of Storms in All Parts of the World,'* published in 1855, he called these storms cyclones, from the Greek word for coil of a snake.

The word cyclone is from the Greek word 'κύκλος', meaning 'circle' or Kyklos meaning 'coils of the snake', describing the rotating movement of the storm. An Egyptian word 'Cykline' meaning to 'to spin' has also been cited as a possible origin. In Greek mythology, Typhoeus or Typhōn was the son of Tartarus and Gaia. He was a monster with many heads, a man's body, and a coiled snake's tail. The king of the gods and god of the sky and weather, Zeus, fought a great battle with Typhoeus and finally buried him under Mount Etna. According to legend, he was the source of the powerful storm winds which caused widespread devastation, loss of many lives and numerous shipwrecks. The Greek word 'typhōn' meaning 'whirlwind' comes from this legend, another possible source for the origin of the English word 'Typhoon.' The term is most often used for cyclones occurring in the Western Pacific Ocean and Indian Ocean. Inaddition, the word is an alteration of the Arabic word, tūfān, meaning hurricane, and the Greek word, typhōn, meaning violent storm and an Egyptian word 'Cykline' meaning to 'to spin.'

The history of the word typhoon presents a perfect example of the long journey that many words made in coming to the English Language vocabulary. It travelled from Greece to Arabia to India, and also arose independently in China, before assuming its current form in our language. The Greek word typhōn, used both as the name of the father of the winds and a common noun meaning "whirlwind, typhoon," was borrowed into Arabic during the Middle Ages, when Arabic learning both preserved and expanded the classical heritage and passed it on to Europe and other parts of the world. In the Arabic version of the Greek word, it was passed into languages spoken in India, where Arabic-speaking Muslim invaders had settled in the eleventh century. Thus the descendant of the Arabic word, passing into English through an Indian language and appearing in English in forms such as touffon and tūfān, originally referred specifically to a severe storm in India.

The modern form of typhoon was also influenced by a borrowing from the Cantonese variety of Chinese, namely the word 'Ty-Fung', and respelled to make it look more like Greek. 'Ty-Fung', meaning literally "great wind," was coincidentally similar to the Arabic borrowing and is first recorded in English guise as tuffoon in 1699. The Cantonese tai-fung and the Mandarin ta-feng are derived from the word jufeng. It is also believed to have originated from the Chinese word 'jufeng.' 'Ju' can mean either 'a wind coming from four directions' or 'scary'; 'feng' is the generic word for wind. Arguably the first scientific description of a tropical cyclone and the first appearance of the word jufeng in the literature is contained in a Chinese book called Nan Yue Zhi (Book of the Southern Yue Region), written around A.D. 470. In that book, it is stated that "Many Jufeng occur around Xi'n County. Ju is a wind (or storm) that comes in all four directions. Another meaning for Jufeng is that it is a scary wind. It frequently occurs in the sixth and seventh month (of the Chinese lunar calendar; roughly July and August of the Gregorian calendar). Before it comes it is said that chickens and dogs are silent for three days. Major ones may last up to seven days. Minor ones last one or two days. These are called heifeng (meaning black storms/winds) in foreign countries." European travellers to China in the sixteenth century took note of a word sounding like typhoon was used to denote severe coastal windstorms. On the other hand, typhoon was used in European texts and literature around 1500, long before systematic contact with China was established. It is possible that the European use of this word was derived from Typhon, the draconian earth demon of Greek Legend. The various forms of the word from these different countries coalesced and finally became typhoon, a spelling that officially first appeared in 1819 in Percy Bysshe Shelley's play 'Prometheus Unbound.' This play was concerned with the torments of the Greek mythological figure Prometheus and his suffering at the hands of Zeus.

In Yoruba mythology, *Oya*, the female warrior, was the goddess of fire, wind and thunder. When she became angry, she created tornadoes and hurricanes. Inaddition, to ward off violent and tropical downpours, Yoruba priests in southwestern Nigeria held ceremonies around images of the thunder and lightning god Sango to protect them from the powerful winds of hurricanes. In ancient Egyptian legend, Set was regarded as the god of storms. He was associated with natural calamities like hurricanes, thunderstorms, lightning, earthquakes and eclipses. In Iroquois mythology, Ga-oh was the wind giant, whose house was guarded by several animals, each representing a specific type of wind. The Bear was the north wind who brought winter hurricanes, and he was also capable of crushing the world with his storms or destroying it with his cold air. In Babylonian mythology, Marduk, the god of gods, defeated the bad tempered dragon goddess Tiamat with the help of a hurricane. When the other gods learned about Tiamat's plans to destroy them, they turned to Marduk for help. Armed with bows and arrows, strong winds and a powerful hurricane, Marduk captured Tiamat and let the hurricane winds fill her jaws and stomach. Then he shot an arrow into her belly and killed her and then became the lord of all the gods.

The Meso-American and Caribbean Indians worshipped many gods. They had similar religions based on the worship mainly agricultural and natural elements gods, even though the gods' names and the symbols for them were a bit different. People asked their gods for good weather, lack of hurricanes, abundant crops and good health or for welfare. The main Inca god was the creator god *Viracocha*. His assistants were the gods of the Earth and the sea. As farming occupied such an important place in the region, the 'earth mother' or earth goddess was particularly important. The Aztecs, Mayas, Taínos and other Indians adopted many gods from other civilizations. As with the Mayans, Aztecs and Taínos, each god was connected with some aspects of nature or natural forces and in each of these religions, hurricanes or the fear of them and the respect for them played a vital part of their worship. The destructive power of storms like hurricanes inspires both fear and fascination and it is no surprise that humans throughout time have tried to control these storms. Ancient tribes were known to make offerings to the weather gods to appease them. People in ancient times believed that these violent storms were brought on by angry weather gods. In some cultures, the word for hurricane means 'storm god', 'evil spirit', 'devil' or 'god of thunder and lightning.'

The natives of the Caribbean and Central America had a healthy respect for hurricanes and an uncanny understanding of nature. According to their beliefs and myths, the wicked gods Huracán, Hurrikán, Hunraken, and Jurakan annually victimized and savagely ravaged their homes, inflicting them with destructive winds, torrential rainfall and deadly floods. These natives were terrified whenever these gods made an appearance. They would beat drums, blew conch shells, shouted curses, and did everything possible to thwart these gods and drive them away. Sometimes they felt they were successful in frightening them off and at other times their fury could not be withstood and they suffered the consequences. Some of these natives depicted these fearsome deities on primitive carvings as a hideous creature with swirling arms, ready to release his winds and claim its prey.

There are several theories about the origin of the word *Hurricane*; some people believe it originated from the Caribbean Arawak-speaking Indians. It is believed that these Indians named their storm god 'Huracán' and over time it eventually evolved into the English word *Hurricane*. Others believed that it originated from the fierce group of cannibalistic Indians called the Caribs but according to some historians this seems like the least likely source of this word. Native people throughout the Caribbean Basin linked hurricanes to supernatural forces and had a word for these storms which often had similar spellings but they all signified death and destruction by some evil spirit and the early European colonial explorers to the New World picked up the native names. Infact, one early historian noted that the local Caribbean Indians in preparation for these storms often tied themselves to trees to keep from being blown away from the winds of these powerful storms. According to one early seventeenth-century English account, Indians on St. Christopher viewed 'Hurry-Cano' as a "tempestuous spirit." These ancient Indians of this region personalized the hurricane, believing that it was bearing down on them as punishment by the gods for something they had done-or not done. These days, there is more science and less superstition to these powerful storms of nature called hurricanes. Yet we humanize hurricanes with familiar names, and the big ones become folkloric and iconic characters, their rampages woven into the histories of the Caribbean, North and Central American coastal towns and cities.

A next popular theory about the hurricane's origin is that it came from the Mayan Indians of Mexico who had an ancient word for these storms, called 'Hurrikán' (or 'Huracán'). In Mayan mythology, 'Hurrikán' ("one legged") was a wind, storm and fire god and one of the creator deities who participated in all three attempts of creating humanity. 'Hurrikán' was the Mayan god of big wind, and his image was chiseled into the walls of the Mayan temples. He was one of the three most powerful forces in the pantheon of deities, along with Cabrakán (earthquakes) and Chirakán (volcanoes). He also caused the Great Flood after the first humans angered the gods. He supposedly lived in the windy mists above the floodwaters and repeated "earth" until land came up from the seas. In appearance he has one leg, the other being transformed into a serpent, a zoomorphic snout or long-nose, and a smoking object such as a cigar, torch holder or axe head which pierces a mirror on his forehead.

Actually, the first human historical record of hurricanes can be found in the ancient Mayan hieroglyphics. Infact, a powerful and deadly hurricane struck the Northern Yucatán in 1464 wiping out most of the Mayan Indian population of that area. According to Mayan mythology, the Mayan rain and wind god, Chac, sent rain for the crops. But he also sent hurricanes, which destroyed crops and flooded villages. The Mayans hoped that if they made offerings to Chac (including human sacrifices), the rains would continue to fall, but the hurricanes would cease. Every year the Mayans threw a young woman into the sea as a sacrifice to appease the god Hurrikán and a warrior was also sacrificed to lead the girl to Hurrikán's underwater kingdom. Also, one of the sacrifices in honour of this god was to drown children in wells. In some Maya regions, Chac the god of rain and wind was so important that the facades of their buildings were covered with the masks of Chac. Infact, at its peak, it was one of the most densely populated and culturally dynamic societies in the world but still they always built their homes far away from the hurricane prone coast.

By customarily building their major settlements away from the hurricane-prone coastline, the Mayan Indians practiced a method of disaster mitigation that, if rigorously applied today, would reduce the potential for devastation along coastal areas. The only Mayan port city discovered to date is the small to medium sized city of Tulum, on the east coast of the Yucatán Peninsula south of Cancun. Tulum remained occupied when the Spaniards first arrived in the sixteenth century and its citizens were more prepared for the storms than for the Spaniards. As the many visitors to these ruins can see, the ceremonial buildings and grounds of the city were so skillfully constructed that many remain today and withstanding many hurricanes. The Indians of Guatemala called the god of stormy weather 'Hunrakán.' Of course, the Indians did not observe in what period of the year these hurricanes could strike their country; they believed that the devil or the evil spirits sent them whenever they pleased. Their gods were the uncontrollable forces of nature on which their lives were wholly dependent, the sun, the stars, the rains and the storms.

The Taínos were generally considered to be part of the Taíno-Arawak Indians who travelled from the Orinoco-Amazon region of South America to Venezuela and then into the Caribbean Islands of the Dominican Republic, Haiti, the Bahamas, Jamaica, Puerto Rico, and as far west as Cuba. The word 'Taíno' comes directly from Christopher Columbus because they were the indigenous set of people he encountered on his first voyage to the Caribbean and they called themselves 'Taíno' meaning 'good' or 'noble' to differentiate themselves from their fierce enemies-the Carib Indians. This name applied to all the Island Taínos including those in the Lesser Antilles. Locally, the Taínos referred to themselves by the name of their location. For example, those in Puerto Rico referred to themselves as Boricua which means 'people from the island of the valiant noble lords' their island was called Borike'n meaning 'Great land of the valiant noble lord' and those occupying the Bahamas called themselves 'Lucayo' or 'Lucayans' meaning 'small islands.' Another important consequence of their navigation skills and their canoes was the fact that the Taínos had contact with other indigenous groups of the Americas, including the Mayas of Mexico and Guatemala. What is the evidence to suggest that the Taínos had contact with the Mayan culture? There are many similarities between the Mayan god, 'Hurrikán' and Taíno god 'Huracán' also, similarities in their ballgames, and similarities in their social structure and social stratification. Inaddition, the Meso-Indians of Mexico also flattened the heads of their infants in a similar fashion to the Island based Arawaks and their relatives.

The Taíno-Arawaks believed in two supreme gods, one male, and the other female. They also believed that man had a soul and after death he would go to a paradise called *Coyaba* where the natural weather elements such as droughts and hurricanes would be forgotten in an eternity of feasting and dancing. In the Taíno Indians culture, they believed in a female zemí (spirit) named Guabancex who controlled hurricanes among other things but when angered she sent out her herald Guataba to order all the other zemis to lend her their winds and with this great power she made the winds and the waters move and cast houses to the ground and uprooted trees. They also believed that sickness, or misfortunes such as devastating hurricanes were the works of malignant or highly displeased zemis and good fortune was a sign that the zemis were pleased. To keep the zemis pleased, great public festivals were held to propitiate the tribal zemis, or simply in their honour. On these occasions everyone would be well-dressed in elaborate outfits and the cacique would lead a parade beating a wooden drum. Gifts of the finest cassava were offered to the zemis in hopes that the zemis would protect them against the four chief scourges of the Arawaks' existence: fire, sickness, the Caribs and most importantly devastating hurricanes. The language of the Taínos was not a written one, and written works from them are very scarce. Some documentation of their lifestyles may be found in the writings of Spanish priests such as Bartholomew de Las Casas in Puerto Rico and the Dominican Republic during the early 16th century. Some of the Taíno origin words were borrowed by the Spanish and subsequently found its way into the English Language, and are today modern day reminders of this once proud and vigorous race of people. These words include; avocado, potato, buccaneer, cay, manatee, maize, guava, *barbacoa* (barbecue), *cacique* (chief), jamaca (hammock), Tabacú (tobacco), caniba (cannibal), *canoa* (canoe), Iguana (lizard), and *huracán* or *huruká* (hurricane). Interestingly, the islands of Inagua and Mayaguana here in the Bahamas both derived their names from the Arawak word 'Iguana.'

In the Taíno culture, it was said that when the hurricane was upon them, these people would shut themselves up in their leaky huts and shouted and banged drums and blew shell trumpets to keep the evil spirits of the hurricane from killing them or destroying their homes and crops. According to Taíno legend, the goddess Atabei first created the earth, the sky, and all the celestial bodies. The metaphor of the sacred waters was included because the Taínos attributed religious and mythical qualities to water. For example, the godess, Atabei, was associated with water. She was also the goddess of water. Yocahú, the supreme deity, was also associated with water. Both of these deities are called *Bagua*, which is water, the source of life. This image of water as a sacred entity was central to their beliefs. They were at the mercy of water for their farming. Without rain, they would not be able to farm their *conucos*. They prayed to the twin gods of rain and fair weather so that they would be pleased and prayed to these gods to keep the evil hurricane away from their farms and homes. To continue her (Atabei) work, she bore two sons, Yucaju and Guacar. Yucaju created the sun and moon to give light, and then made plants and animals to populate the earth. Seeing the beautiful fruits of Yucaju's work, Guacar became jealous and began to tear up the earth with powerful winds, renaming himself Jurakan, the god of destruction. Yucaju then created Locuo, a being intermediate between a god and a man, to live in peaceful harmony with the world. Locuo, in turn, created the first man and woman, Guaguyona and Yaya. All three continued to suffer from the powerful winds and floods inflicted by the evil Jurakán. It was said that the god Jurakán, was perpetually angry and ruled the power of the hurricane. He became known as the god of strong winds, hence the name today of hurricane. He was feared and revered and when the hurricanes blew, the Taínos thought they had displeased Jurakán.

The origin of the name "Bahamas" is unclear in the history of these islands. Some historians believe it may have been derived from the Spanish word *baja mar*, meaning lands of the *'shallow seas'*; or the Lucayan Indian word for the Island of Grand Bahama, *ba-ha-ma* meaning *'large upper middle land.'* The seafaring Taíno people moved into the uninhabited Southeastern Bahamas from the islands of Hispaniola and Cuba sometime around 1000-800 A.D. These people came to be known as the Lucayans. According to various historians, there were estimated reports of well over 20,000 to 30,000+ Lucayans living in the Bahamas at the time of World famous Spanish Explorer

Christopher Columbus' arrival in 1492. Christopher Columbus's first landfall in the New World was on an island called San Salvador which is generally accepted to be present-day San Salvador (also known Watlings Island) in the Southeastern Bahamas. The Lucayans called this island Guanahaní but Columbus renamed it as San Salvador (Spanish for "Holy Saviour"). However, Columbus's discovery of this island of San Salvador is a very controversial and debatable topic among historians, scientists and lay-people alike and even to this day some of them still suggest that Columbus made his landfall in some other island in the Bahamas, such as, Rum Cay, Samana Cay, Cat Island and some even suggested he landed as far south as Grand Turk, Grand Caicos. However, it still remains a matter of debate and mystery within the archeological and scientific community. Regrettably, that question may never be solved, as Columbus's original log book has been lost for centuries, and the only evidence is in the edited abstract made by Father Bartholomew Las Casas.

In the Bahamas, Columbus made first contact with the Lucayans and exchanged goods with them. The Lucayans-a word that meant 'meal-eaters' in their own language, from their dependence upon cassava flour made from bitter manioc root as their staple starch food. They were sub-Taínos of the Bahamas and believed that all their islands were once part of the mainland of America but had been cut off by the howling winds and waves of the hurricanes. The Lucayans (the Bahamas being known then as the Lucayan Islands) were Arawakan People who lived in the Bahamas at the time of Christopher Columbus landfall on October 12, 1492. Sometime between 1000-800 A.D. the Taínos of Hispaniola pressured by over-population and trading concerns migrated into the southeastern islands of the Bahamas. The Taínos of Cuba moved into the northwestern Bahamas shortly afterwards. They are widely thought to be the first Amerindians encountered by the Spanish. Early historical accounts describe them as a peaceful set of people and they referred to themselves as 'Lucayos,' 'Lukku Kairi' or 'Lukku-Cairi' meaning 'small islands' or 'island people' because they referred to themselves by the name of their location.

Before Columbus arrived to the Bahamas, there were about 20,000 to 30,000+ Lucayans, but because of slavery, diseases such as smallpox and yellow fever (to which they had no immunity), and other hardships brought about by the arrival of the Europeans, by 1517, they were virtually non-existent. Infact, when Spanish Conquistador Ponce de Leon visited these islands in 1513 in search of the magical 'Fountain of Youth,' he found no trace of these Lucayan Indians, with the exception of one elderly Indian woman. These Indians of the Caribbean and Central America lived in one of the most hurricane prone areas of the earth; as a result most of them built their temples, huts, pyramids and houses well away from the hurricane prone coastline because of the great fear and respect which they had for hurricanes. Many early colonists in the Caribbean took solace by displaying a Cord of Saint Francis, a short length of rope with three knots with three turns apiece, in their boats or homes as a protective talisman during the hurricane season. According to tradition, if these residents untied the first knot of the Cord, winds would pick up but only moderately. Winds of 'half a gale' resulted from untying the second knot. If all three knots were untied, winds of hurricane strength were produced.

Similar accounts also emerged from encounters with the Carib Indians. In old historical accounts these Indians were referred to by various names such as, *'Caribs' 'Charaibes' 'Charibees'* and *'Caribbees'* and they were a mysterious set of people who migrated from the Amazon jungles of South America. They were a tribe of warlike and cannibalistic Indians who migrated northwards into the Caribbean in their canoes overcoming and dominating an earlier race of peaceful set of people called the Arawaks. Ironically, the region became known as the Caribbean, named after these fierce Indians. Their practice of eating their enemies so captured the imagination of the Europeans that the Caribbean Sea was also named after these Indians. The English word 'cannibal' is derived from one of the terms, 'Caniba' used by the Arawaks to refer to the Caribs eating the flesh of their enemies. Their raids were made over long distances in large canoes and had as one of their main objectives was to take the Arawak women as their captives, wives and slaves. While on the other hand, the captured Arawak men were tortured and killed and then barbecued and eaten during an elaborate ceremony. The French traveller Charles de Rochefort wrote that when these Caribs Indians heard the thunder clap, they would *"make all the haste they can to their little houses, and sit down on low stools about the fire, covering their faces and resting their heads on their hands and knees, and in that posture they fall a weeping and say...Maboya is very angry with them: and they say the same when there happens a Hurricane."*

The Caribs were terrified of spilling fresh water into the sea because they believed that it aroused the anger of hurricanes. They had no small stone gods but believed in good and powerful bad spirits called 'Maboya' which caused all the misfortunes of their lives. They even wore carved amulets and employed medicine men to drive the evil Maboya away. When a great and powerful storm began to rise out of the sea, the Caribs blew frantically into the air to chase it away and chewed manioc bread and spat it into the wind for the same purpose. When that was no use, they gave way to panic and crouched in their communal houses moaning, with their arms held over their heads. They felt that they were reasonably safe there because they fortified their houses with corner posts dug deep into the ground. They also believed that beyond the Maboya were great spirits, the male sun, and the female moon. They believed that the spirits of the stars controlled the weather. They also believed in a bird named Savacou which was sent out by the angry Maboya to call up the hurricane, and after this task was finished this bird would then be transformed into a star.

Several elderly Carib Indians stated that hurricanes had become more frequent in the recent years following the arrival of the Europeans to the Caribbean, which they viewed as punishment for their interactions with the Europeans. Infact, as early as 1630s, English colonists reported that Carib Indians knew when storms would strike by the number of rings that appeared around the moon: three rings meant the storm would arrive in three days, two rings meant two days and one ring meant the storm would arrive in one day. Of course, the connection between such signs and the onset of hurricanes was indeed a very unreliable way to predict the onset of hurricanes. The Carib Indians while raiding islands in the Caribbean would kill off the Arawak men and took the Arawak women as wives and mothers to their children. Infact, when the Europeans came to the Caribbean, they found that many Carib women spoke the Taíno language because of the large number of female Taíno captives among them. So it is speculated that a word like 'Hurricane' was passed into the Carib speech and this was how these fierce people learned about the terror of these savage storms. Native Indians of the West Indies often engaged in ritual purification and sacrifice and offered songs and dances to help ward off hurricanes.

An Aztec myth tells that when the gods created the world, it was dark and cold. The youngest of the gods sacrificed himself to create a sun. But it was like him, weak, dim and feeble. Only when more powerful gods offered themselves did the sun blaze into life and shine brightly on them. However, there was one disadvantage, and that was that these gods needed constant fuel, human lives and the Aztecs obliged. They offered tens of thousands of human sacrifices a year, just to make sure that the sun rose each morning and to prevent natural disasters such as, devastating hurricanes from destroying their communities and villages. The Aztec god Tezcatlipoca (meaning Lord of the Hurricane) was believed to have special powers over hurricane winds, as did the Palenque god Tahil (Obsidian Mirror) and the Quiché Maya sky god Huracán. The Aztec god Tezcatlipoca was feared for his capricious nature and the Aztecs called him Yaotl (meaning 'Adversary'). Inaddition, Tonatiuh was the Aztec Sun god and the Aztecs saw the sun as a divinity that controlled the weather, including hurricanes and consequently, all human life form. The Aztecs of Mexico, in particular built vast temples to the sun God Tonatiuh, and made bloody sacrifices of both human and animal, to persuade him to shine brightly on them and in particular not send any destructive hurricanes their way and to allow prosperity for their crops. When they built these temples, they were constructed according to the earth's alignment with the sun but most importantly they were always constructed with hurricanes in mind and away from the hurricane prone coastline.

The Aztec people considered Tonatiuh the leader of Tollán, their heaven. He was also known as the fifth sun, because the Aztecs believed that he was the sun that took over when the fourth sun was expelled from the sky. Mesoamerican creation narratives proposed that before the current world age began there were a number of previous creations, the Aztec account of the five suns or world ages revealed that in each of the five creations the earth's inhabitants found a more satisfactory staple food than eaten by their predecessors. In the era of the first sun, which was governed by Black Tezcatlipoca, the world was inhabited by a race of giants who lived on acorns. The second sun, whose presiding god was a serpent god called Quetzatzalcóatl who saw the emergence of a race of primitive humans who lived on the seeds of the mesquite tree. After the third age, which was ruled by Tláloc, in which people lived on plants that grew on water, such as the water lily, people returned to a diet of wild seeds in the fourth age of Chalchiúhtlicue. It was only in the fifth and current age, an age subject to the sun god Tonatiuh that the people of Mesoamerica learned how to plant and harvest maize. According to their cosmology, each sun was a god with its own cosmic era. According to the Aztecs, they were still in Tonatiuh's era and according to the Aztec creation mythology, the god demanded human sacrifice as a tribute and without it he would refuse to move through the sky, hold back on the rainfall for their crops and would send destructive hurricanes their way. It is said that some 20,000 people were sacrificed each year to Tonatiuh and other gods, though this number however, is thought to be highly inflated either by the Aztecs, who wanted to inspire fear in their enemies, or the Spaniards, who wanted to speak ill of the Aztecs. The Aztecs were fascinated by the sun so they worshiped and carefully observed it, and had a solar calendar second only in accuracy to the Mayans.

It was Captain Fernando de Oviedo who gave these storms their modern name when he wrote "*So when the devil wishes to terrify them, he promises them the 'Huracan,' which means tempest.*" The Portuguese word for them is Huracao which is believed to have originated from the original Carib word Huracán. The Native American Indians had a word for these powerful storms, which they called 'Hurucane' meaning 'evil spirit of the wind.' When a hurricane approached the Florida coasts, the medicine men of the North American Indians worked frantic incantations to drive the evil hurricane away. Many other sub-culture Indians had similar words for these powerful storms which they all feared and respected greatly. For example, The Galibi Indians called these hurricanes Yuracan, Giuana Indians called them Yarukka and other similar Indian names were Hyrorokan, aracan, urican, huiranvucan, Yurakon, Yuruk or Yoroko. As hurricanes were becoming more frequent in the Caribbean, many of the colonists and natives of this region had various words and spellings all sounding phonetically similar for these powerful storms. The English called them, 'Haurachana', 'Uracan', 'Herocano' 'Harrycane', and 'Hyrracano.' The Spanish called them

'Huracán'and 'Furicane'and the Portuguese called them, 'Huracao' and 'Furicane.' The French had for a long time adapted the Indian word called 'Ouragan' and the Dutch referred to them as 'Orkan.' These various spellings were used until the word 'hurricane' was finally settled on in the English Language.

Christopher Columbus on his first voyage managed to avoid encountering any hurricanes but it wasn't until his later voyages that he encountered several hurricanes that disrupted his voyages to the New World. In fact, Christopher Columbus himself weathered at least three of these dangerous storms. By 1495, the small town of Isabella, founded by Columbus on Hispaniola, became the first European settlement destroyed by a hurricane. The Spaniards who accompanied Columbus on his four voyages to the New World took back to Europe with them a new concept of what a severe storm could be and, naturally, a new word of Indian origin. It seems that the Indian word was pronounced 'Furacán' or 'Furacánes' during the early years of discovery and colonization of America. Peter Martyr, one of the earliest historians of the New World, said that they were called by the natives 'Furacanes', although the plural is obviously Spanish. The Rev. P. du Tertre, (1667) in his great work of the middle of the seventeenth century, wrote first 'ouragan', and later 'houragan.'

After 1474 some changes in the Spanish language were made. For instance, words beginning with 'h' were pronounced using the 'f' consonant.' The kingdoms of Aragon and Castile were united in 1474, before the discovery of America, and after that time some changes in the Spanish language were made. One of them involved words beginning with the letter 'h.' In Aragon they pronounced such words as 'f'. As Menéndez Pidal said, 'Aragon was the land of the 'f', but the old Castilian lost the sound or pronunciation, so that Spanish Scholar Nebrija (Nebrija wrote a grammar of the Castilian language, and is credited as the first published grammar of any Romance language) wrote, instead of the lost 'f', an aspirated 'h.' Menéndez wrote concerning the pronunciation of the word 'hurricane' and its language used by Fernando Colón, son of Christopher Columbus "Vacillation between 'f' and 'h' is very marked predominance of the 'h.' And so, the 'h' became in Spanish a silent letter, as it still is today." Father Bartholomew Las Casas, referring to one of these storms wrote: "*At this time the four vessels brought by Juan Aguado were destroyed in the port (of Isabella) by a great tempest, called by the Indians in their language 'Furacán.' Now we call them hurricanes, something that almost all of us have experienced at sea or on land...* "Infact, Las Casas, outraged by the brutal treatment of the Indians on Hispaniola, declared that the wrath of the hurricane which struck Hispaniola was the judgment of God on the city and the men who had committed such sins against humanity. All other European languages coined a word for the tropical cyclone, based on the Spanish 'Huracán.' Gonzalo Fernandez de Oviedo (Oviedo y Valdes, 1851, Book VI, Ch. III) is more explicit in his writings concerning the origin of the word 'hurricane.' He says: *"Hurricane, in the language of this island, properly means an excessively severe storm or tempest; because, in fact, it is only a very great wind and a very great and excessive rainfall, both together or either these two things by themselves."* Oviedo further noted that the winds of the *'Huracán'* were so *"fierce that they topple houses and uproot many large trees."*

Even in the English Language the word 'hurricane' evolved through several variations, for example, William Shakespeare mentioned it in his play 'King Lear' where he said *"Blow, winds, and crack your cheeks! Rage! Blow! You catracts and hurricanes, spout till you have drench'd out steeples, drown'd the cocks!"* As stated earlier, Christopher Columbus did not learn on his first voyage, the voyage of discovery, of the existence of such terrible 'tempests' or 'storms.' He had the exceptional good fortune of not being struck by any of them during this voyage. The Indians, while enjoying pleasant weather had no reason for speaking about these storms to strangers who spoke a language which they could not understand. Naturally, Columbus did not say one word about these awful storms in his much celebrated letter *"The letter of Columbus on the Discovery of America."* However, on his second voyage things were quite different. After arriving on November 3, 1493, at an island in the Lesser Antilles which he named Dominica, Columbus sailed northward and later westward, to Isabella Hispaniola, the first city in the New World, at the end of January, 1494. Then in June of that year, 1494, Isabella was struck by a hurricane, the first time that European men had seen such a terrible storm. Surely, for the first time, they heard the Taíno Indians, very much excited; extending their arms upward, and shouting: *"Furacán! Furacán!"* when the storm commenced. We can indeed say that it was that moment in history, when the word *'Hurricane'* suddenly appeared to the Europeans. Columbus was not at that time in Isabella because he was sailing near the Isle of Pines, Cuba. So his companions of the ships *'Marigalante'* and *'Gallega'* were the first white men who heard these words spoken that were applied to a phenomenon of the New World and of Indian origin. Knowledge of 'Furacanes,' both the word and the terrifying storms it described, remained limited to Spanish speakers until 1555, when Richard Eden translated Columbus's ship report and other Spanish accounts of the New World, making it the first time it appeared in the English vocabulary.

In October of 1495, probably in the second half of the month, another hurricane struck Isabella, which was much stronger than the first. It finally gave Columbus, who was there at the time, the opportunity of knowing what a hurricane was, and of hearing the Indians shouting the same word with fear and anxiety on their faces, on account of these terrible storms of the tropics, which they believed were caused by evil spirits. Christopher Columbus later declared that "*nothing but the service of God and the extension of the monarchy*" would induce him to expose himself to such danger from these storms again. *'The Niña'* was the only vessel which was the smallest, oldest and the most fragile at the time but amazingly withstood that hurricane, the two other ships of Columbus, ' *The San Juan'* and ' *The Cordera,'* were in the harbour and were lost or badly damaged by this hurricane. Columbus gave orders to have one repaired and another ship known as *India* constructed out of the wreck of the ones which had been destroyed, making it the first ship built in the Caribbean by Europeans.

In 1502 during his fourth voyage, Columbus warned the Governor of Santo Domingo of an approaching hurricane, but he was ignored; as a result a Spanish treasure fleet set sailed and lost 21 of 30 ships with 500 men. Columbus had a serious disagreement with the bureaucrats appointed by Spain to govern the fledgling colonies in the Caribbean to extract gold, pearl and other precious commodities from the native Indians. Among the more unfriendly of these exploiters was Don Nicolas de Orvando, the Governor of Hispaniola, with whom Columbus had been forbidden to have any contact with by the request of his Spanish sovereigns. But as Columbus approached Santa Domingo, he recognized the early signs of an approaching hurricane, such as ocean swells and a veil of cirrostratus overhead. Concerned for the safety of his men and ships, he sent a message to Governor Orvando begging him to be allowed to seek refuge in Santa Domingo Harbour. Columbus had observed that the Governor was preparing a large fleet of ships to set sail for Spain, carrying large quantities of gold and slaves, and warned him to delay the trip until the hurricane had passed. Refusing both the request and the advice, Orvando read Columbus's note out loud to the crew and residents, who roared with laughter at Columbus's advice. Unfortunately, the laughter was very short-lived and Orvando's ships left port only to their own demise when 21 of the 30 ships were lost in a hurricane between Hispaniola and Puerto Rico.

English explorers and privateers soon contributed their own accounts of encounters with these storms. Famous English explorer Sir John Hawkins wrote his own encounters with these storms. Sir John Hawkins wrote that he left Cartagena in late July 1568 *"Hoping to have escaped the time of their stormes…which they call Furicanos."* Hawkins did not leave soon enough, and he and his ships were bashed by an *"extreme storme"* as he referred to it, lasting several days. English Explorer Sir Francis Drake encountered several major hurricanes while sailing the dangerous seas of the Americas and the Atlantic Ocean and in most cases these encounters changed the course of history. One of his most famous encounters was with a major hurricane while anchored near the ill-fated Roanoke colony in present day North Carolina in June of 1586. There was no greater thorn in the side of the Spanish than Francis Drake. His exploits were legendary, making him a hero to the English but a simple pirate to the Spaniards and for good reasons because he often robbed them of their valuable treasures. To the Spanish, he was known as *El Draque*, "the Dragon"; "Draque" is the Spanish pronunciation of "Drake". As a talented sea captain and navigator, he attacked their fleets and took their ships and treasures. He raided their settlements in America and played a major role in the defeat of the greatest fleet ever assembled, the "Spanish Armada."

No other English seaman brought home more wealth or had a bigger impact on English history than Drake. At the age of 28 he was trapped in a Mexican port by Spanish war ships. He had gone there for repairs after an encounter with one of his first major hurricanes at sea.

Drake escaped but some of the sailors left behind were so badly treated by the Spanish that he swore revenge. He returned to the area in 1572 with two ships and 73 men. Over the next fifteen months he raided Spanish towns and their all important Silver train across the isthmus from Panama. Other English accounts reported ships damaged or lost in storms characterized by extreme wind and rain, some of which were definitely hurricanes. The English (including Drake and Hawkins) had a great respect for hurricanes, to such an extent that, as the hurricane season was understood to be approaching, more and more pirates went home or laid up their ships in some sheltered harbour until the last hurricane had passed and was replaced by the cool air of old man winter.

Probably those that first discovered the period of the year in which hurricanes developed were Spanish priest, officers of the navy or army, or civilians that had lived for a long time in the Caribbean. By the end of the sixteenth century they should have already known the approximate period that these hurricanes occurred. The Roman Catholic Church knew early on that the hurricane season extended at least from August to October because the hierarchy ordered that in all of the churches in the Caribbean to say a special prayer to protect them from these deadly hurricanes. The prayer which had to be said was: '*Ad repellendas tempestates,*' translated to mean '*for the repelling the hurricanes or tempest.*' It was also ordered that the prayer should be said in Puerto Rico during August and September and in Cuba in September and October. This indicates that it was known that hurricanes were more frequent in those islands during the months mentioned. Eventually, West Indian colonists through first hand experience with these storms gradually learned that hurricanes struck the Caribbean within a well-defined season. Initially, those early colonists believed that hurricanes could strike at any time, but by the middle of the seventeenth century most recognized that there was a distinct hurricane season. This was because the hurricanes simply occurred too frequent within a particular time period for them to remain strange and unusual in their eyes. Numerous letters and reports written by colonists specifically discussed the period between July and October as the '*time of hurricanes.*'

CHAPTER TWO

The Naming Of Hurricanes

Atlantic Tropical Cyclone Names

2009	2010	2011	2012	2013	2014
Ana	Alex	Arlene	Alberto	Andrea	Arthur
Bill	Bonnie	Bret	Beryl	Barry	Bertha
Claudette	Colin	Cindy	Chris	Chantal	Cristobal
Danny	Danielle	Don	Debby	Dorian	Dolly
Erika	Earl	Emily	Ernesto	Erin	Edouard
Fred	Fiona	Franklin	Florence	Fernand	Fay
Grace	Gaston	Gert	Gordon	Gabrielle	Gustav
Henri	Hermine	Harvey	Helene	Humberto	Hanna
Ida	Igor	Irene	Isaac	Ingrid	Ike
Joaquin	Julia	Jose	Joyce	Jerry	Josephine
Kate	Karl	Katia	Kirk	Karen	Kyle
Larry	Lisa	Lee	Leslie	Lorenzo	Laura
Mindy	Matthew	Maria	Michael	Melissa	Marco
Nicholas	Nicole	Nate	Nadine	Nestor	Nana
Odette	Otto	Ophelia	Oscar	Olga	Omar
Peter	Paula	Philippe	Patty	Pablo	Paloma
Rose	Richard	Rina	Rafael	Rebekah	Rene
Sam	Shary	Sean	Sandy	Sebastien	Sally
Teresa	Tomas	Tammy	Tony	Tanya	Teddy
Victor	Virginie	Vince	Valerie	Van	Vicky
Wanda	Walter	Whitney	William	Wendy	Wilfred

Courtesy of NOAA

Hurricanes are the only weather disasters that have been given their own iconic names, such as, Hurricane Andrew, Gilbert, Katrina, Camille or Mitch. No two hurricanes are the same but like people; they share similar characteristics but yet still they have their own unique stories to tell. The naming of storms or hurricanes has undergone various stages of development and transformation. Initially, the word 'Hurricane' accompanied by the year of occurrence was used, for example, *'the Great Hurricane of 1780'* which killed over 22,000 persons in Martinique, Barbados and St. Eustatius. Another example was *'the Great Storm of 1703'* whose incredible damage of the British Isles was expertly detailed by Robinson Crusoe's author, Daniel Defoe. The naming scheme was substituted by a numbering system (e.g. Hurricane #1, #2, #3 of 1929 etc…) however; this became too cumbersome and confusing, especially when disseminating information about two or more storms within the same geographical area or location.

For the major hurricanes of this region, they were often named after the particular country or city they devastated. This was especially true for severe hurricanes which made their landing somewhere in the Caribbean. Two notable examples were, *'the Dominican Republic Hurricane of 1930'* which killed over 8,000 persons in the Dominican Republic and *'the Pointe-a-Pitre Hurricane of 1776'* which devastated the country of Guadeloupe and killed over 6,000 persons and devastated it's largest city and economic capital of Pointe-a-Pitre. In some cases they were even named after the holiday on which they occurred, for example, *'the Great Labour Day Hurricane of 1935.'* The *Great Labour Day Hurricane of 1935* was the strongest tropical cyclone during the 1935 North Atlantic hurricane season. This compact and intense hurricane caused extensive damage in the Bahamas and the upper Florida Keys. To this day, the Great Labour Day Hurricane of 1935 is the strongest hurricane to have ever strike the United States in terms of barometric pressure. The Great Labour Day Hurricane was the most intense hurricane known to have struck the United States, and it is one of the strongest recorded landfalls worldwide. It was the only hurricane known to have made landfall in the United States with a minimum central pressure below 900 mbar; only two others have struck the United States with winds of Category 5 strength on the Saffir-Simpson Scale. It remains the third-strongest North Atlantic hurricane on record, and it was only surpassed by Hurricane Gilbert (888mbar) in 1988 and Hurricane Wilma (882Mbar) in 2005. In total, at least 408 people were killed by this hurricane.

In some cases they were named after the ship which experienced that particular storm. Two notable examples were: - *'The Racer's Storm of 1837'* and *'The Sea Venture Hurricane of 1609.'* The *1837 Racer's Storm* was a very powerful and destructive hurricane in the 19th century, causing 105 deaths and heavy damage to many cities on its 2,000+ mile path. *The Racer's Storm* was the 10th known tropical storm in the 1837 North Atlantic hurricane season. *The Racer's Storm* was named after the British war ship *HMS Racer* which encountered the storm in the extreme northwest Caribbean on September 28th. Another example was *The Sea Venture Hurricane of 1609*. In July 28th of 1609, a fleet of seven tall ships, with two pinnaces in tow carrying 150 settlers and supplies from Plymouth, England to Virginia to relieve the starving Jamestown colonists was struck by a hurricane en route there. They had been sent by the Virginia Company of London to fortify the Jamestown settlement. *The Sea Venture* was grounded at Bermuda which for some time was called *Somers Island* after the ship's captain, Admiral Sir George Somers. After being struck by this hurricane, *The Sea Venture* sprung a leak and everyone on board worked frantically to save this ship and their lives by trying to pump the water out of the hull of the ship. They tried to stem the flow of water coming onto the ship by stuffing salt beef and anything else they could find to fit into the leaks of the ship. After this proved futile most of the crew simply gave up hope, falling asleep where they could, exhausted and aching from their relentless but futile efforts. But just as they were about to give up and face the grim reality that they would be loss to the unforgiving Atlantic Ocean, they spotted the island of Bermuda. Somers skillfully navigated the floundering *Sea Venture* onto the reef about half a mile to the leeward side of Bermuda. They used the ship's long boat to ferry the crew and passengers ashore.

The passengers of the shipwrecked *Sea Venture* became Bermuda's first inhabitants and their stories helped inspire William Shakespeare's writing of his final play '*The Tempest*' making it perhaps the most famous hurricane in early American history. Most of those venturing to the New World had no knowledge of the word or the actual storm.

The lead ship, the three-hundred-ton *Sea Venture*, was the largest in the fleet and carried Sir Thomas Gates, the newly appointed governor of the colony, and Sir Georges Somers, admiral of the Virginia Company. It is interesting to note that Shakespeare did not name his play '*The Hurricane.*' He actually did know the word "*hurricano*" because it appears in two earlier plays, *King Lear* and *Troilus and Cressida*. Maybe he recognized that such a title would be confusing and unfamiliar to most of his audience, so he chose a more familiar word '*The Tempest*' instead. Though the island was uninhabited, Spaniards had visited Bermuda earlier and set ashore wild pigs. The shipwrecked passengers fed on those wild pigs, fish, berries and other plentiful game on the island. Although they yearned to stay in that island paradise they managed to make two vessels out of what was left of the *Sea Venture* and ten months later they set sailed for Jamestown. However, some persons remained on the island and became the first colonists of that island, including Admiral Sir George Somers who initially left with the other Jamestown passengers but eventually returned and died on that island.

In some instances, hurricanes were named after important persons within this region; one such storm was, the '*Willoughby Gale of 1666.*' The word 'Gale' during these colonial times was often interchanged with the word 'hurricane' but they often meant the same thing-a hurricane and not the official term we now use today for the definition of a Gale. This storm was named after the British Governor of Barbados, Lord Francis Willoughby who lost his life aboard the flagship *Hope* along with over 2,000 of his troops in his fleet in this hurricane. He was appointed Governor of Barbados by Charles II in May of 1650 and attempted to negotiate the strained politics of that island, which also experienced a division between the Royalists and Parliamentarians. His last act on behalf of the English Crown came in July 1666 when, having learned of the recent French seizure of St. Kitts, he formed a relief force of two Royal Navy Frigates, twelve other large vessels (including commandeered merchant ships), a fire ship, and a ketch, bearing over 2,000 men. He planned to proceed north to Nevis, Montserrat, and Antigua to gather further reinforcements before descending on the French. Leaving Barbados on July 28, his fleet waited for the French just off the coast of Martinique and Guadeloupe, where he sent a frigate to assault the harbour and ended up capturing two French merchant vessels on August 4. This success could not be exploited however as that night most of his force was destroyed by a strong hurricane, including the flagship *Hope*, from which Willoughby drowned in this ship during the storm. This hurricane occurred in 1666 and was a very intense storm which struck the islands of St. Kitts, Guadeloupe, and Martinique. The fleet was actually caught by surprise by this hurricane after leaving Barbados en-route to St. Kitts and Nevis to aid the colonists there to help battle against the French attacks. After the storm, only two vessels from this fleet were ever heard from again and the French captured some of these survivors. All of the vessels and boats on the coast of Guadeloupe were dashed to pieces. For a period in the late seventeenth century, some colonists referred to especially powerful and deadly hurricanes as "Willoughby Gales." Personal names were also used elsewhere in this region, for example, *'Saxby's Gale'* which occurred in Canada in 1869, and was named after a naval officer who was thought to have predicted it.

Another example was, the *Daniel Defoe Hurricane of 1703* which occurred in November of 1703 and moved from the Atlantic across to southern England. It was made famous by an obscure political pamphleteer, Daniel Defoe. It was six years before he wrote the world famous book *Robinson Crusoe.* At the time the hurricane struck, he needed money so the storm gave him the idea of collecting eye-witness accounts of the storm and publishing it in a pamphlet. He printed and sold this pamphlet under the very strange and exceptionally long title of *'the storm or collection of the Most Remarkable Casualties and Disasters which happened in the late Dreadful Tempest both by Sea and Land.'* In total, around 8,000 sailors lost their lives, untold numbers perished in the floods on shore, and 14,000 homes, 400 windmills and 16,000 sheep were destroyed. Some of the windmills burned down, because they turned so fast in the fierce winds that friction generated enough heat to set them on fire. The damage in London alone was estimated to have cost £2 million (at 18th century prices).

Another example was, the *Benjamin Franklin Hurricane of October 1743,* which affected the Northeastern United States and New England, brought gusty winds and rainy conditions as far as Philadelphia, and produced extensive flooding in Boston. This was the first hurricane to be measured accurately by scientific instruments. John Winthrop, a professor of natural philosophy at Harvard College, measured the pressure and tides during the storm passage. This storm, which wasn't particularly powerful but was memorable because it garnered the interest of future patriot and one of the founders of the United States, Benjamin Franklin, who believed the storm was coming in from Boston. However, it was going to Boston. Benjamin Franklin had planned to study a lunar eclipse one evening in September 1743, but the remnants of this hurricane ruined his evening. His curiosity aroused, Franklin gathered additional details about the storm and learned that the storm had moved up the Atlantic seaboard and against the surface winds. Thus science took the first step toward a basic understanding of hurricane.

Benjamin Franklin is also popularly known for his off the wall weather experiment where during a thunderstorm, in 1752, he carried out a dangerous experiment to demonstrate that a thunderstorm generates electricity. He flew a kite, with metal objects attached to its string, high in the sky into a thunderstorm cloud (Cumulonimbus). The metal items produced sparks, proving that electricity had passed along the wet string. After discovering that bolts of lightning were in fact electricity, with this knowledge Franklin developed the lightning rod to allow the lightning bolt to travel along the rod and safely into the ground. This discovery by Franklin is still used even to this day all over the world. A year later after Benjamin Franklin's kite flight, Swedish physicist G.W. Richmann conducted a similar experiment following Franklin's instructions to the letter, and as fate would have it, he was struck by a lightning which killed him instantly. Sailing home from France on the fifth of September, 1789, after his great years as a US Ambassador, Benjamin Franklin experienced a storm which may have been the same storm which devastated Dominica. He was eighty years old and suffering from "the Stone" but was busy observing the temperatures of the sea water, which would eventually lead to his discovery of the Gulf Stream.

One final example was, the *Alexander Hamilton Hurricane of 1772*, because he experienced a powerful and deadly hurricane growing up as a boy living in the Caribbean on the island of St. Kitts in the Leeward Islands. He later on in life became the confidential aide to George Washington and his greatness rests on his Federalist influence on the

American Constitution and much as on his financial genius as the first United States Secretary of the Treasury. Today he is featured on the U.S. ten dollar bill and he is one of two non-presidents featured on currently issued U.S. bills. The other is Benjamin Franklin who is found on the U.S. $100 bill. A westward moving hurricane hit Puerto Rico on August 28. It continued through the Caribbean, hitting Hispaniola on the 30th and later Jamaica. It moved northwestward through the Gulf of Mexico, and hit just west of Mobile, Alabama on the 4th. Many ships were destroyed in the Mobile area, and its death toll was very severe. In Pensacola, it destroyed most of the wharves. The most devastation occurred in the vicinity of Mobile and the Pasca Oocola River. All shipping at the Mouth of the Mississippi was driven into the marshes; this included the ship *El Principe de Orange* from which only 6 survived. This storm was famously described by Alexander Hamilton, who was living on the island of St. Croix at the time, and wrote a letter about it to his father in St. Kitts. The letter was so dramatic and moving that it was published in newspapers locally on the island and first in New York and then in other states (please see my book *'Rediscovering Hurricanes'* for a complete copy of this letter), and the locals on St. Kitts raised money to have him brought to America to receive a formal education to make good use of his intellectual abilities. This was because, this letter created such a sensation that some planters of St. Kitts, in the midst of the hurricane devastation, took up a collection to send him to America for better schooling because they saw in him great potential. By 1774 he was a student at King's College, now Columbia University, in New York. On St. Kitts, the damage was considerable and once again, many houses were flattened, and there were several fatalities and many more injuries. Total damage from this storm alone was estimated at £500,000 on St. Kitts. The second storm struck just three days later causing even more significant damage to the few remaining houses on this island already battered by the previous storm in 1772.

Several claimants have been put forth as the originators of the modern tropical cyclone 'naming' system. However, it was forecaster Clement Lindley Wragge, an Australian meteorologist who in 1887 began giving women's names, names from history and mythology and male names, especially names of politicians who offended him to these storms before the end of the 19th century. He was a colourful and controversial meteorologist in charge of the Brisbane, Australia Government weather office. He initially named the storms after mythological figures, but later named them after politicians he didn't like. For example, Wragge named some of these storms using biblical names such as, Ram, Raken, Talmon, and Uphaz or the ancient names of Xerxes and Hannibal. Wragge even nicknamed one storm Eline, a name that he thought was reminiscent of *'dusty maidens with liquid eyes and bewitching manners.'* Most ingeniously, he gained a measure of personal revenge by naming some of the nastiest storms with politicians' names such as Drake, Barton, and Deakin. By properly naming a hurricane, he was able to publicly describe a politician (perhaps a politician who was not too generous with the weather-bureau appropriations) as *'causing great distress'* or *'wandering aimlessly about the Pacific.'* By naming these storms after these hated politicians he could get a degree of revenge on them without suffering any repercussions from them. During his last days in office, he fought with the Australian Government over the right to issue national forecasts and he lost, and was fired in 1902.

For a while, hurricanes in the West Indies were often named after the particular Saint's day on which the hurricane occurred. As Christianity took hold in the West Indies, the naming system of storms here in the Caribbean was based on the Catholic tradition of naming these storms with the 'Saint' of the day (e.g. San Ciprian on September 26th). This system for naming them was haphazard and not really a system at all. According to Historian Alejandro Tapia, the first hurricane to be named with the Saint of the day was the *Hurricane of San Bartolomé* which devastated Puerto Rico and the Dominican Republic on August 24th and 25th of 1568. The earlier tropical cyclones were simply designated by historians' years later after their passages. One example of a great storm named after a Saint of the day was, *'Hurricane San Felipe'* which struck Puerto Rico on 13th September 1876. Another example was *'Hurricane San Felipe the Second'* which occurred strangely enough on the very same date 52 years later on 13th September of 1928 and was responsible for well over 3,433 deaths. Another hurricane named the *Hurricane of Santa Elena* struck Puerto Rico on 18th August, 1851 and then there was the *'Hurricane of Santa Ana'* (in English, Saint Anne) which struck Puerto Rico and Guadeloupe on 26th July of 1825 and killed over 1,300 persons. In addition, there was the *'Hurricane of San*

Ciriaco' which killed 3,369 persons in Puerto Rico on 8ᵗʰ August of 1899 (feast day of Saint Cyriacus) and remains one of the longest duration tropical storms(28 days) to hit the Caribbean or anywhere in the world. This tradition of naming storms that way officially ended with Hurricane Betsy in 1956 which is still remembered as the *'Hurricane of Santa Clara.'* However, years later with the passage of Hurricane Donna in 1960, the storm was recognized as the *'Hurricane of San Lorenzo.'* At this time, only the major hurricanes were given names so most storms especially the minor storms before 1950 in the North Atlantic never received any kind of designation. This is why these hurricanes in 1926 were never named but were simply referred to as *'The Great Nassau Hurricane of 1926'* or *'The Great Miami Hurricane of 1926'* after the cities they devastated. The word 'Great' simply meant that the hurricane was a powerful storm and that it had sustained winds of 136 mph or greater and a Minimum Central Pressure of 28.00 inches or less (see later chapter on the classification of hurricanes).

Later, latitude-longitude positions were used. At first they listed these storms by the latitude and longitude positions where they were first reported. This was cumbersome and confusing. For example, a name like *'Hurricane 12.8ºN latitude and 54.7ºW longitude'* was very difficult to remember, and it would be easy to confuse this storm with another that was seen two months later, but almost at the same location. In addition, this posed another significant problem, in the 1940's when meteorologists began airborne studies of tropical cyclones, ships and aircrafts communicated mainly in Morse code. This was ok for the letters of the alphabet, but it was not very good at dealing with numbers because it was slow and caused confusion among its users. In this region, these early storms were often referred to as Gales, Severe Gales, Equinoctial Storms, or Line Storms. The latter two names referred to the time of the year and the location from which these storms were born (referring to the Equatorial line). However, experience has shown that using distinctive names in communications is quicker and less subject to error than the cumbersome latitude-longitude identification methods. The idea was that the names should be short, familiar to users, easy to remember and that their use would facilitate communications with millions of people of different ethnic races threatened by the storm. This was because a hurricane can last for a week or more, and there can be more than one storm at a time, so weather forecasters starting naming these storms so that there would be absolutely no confusion when talking about a particular storm.

The first US named hurricane (unofficially named) was Hurricane George in 1947 and the second hurricane unofficially named was Hurricane Bess (named for the outspoken First Lady of the USA, Bess Truman, in 1949). The third was nicknamed by the news media 'Hurricane Harry' after the then President of the United States Harry Truman. United States Navy and Air Force meteorologists working in the Pacific Ocean began naming tropical cyclones during World War II, when they often had to track multiple storms. They gave each storm a distinctive name in order to distinguish the cyclones more quickly than listing their positions when issuing warnings. Towards the end of World War II, two separate United States fleets in the Pacific lacking sufficient weather information about these storms were twice badly damaged when they sailed directly into them resulting in massive causalities. Three ships were sunk, twenty one were badly damaged, 146 planes were blown overboard, and 763 men were lost. One of the results that came out of these tragedies was the fact that Army and Navy planes were then ordered to start tracking and studying these deadly storms, so as to prevent similar disasters like those ones from occurring again. During World War II this naming practice became widespread in weather map discussions among forecasters, especially Air Force and Navy meteorologists who plotted the movements of these storms over the wide expanses of the Pacific Ocean. These military meteorologists started naming these storms after their wives and girlfriends; however, this practice didn't last too long for whatever reason, but my guess is that those women rejected or took offense to being named after something that was responsible for so much damage and destruction.

An early example of the use of a woman's name for a storm was in the best selling pocketbook novel "Storm" by George R. Stewart, published by Random House in 1941, and has since been made into a major motion picture by Walt Disney further promoting the idea of naming storms. It involved a young meteorologist working in the San Francisco Weather Bureau office tracking a storm, which he called *Maria*, from its birth as a disturbance in the North Pacific to its death over North America many days later. He gave it a name because he said that he could easily say 'Hurricane Maria' rather than, *'the low pressure center which at 6pm yesterday was located at latitude one-seventy four degrees east and longitude forty-three degrees north'* which he considered too long and cumbersome. As Stewart detailed in his novel, *'Not since at any price would the Junior Meteorologist have revealed to the Chief that he was bestowing names-and girls' names-upon those great moving low-pressure areas.'* He unofficially gave the storms in his book women names such as, Lucy, Katherine and Ruth after some girls he knew because he said that they each had a unique personality. It is not known whether George Stewart was indeed the inspiration for the trend toward naming hurricanes which came along later in the decade, but it seems likely.

In 1950 military alphabet names (e.g. Able, Baker, Charley, Dog, Easy, Fox etc...) were adopted by the World Meteorological Organization (WMO) and the first named Atlantic hurricane was Able in 1950. The Joint Army/Navy (JAN) Phonetic Alphabet was developed in 1941 and was used by all branches of the United States military until the promulgation of the NATO phonetic alphabet in 1956, which replaced it. Before the JAN phonetic alphabet, each branch of the armed forces used its own phonetic alphabet, leading to difficulties in inter-branch communications. This naming method was not very popular, and caused a lot of confusion because officials soon realized that this naming convention would cause more problems in the history books if more than one powerful Hurricane Able made landfall and caused extensive damage and death to warrant retirement. This was because hurricanes that have a severe impact on the lives or the economy of a country or region and are remembered generations after the devastation they caused, and some go into weather history, so distinguishing one storm name from another was essential for the history books. The modern naming convention came about in response to the need for unambiguous radio communications with ships and aircrafts. As air and sea transportation started to increase and meteorological observations improved in number and quality, several typhoons, hurricanes or cyclones might have to be tracked at any given time. To help in their identification, in 1953 the systematic use of only regular women names were used in alphabetical order and this lasted until 1978. The 1953's Alice was the first real human-named storm. Beginning in 1960, four semi-permanent sets of names were established, to be re-cycled after four years. This list was expanded to ten sets in 1971, but before making it through the list even once; these sets were replaced by the now familiar 6 sets of men and women names.

This naming practice started in the Eastern Pacific in 1959 and in 1960 for the remainder of the North Pacific. It is interesting to note that in the Northwest Pacific Basin the names, by and large, are not personal names. While there are a few men and women names, the majority of the Northwest Pacific tropical cyclone names are of flowers, animals, birds, trees, or even foods while some are just descriptive adjectives. Inaddition, the names are not allotted in alphabetical order but are arranged by the contributing nation with the countries being alphabetized. For example, the Cambodians have contributed Naki (a flower), Krovanh (a tree) and Damrey (an elephant). China has submitted names such as Yutu (a mythological rabbit), Longwang (the dragon king and god of rain in Chinese mythology), and Dainmu (the mother of lightning and the goddess in charge of thunder). Micronesian typhoon names include Sinlaku (a legendary Kosrae goddess) and Ewiniar (the Chuuk Storm god).

In the North Atlantic Basin in 1979, gender equality finally reached the naming of hurricanes when thousands of complaints written to the WMO and feminists groups in the USA and worldwide urged the WMO to add men's names, hence both men and women names were used alternately and this practice is still in use today. Hurricane Bob was the first North Atlantic storm named after a man in the 1979 hurricane season, however it was not retired (it would eventually be retired in the 1991 hurricane season). Hurricane David was the second storm named after a man and it was the first male storm to be retired in the North Atlantic Region thanks in part to the great death toll and substantial damage it inflicted to the countries of Dominica, the Dominican Republic and the Bahamas during the last week of August and the first week of September in 1979. Also, since 1979, the lists now includes names from non-English speaking countries within this region, such as Dutch, French and Spanish names which also have a large presence here in the Caribbean. This is done to reflect the diversity of the different ethnic languages of the various countries in this region, so the names of Spanish, French, Dutch, and English persons are used in the naming process. The names of storms are now selected by a select committee from member countries of the World Meteorological Organization that falls within that particular region of the world, and we here in the Caribbean comes under Region IV for classification purposes. This committee meets once a year after the hurricane season has passed and before the beginning of the new hurricane season to decide on which names that are to be retired and to replace those names with a new set of names when and where necessary.

The practice of giving different names to storms in different hurricane basins has also led to a few rare circumstances of name-changing storms. For example, in October of 1988, after Atlantic Hurricane Joan devastated Central America, it proceeded to move into the Pacific and became Pacific tropical storm Miriam. Hurricane Joan was a powerful hurricane which caused death and destruction in over a dozen countries in the Caribbean and Central America. Another example was Hurricane Hattie, which was a powerful Category 5 hurricane that pounded Central America on Halloween during the 1961 North Atlantic hurricane season. It caused $370 million in damages and killed around 275 persons. Hattie is the only hurricane on record to have earned three names (Hattie, Simone, Inga) while crossing into different basins twice. Hattie swept across the Caribbean and came ashore in the town of Belize City, British Honduras (now called Belize), on October 31. It was a strong Category 4 hurricane at landfall, having weakened from a Category 5 just offshore. After making landfall, its remnants crossed over into the Pacific and attained tropical storm status again under the name Simone. In a remarkable turn of events, after Simone itself made landfall, its remnants crossed back over to the Gulf of Mexico, where the storm became Tropical Storm Inga before dissipating. However, it is debatable whether Inga in fact formed from the remnants of Simone at all.

It is interesting to note here that the letters Q, U, X, Y, and Z are not included in the hurricane list because of the scarcity of names beginning with those letters. However, in other regions of the world some of these letters are used, for example; only "Q" and "U" are omitted in the Northeastern Pacific Basin. When a storm causes tremendous damage and death, the name is taken out of circulation and retired for reasons of sensitivity and replaced with a name of the same letter and of the same gender and if possible, the same language as the name being retired (e.g. neither Hurricane Andrew in 1992 nor Hurricane Katrina in 2005 will ever be used again). The name used the most (at least with the same spelling is Arlene (seven times), while Frances and Florence have been used seven and six times respectively. However, considering different spellings of the same name, Debbie/Debby has been used seven times, and Anna/Ana has been used eight times. The first name to be called into use five times was Edith, but that name hasn't been used since 1971. After the 1996 season, Lilly has the distinction of being the first 'L' name to be used three times, while Marco is the first 'M' name to be used more than once. The name Kendra was assigned to a system in the 1966 hurricane season, but in post-season analysis it was decided it had not been a bona fide tropical storm. This storm marked the birth of reclassification of storms in the post-hurricane season (Hurricane Andrew was a storm that was reclassified from a Category Four hurricane to a Category Five hurricane in the off season). In only two years (2005, 1995) have names beginning with the letter 'O' and beyond have been used, but there have been several other years in which more than 14 storms have been tracked such as: 1887-17 storms, 1933-21 storms, 1936-16 storms, 1969-17 storms, 1995-19 storms and 2005-28 storms. The first three of these years were well before the naming of storms began, but 1969 requires an explanation. This was early in the era of complete satellite coverage, and forecasters were still studying the evolution of non-tropical systems (sub-tropical) into warm-core, tropical-type storms. Several systems that year were not named as tropical because they began at higher latitudes and were initially cold-cored. Formal classification of subtropical(hybrid type) cyclones and public advisories on them began in 1972, and a few years later, a review was made of satellite imagery from the late 60's and early 70's and several of these systems were included as tropical storms. In fact, two of the storms added in 1969 were hurricanes, so 1969 now stands as having 12 hurricanes.

Whenever a hurricane has had a major impact, any country affected by the storm can request that the name of the hurricane be 'retired' by agreement of the World Meteorological Organization (WMO). Prior to 1969, officially, retiring a storm name actually meant that it cannot be reused for at least 10 years, to facilitate historic references, legal actions, insurance claim activities, etc. and to avoid public confusion with another storm of the same name. But today these storms are retired indefinitely and if that happens, a gender name is selected in English, Dutch, Spanish or French for North Atlantic Storms. Other than that, the names are repeated every six years. It is interesting to note here that there hasn't been a case in the North Atlantic, where after 10 years of a name being 'retired' it was placed back on the list or re-used. Those hurricanes that have their names retired tend to be exceptionally destructive storms that often become household names in the regions they affected. When that list of names is exhausted, the Greek Alphabet (Alpha, Beta, Gamma, Delta, Epsilon, Zeta, Eta, Theta, Iota, Kappa and Lambda) is used but so far it has only been used once in either the Pacific or the Atlantic Basins, which was in the Atlantic Hurricane Season of 2005 (it is important to note here that there were a few subtropical storms which used the Greek Alphabet in the 1970's but they were really not truly tropical in nature).

If a storm forms in the off-season, it will take the next name on the list based on the current calendar date. For example, if a tropical cyclone formed on December 29th, it would take the name from the previous season's list of names. If a storm formed in February, it would be named from the subsequent season's list of names. Theoretically, a hurricane or tropical storm of any strength can have its name retired; retirement is based entirely on the level of damage and death caused by a storm. However, up until 1972 (Hurricane Agnes), there was no Category 1 hurricane which had its name retired, and no named tropical storm had its name retired until 2001 (Tropical Storm Allison). Allison is the only tropical storm to have its name retired without ever having reached hurricane strength. This is at least partially due to the fact that weaker storms tend to cause less damage, and the few weak storms that have had their names retired caused most of their destruction through heavy rainfall rather than winds. While no request for retirement has ever been turned down, some storms such as Hurricane Gordon in 1994 caused a great deal of death and destruction but nonetheless was not retired as the main country affected-Haiti did not request retirement. Hurricane Gordon in 1994 killed 1,122 persons in Haiti, and 23 deaths in other nations. Damage in the United States was estimated at $400 million, and damages in Haiti and Cuba were severe. Despite the tremendous damage caused, the name 'Gordon' was not retired and was reused in both the 2000 and 2006 North Atlantic hurricane seasons. Since 1953, 68 storms have had their names retired. Of these, two (Carol and Edna) were reused after the storm for which they were retired but were later retroactively retired, and two others (Hilda and Janet) were included on later lists of storm names but were not reused before being retroactively retired. Before 1979, when the first permanent six-year storm name list began, some storm names were simply not used anymore. For example, in 1966, 'Fern' was substituted for 'Frieda,' and no reason was cited.

In the Atlantic Basin in most cases, a tropical cyclone retains its name throughout its life. However, a tropical cyclone may be renamed in several situations. First, when a tropical storm crosses from the Atlantic into the Pacific, or vice versa, before 2001 it was the policy of National Hurricane Center (NHC) to rename a tropical storm which crossed from Atlantic into Pacific, or vice versa. Examples included Hurricane Cesar-Douglas in 1996 and Hurricane Joan-Miriam in 1988. In 2001, when Iris moved across Central America, NHC mentioned that Iris would retain its name if it regenerated in the Pacific. However, the Pacific tropical depression developed from the remnants of Iris was called Fifteen-E instead. The depression later became Tropical Storm Manuel. NHC explained that Iris had dissipated as a tropical cyclone prior to entering the eastern North Pacific Basin; the new depression was properly named Fifteen-E, rather than Iris. In 2003, when Larry was about to move across Mexico, NHC attempted to provide greater clarity: *"Should Larry remain a tropical cyclone during its passage over Mexico into the Pacific, it would retain its name. However, a new name would be given if the surface circulation dissipates and then regenerates in the Pacific."* Up to now, it is extremely rare for a tropical cyclone to retain its name during the passage from Atlantic to Pacific, or vice versa. Second, in situations where there are uncertainties of the continuation of storms. When the remnants of a tropical cyclone redevelop, the redeveloping system will be treated as a new tropical cyclone if there are uncertainties of the continuation, even though the original system may contribute to the forming of the new system. One example is the remnants of Tropical Depression #10 reforming into Tropical

Depression #12 from the 2005 season which went on to become the powerful and deadly Hurricane Katrina. Another example was a storm which had the most names as stated earlier; in 1961 there was one tropical storm which had three lives and three names. Tropical Storm Hattie developed off the Caribbean Coast of Nicaragua on October 28, 1961, and drifted north and west before crossing Central America at Guatemala. It re-emerged into the Pacific Ocean on November 1 and was re-christened Simone. Two days later it recurved back towards the coastline of Central America and crossed over into the Atlantic via Mexico, re-emerging into the Gulf of Mexico as Inga.

CHAPTER THREE

The Anatomy of Hurricanes

Many early ideas and concepts about the origin and structure of hurricanes were well founded in observations and reasons, while others were long held traditions and beliefs. Sometimes there was a connection between traditional ideas and scientific thoughts. For example, most persons before the invention of modern meteorological offices and instruments, often predicted the onset of a hurricane by observing the tidal changes before the storm, something that is still practiced today but on a more refined and scientific level and it is now referred to as the 'storm surge.' To understand how hurricanes work, and to improve forecasts, meteorologists need detailed information from the heart of the storm. During the more recent hurricane seasons, considered to be some of the most active Atlantic seasons on record, meteorologists investigated hurricanes from top to bottom and from side to side to get as much information about these storms as possible. By using this information, they can gather vital information about the anatomy of hurricanes which can ultimately lead to a greater improvement in hurricane forecasting and evacuation plans, which can ultimately result in saving many more lives and reduced property damages. Known simply as hurricanes in this region and tropical cyclones by meteorologists, they claim more lives and cause more damage each year than any other storm or weather phenomena combined. When a full-blown hurricane strikes, trees are ripped up, power lines are torn down and buildings flattened and totally destroyed by raging winds, gusting up to 200 mph. Large areas are swamped by torrential rain, and coastal regions can be completely devastated by the storm surge. Here in the North Atlantic Hurricane Basin, we are affected by an average of 10 tropical storms and of this total six to eight become hurricanes per year and two to three of these becomes major hurricanes, but there are wide variations from this figure, for example, in 2005 there was a record twenty eight tropical storms and 14 of those became hurricanes, but in 1929 and 1930 there were only three and two hurricanes respectively in those years.

The summer solstice, June 21, marks the official beginning of summer north of the Equator, and is the longest day of the year. It is not, however the hottest day of the year. This is because a phenomenon known as 'seasonal temperature lag,' the hottest time of the year lags behind the time you might logically expect to encounter it. This is because the earth is slow to absorb and release heat energy, during the late summer months it gets showered with more energy from the sun than it can immediately re-radiate back into space. The temperature keeps building as long as the earth keeps absorbing more energy than it loses, with the peak coming well after the summer solstice has passed. With the coming of autumn and shorter days, the earth catches up, and starts radiating heat energy back into space faster than the sun can pour it on. That's when the temperature starts to fall. It continues to fall reaching its low well after the winter solstice, until the next spring when the heat starts building again. This seasonal lag in temperature has a great effect on the formation of hurricanes in the North Atlantic. Ocean waters cover about 75% of the tropics, and this water reflects only about 5% of the solar energy reaching it. The rest is absorbed and this vast quantity of energy that both warms the water and evaporates large amounts of it to create the typically warm and humid tropical climate.

Hurricanes may reach the Caribbean between June and November, but they are most common in August and September where on average 84 % of these deadly storms occur. The reason for this simple; in the summer water must be absorbed by three times as much energy as compared to the land, in order to have the same ambient temperature. In addition, the winds must continually perturb the ocean, thereby allowing the colder waters from the deep to mix with the surface waters. This oceanic lag postpones the meteorological onset of summer by a month beyond its astronomical onset, so because of this factor, the warmer months are late July, August and early September rather than in June the astronomical date for summer. In other words, it takes several more weeks for the oceans to reach their warmest temperatures of 26.5 Celsius or greater. Inaddition, the atmospheric circulation in the tropics also reaches its most pronounced and favorable conditions for tropical cyclone development at the same time. As a result of these factors, it is one of the reasons why most of the hurricanes form in late July, August and early September rather than in June. But from a personal perspective, meteorologists have learned that hurricanes don't usually go by the rules of scientific law or statistics because they seem to have a mind of their own at times. Pick up any text book on hurricanes and it will tell you that the one place where hurricanes do not form is in the South Atlantic Ocean. The atmosphere does not provide enough spin near the surface to get them started, the sea surface temperature is not warm enough to support hurricanes and winds higher in the atmosphere tend to shear off any that do make a start. Hence, it was with some amazement that meteorologists from around the world watched the first ever recorded hurricane (officially in the South Atlantic they are called 'cyclones' but for uniformity and clarity I will use the word 'hurricane') to develop off the east coast of Brazil in the last week of March, 2004. Initially the storm did not look much like a hurricane, but gradually it developed some common characteristics with some of its counterparts which develop in the North Atlantic Ocean; it acquired enough characteristics to convince the majority of the world's tropical cyclone experts that it was indeed a hurricane even though it occurred outside of traditional hurricane basins and was called Hurricane Catarina.

In the North Atlantic there are four different types of hurricanes that influence us in some way or the other. The first is the Cape Verde Type hurricane which as it name suggests originates off the African Coast in the vicinity of the Cape Verde Islands initially moving in a westerly direction and then in a west-northwest to a northwesterly track as it makes it way through the Caribbean. The Cape Verde Islands is an archipelago about 400 miles off the West African Coast and are volcanic in nature. It was colonized by Portugal in the fifteenth century and became an independent country in 1975. At one point in their history, these islands served as an outpost station for the movement of African slaves on the 'Middle Passage' to the Americas. This type of hurricane forms over the Atlantic mainly during the early part of the season, June thru mid September months when the easterly waves are most dominant and prominent features in the Caribbean region. At the beginning and the middle of the hurricane season, storms also tend to form near the Bahamas and this type has come to be known as '*Bahama Buste*rs' according to world renowned Professor William Gray from Colorado State University. An example of this type was Hurricane Katrina in 2005 which formed just east to the Bahamas and moved initially westward and then northwestward into the Gulf of Mexico and then over Louisiana. Then there is the Gulf of Mexico type, which as it names suggest originates in the Gulf of Mexico and travels northward from its inception and mainly influences Latin America, and the Gulf Coast of the United States. Finally, there is the western Caribbean type which forms during the early and late parts of the hurricane season and forms in the most favoured location near the Gulf of Honduras mainly in May and June and mid-September thru late November. The formations of these cyclones are due in part to the seasonal movement of the Inter-Tropical Convergence Zone, also known as the Equatorial Trough. From its inception this type of hurricane seems to take a northward movement, which normally takes a track over the island of Cuba and into the Bahamas, the severity of which is influenced by how long the cyclone remains over the mountainous terrain of Cuba.

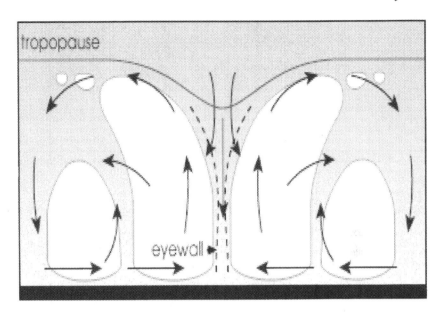

B)

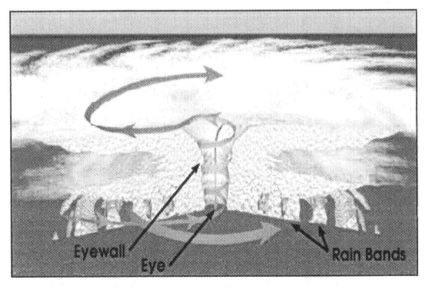

A) Cross-sectional view into a hurricane (Courtesy of NOAA)

B) Hurricanes form when the energy released by the condensation of moisture in rising air causes a chain reaction. The air heats up and rises further, which leads to more condensation. The air flowing out of the top of this 'Chimney' drops towards the ground, forming powerful winds. (Graphic by Robert Simmons, NASA GSFC)

The nature of hurricanes varies with their age, size and position, but the following features generally characterize most fully developed hurricanes: -

- They are tropical, meaning that they are generated in tropical areas of the ocean near the Equator.

- They are cyclonic, meaning that their winds which weaken with height swirl around a central *eye*. Wind direction is counterclockwise (west to east) in the Northern Hemisphere and clockwise (east to west) in the Southern Hemisphere.

- They are low-pressure systems. The eye of a hurricane is always a low-pressure area and in this area air sinks at the center of the hurricane. The lowest barometric pressures ever recorded on earth have occurred inside hurricanes.

- The winds swirling around the center of the storm have a sustained speed of at least 74 mph.

- Their main source of energy is from latent heat of condensation

Size:

In the Caribbean, the average diameter of a well-developed hurricane is between 100 to 500 miles, but some have reached diameters of 800 miles. The diameter of the eye, or calm centre, of a well-developed hurricane is on average between 10 to 20 miles across. The largest eye ever observed was 56 miles in radius, which was measured from a reconnaissance aircraft during Tropical Cyclone Kerry in the Coral Sea, off the north-east coast of Australia on February 21, 1979. The size of a typical tropical cyclone can vary considerably depending on the extent of the wind and rain fields. Typhoon Tip in October of 1979 is considered the largest tropical cyclone on record at 1350 miles (2170 km) wide. The storm weakened greatly before landfall, but still caused widespread flood damage across most of Japan during the 1979 Pacific typhoon season. Tip is sometimes regarded as the first known 'Super Typhoon.' While Cyclone Tracy in December of 1974 is the smallest tropical cyclone on record at only 60 miles (96 km) wide, it is sometimes referred to as a 'midget' hurricane. Cyclone Tracy was a tropical cyclone which devastated the city of Darwin, Australia, from December 24 to December 25, 1974. After forming over the Arafura Sea, the storm moved southward and affected the city with Category 4 winds on the Australian cyclone intensity scale and the Saffir-Simpson Hurricane Scale, although there is evidence to suggest that it had reached Category 5 when it made landfall.

Speed:

Like a top spinning swiftly around its axis and 'walking' slowly across the floor, the forward movement of the entire mass of a hurricane is relatively slow compared to the speed of its rotating winds. Hurricanes generally move at a speed of between 10 to 15 miles per hour, but sometimes these storms can go much faster than their average speeds or even remain stationary over one spot for a while. In the Atlantic, the average hurricane moves about 300 to 400 miles a day or about 3,000 miles in its average nine-day life. However, some hurricanes can last three weeks and travel 10,000 miles. The longest-lived tropical storm in the Atlantic Basin history was the third storm of the 1899 season, known as the San Ciriaco Hurricane after a town it devastated on the island of Puerto Rico and was a storm for a total of 33 days from August 3rd until September 4th 1899 (This however, was before the days of satellite coverage so this can never really be officially confirmed). Another example, tropical Storm Ginger in 1971 spun around in the open ocean for 27.25 days in the Atlantic. However, officially the longest lasting and furthest travelling cyclone ever observed was Hurricane/Typhoon John (it crossed the International Date Line twice, it changed status from hurricane to typhoon and back to a hurricane) which lasted a total of 31 days in the 1994 hurricane season.

Movement:

The movements of hurricanes are subject to pressure systems of the surrounding atmosphere, as well as the influence of prevailing winds and of the spinning Earth. While some hurricanes travel in a general curved or parabolic path, others change course quite abruptly. They have been known to reverse direction, zig-zag, turn back around towards the Equator, make loops, stall, return to the same area, and move in every direction of the compass. These changes usually occur as the storm passes through areas of light and variable winds between the prevailing easterlies and westerlies. They are also influenced by the presence of highs and lows. High pressure areas act as barriers, and if a high is well developed, its outward-spiraling flow will guide the hurricane around its edges. Low pressures, on the other hand, can tend to draw the hurricane system toward their slowly inward rotating winds. With all these pushes and pulls, the hurricane can follow a seemingly erratic route.

Winds:

Of all the tropical cyclone damaging agents, strong winds are perhaps the best understood of all of them. Damaging winds will accompany any hurricane, no matter what category it is. A hurricane by definition has winds of at least 74 miles per hour. This wind speed alone is enough to cause great damage to poorly constructed signage and knock over some of the sturdiest trees and other vegetation. Obviously, the stronger the hurricane (higher winds), the more potential there is for wind damage to exists. The fierce winds which blow in an anti-clockwise direction around the centre of the central calm in the northern hemisphere may reach 100 to 200 mph. Wind speeds are the greatest near the surface around the central calm or eye. The energy released in a normal hurricane is great. An average hurricane winds are so great that it is equipped with some 1.5 trillion watts of power in its winds which if converted to electricity would be equivalent to about half of the world's entire electrical generating capacity. In fact, in a single day, a hurricane can release the amount of energy necessary to supply all of the United States electrical needs for about six months. One second of a hurricane's energy is equivalent to about ten Hiroshima atomic bombs and in total, a single hurricane during its lifetime can dissipate more energy than that contained in thirty thousand atomic bombs. The hurricane which hit Galveston, Texas, in September, 1900, during its lifespan had sufficient energy to drive all the power stations in the world for four years. A large hurricane stirs up more than a million miles of atmosphere every second.

The force of the wind can quickly decimate the tree population, downed power lines and utility poles, knock over signs, and may be strong enough to destroy some homes and buildings. Flying debris can also cause damage, and in cases where people are caught outdoors, injuries and death can prevail. When a hurricane first makes landfall, it is common for tornadoes to form which can cause severe localized wind damage. In most cases, however, wind is a secondary cause of damage. Storm surge is normally the primary cause. The right front quadrant is strongest side of the hurricane, this is the area where there is positive convergence, in this quadrant the winds are typically the strongest, the storm surge is highest, and the possibility of tornadoes are the greatest. The right side of a hurricane is the strongest side because the wind speed and the hurricane speed-of-motion are complimentary there; meaning on this side, the wind blows in the same direction as the storm's forward motion. On the left side, the hurricane's speed of motion subtracts from the wind speed because the main bulk of the storm is moving away from it. The storm's angle of attack is a key factor in its impact. Just as in an automobile accident, the highest level of destruction is caused by a hurricane hitting the coastline head-on. If a storm travels up the coast, with its left side brushing the seashore, the most dangerous part of the storm stays offshore and the net effect will be much less damage. The worst-case scenario would be a hurricane arriving onshore at high tide or spring tide. With the ocean level already at its highest point of the day, the storm surge from a category four or five hurricane can add another 15 to 20 feet of water, with abnormally large waves breaking on top of that. Water weighs around 1,700 pounds per cubic yard, and there are very few structures that can stand up to the force a high storm surge can produce.

The Sea Level Atmospheric Pressure:

The atmospheric pressure is defined as the force per unit area exerted against a surface by the weight of the air above the surface. In the tropics this varies by only about 0.3%, but during the passage of the central low pressure of a hurricane, it may fall by 5% or 10% below the average of 29.2 inches or 989 Millibars. Super Typhoon Tip in the Northwest Pacific on October 12, 1979 had the lowest central pressure ever measured in a tropical cyclone of 870mb and powerful Hurricane Wilma in 2005 had the lowest North Atlantic pressure reading of 882mb.

Clouds:

The solid cumulonimbus or rain clouds, which surrounds the core and within the spiral Rainbands, makes up the main part of the hurricane and may extend for a radius of 100 miles around the eye and reach heights of 40,000 to 50,000 feet or more. Within the eye the sky is generally clear and rain-free.

Rainfall:

Virtually all literal use of the word hurricane in literary works evokes violent wind. Yet some of the worst tropical cyclone catastrophes are caused not by winds but by torrential rain (e.g. Hurricane Katrina in 2005). Rainfall associated with hurricanes is both beneficial and harmful. Although the rains contribute to the water needs of the areas traversed by the hurricane, the rains are harmful when the amount is so large as to cause extensive flooding. There are about four factors that determine how much rain will fall in a given place: the amount of water vapour in the air, topography, the vertical extent and duration of the updraft. Curiously, some of the most devastating floods are produced by tropical cyclones of sub-hurricane strength. The torrential rainfall which normally accompanies a hurricane can cause serious flooding. A recent and especially tragic example of this is that of Hurricane Mitch of 1998, the deadliest Atlantic hurricane since the Great Hurricane of 1780. Floods produced by Mitch killed more than 11,000 people in Central America, and the President of Honduras declared that Mitch destroyed 50 years of progress in that country. Whereas, the storm surge and high winds are concentrated near the eye, the rain may extend outward for hundreds of miles away from the center and may last for several days, affecting areas well after the hurricane has diminished or passed over a particular area.

An average of 10 to 15 inches of rain falls over coastal areas during the passage of a well-developed hurricane, but over 20 inches have been recorded and rain may fall at the rate of one inch an hour. In twenty-four hours a record of 32.67 inches fell at Belize City in Belize from Hurricane Keith in 2000, for comparison, the average annual rainfall of Belize is about 74.4 inches. Furthermore, Hurricane Camille dumped over 760 millimeters (30 inches) of rainfall over central Virginia, drowning 109 persons in the process with flash flooding. For comparison, the average annual rainfall of Central Virginia is only about 45.22 inches. The Cedar Key Hurricane of September, 1950, poured nearly 39 inches of rain in one day and night on Yankeetown, Florida, off the Gulf Coast. This 9-day hurricane traced an unusual double loop in the Cedar Keys area, and the coast from Sarasota northward suffered extensive wind and flood damage. The coastal area inland from Yankeetown to Tampa was flooded for several weeks. In 1963 Pacific Hurricane Season, Typhoon Gloria dumped in 49.13 inches of rainfall in Baxin, Taiwan. While in the 1967 Pacific Typhoon Season 65.83 inches felled at Xinliao in Taiwan during a 24 hour period from Typhoon Carla. For comparison, the average annual rainfall of Xinliao, Taiwan is about 85 inches. However, Tropical Cyclone Denise in Foc-Foc in the La Reunion Island on the 7-8th January, 1966 holds a world record of 45 inches in just 12 hours and 71.80 inches of rainfall in 24 hours in the same location for the total amount of rainfall over a particular location from a tropical cyclone.

Eye:

This is the most recognizable feature found within a hurricane and is an area at the center of the hurricane consisting of clears skies but can also have scattered to broken to even overcast clouds. Within the eye, the winds are light, the surface pressure is very low and there is almost no rain and it can have a diameter of 20 to 40 miles across. The eye is the warmest part of the hurricane and has the lowest pressure reading. The eye is the calmest part of the storm because the strong surface winds converging towards the center never actually reach the exact center of the storm, but instead form a cylinder of relatively calm air.

Eyewall:

Adjacent to the eye is the eyewall, a ring or wall of intense thunderstorms that whirl around the storm's center and extend upward to almost 50,000 feet above sea level. Within the eyewall, we find the heaviest rainfall and the strongest winds. This is the most dangerous part of the hurricane and the winds in this area may blow up to 155mph and gusting up to 225mph in severe storms. The winds spiral in a counterclockwise direction into the storm's low-pressure center. In several hurricanes, meteorologists have documented a phenomenon called 'eyewall replacement' in which a second eyewall forms around the eye. The inner eyewall collapses and temporarily weakens the storm. The outer eyewall then contracts and takes its place strengthening the storm again.

Spiral Bands:

Long bands of rain clouds that appear to spiral inward to the eyewall, these are called spiral rainbands or feeder bands and can be hundreds of miles across. Surface winds increase in speed as they blow counterclockwise and inward toward the center. These bands become more pronounced as the storm intensifies, and are fed by the warm oceans.

The Height:

A hurricane may be as much as 9 miles or 50,000 feet high. This is equal to almost twice the height of Mount Everest, the highest mountain on Earth.

Storm Surge:

Violent hurricane winds may produce storm surges of up to 45 feet high at sea, and storm surges of over twenty feet may crash against shores at speeds of up to 40 mph. Long swells may move outwards from the eye of a hurricane for more than 1,000 miles. These long swells are often the first visible signs of an approaching hurricane and are known as the *Storm Surge*. A *storm surge*, also called a *hurricane surge*, is the abnormal rise in sea level caused by wind and pressure forces of a hurricane. It can be extremely devastating, and is in fact a major cause of damage and greatest danger to life during the passage of a hurricane. It is estimated that 75% of all hurricane related deaths and injuries are caused by the storm surge and the remaining 20% of the 25% is simply caused by due negligence. For example, persons out of curiosity venturing out into the peak of the storm and being killed by flying debris or someone stepping on a live wire and getting electrocuted before the 'all-clear' is given.

The storm surge isn't just another wave pushed ahead of a storm; it acts like a gigantic bulldozer that can destroy anything in its path. Think of the storm surge as a moving wall of water weighing millions of tons. The storm surge itself is caused by the wind and pressure 'pushing' the water into the continental shelf and onto the coastline caused by a hurricane. The height of the storm surge is the difference between the observed level of sea surface and its level in the absence of the storm. In other words, the storm surge is estimated by subtracting the normal or astronomical tide from the observed or estimated storm tide. The astronomical tide is the results from the gravitational interactions between the earth, moon, and sun, generally producing two high and two low oceanic tides per day. Should the storm surge coincide with the high astronomical tide, several additional feet could be added to the water level, especially when the sun and moon are aligned, which produces the highest oceanic tides (known as syzygy).

Hurricanes have a vacuum effect on the ocean. The water is pulled toward the hurricane, causing it to 'pile up' like a small mountain. A mound of water forms under the center of a hurricane as the intensely low pressure draws water up. The shape of the shoreline and the ocean bottom has a great deal to do with a storm surge's magnitude. Over the ocean, this mound of water is barely noticeable, but builds up as the storm approaches land. The surge's height as it reaches land depends upon the slope of the ocean floor at the coast. The more gradual the slope, the less volume of sea there is in which the surge can dissipate and further inland the water is displaced. This is why Katrina did so much damage in 2005 and why areas like New Orleans in the United States will continue to remain vulnerable to future hurricanes. This dome of water can be up to 40 to 60 miles long as it moves onto the shoreline near the landfall point of the eye. A cubic yard of sea water weighs approximately 1,700 pounds and this water is constantly slamming into shoreline structures, even well-built structures get quickly demolished because this water acts like a battering ram on these vulnerable shoreline structures.

The highest storm surge ever recorded was produced by the 1899 Cyclone Mahina, which caused a storm surge of over 13 meters (43 feet) at Bathurst Bay, Australia. This value was derived from reanalysis of debris sightings and eyewitness reports, as a result it is controversial within the meteorological community, but clearly a phenomenal storm surge occurred. In the United States, the greatest recorded storm surge was generated by 2005's Hurricane Katrina, which produced a massive storm surge of approximately 9 meters (30 feet) high in the town of Bay St. Louis, Mississippi, and in the surrounding coastal counties, while

Hurricane Camille came in second with 24 feet in 1969. The worst storm surge, in terms of loss of life, was the 1970 Bhola cyclone and in general the Bay of Bengal is particularly prone to tidal surges. In the Bay of Bengal area, often referred to as the "storm surge capital of the world", 142 moderate to severe storm surge events are on record from 1582 to 1991. These surges, some in excess of eight meters (26 feet), have killed hundreds of thousands of people, primarily in Bangladesh. The Caribbean Islands have endured many devastating surges as well. These powerful hurricanes listed above caused very high storm surge. However, worldwide storm surge data is sparse. Hurricanes and the accompanying storm surge they produce can even affect the very depths of the ocean. In 1975 some meteorological and oceanographic instruments were dropped from a research reconnaissance airplane in the Gulf of Mexico showed that Hurricane Eloise disturbed the ocean hundreds of feet down and created underwater waves that persisted for weeks.

Tropical Wave:

This is an inverted trough of low pressure that moves generally westward along with the trade winds. A trough is defined as a region of relative low pressure. Tropical waves occasionally intensify into tropical cyclones. They are also called *Easterly Waves*. The majority of the world's tropical cyclones form from easterly waves.

Tropical Disturbance:

A discrete tropical weather system of apparently organized thunderstorms or convection - generally 100 to 300 miles in diameter - originating in the tropics or subtropics, having a non-frontal migratory character, and maintaining its identity for 24 hours or more. Disturbances associated with perturbations in the wind field and progressing through the tropics from east to west are also known as *Easterly or Tropical Waves*

Tropical Depression:

An organized system of clouds and thunderstorms with a well defined circulation and maximum sustained winds of 20 to 33 knots. The tropical disturbance becomes classified as a tropical depression when a closed circulation is first observed and sustained winds are less than 33 knots or 39 mph.

Tropical storm:

An organized system of strong thunderstorms with a well defined circulation and maximum sustained winds of 34 to 63 knots. At this point the storm is given a name.

Hurricane:

This the term used in North and Central America and the Caribbean to describe a severe tropical cyclone with a well defined circulation and having winds in excess of 64 knots (74mph) and capable of producing widespread wind damage and heavy flooding; Beaufort scale numbers 12 through 17.

Hurricane season:

This is the part of the year having a relatively high incidence of hurricanes. The hurricane season in the Caribbean, North and Central America and Atlantic runs from June 1 to November 30 each year.

Hurricane Alert:

A hurricane alert indicates that a hurricane poses a threat to a specific area or region within 60 hours and residents of the specified area should start to make any necessary preparations.

Hurricane Warning:

A warning is given when it is likely that a hurricane will strike a specific area within 24 hours. At this point residents should have completed the necessary preparations for the storm.

Hurricane Watch:

A hurricane watch indicates that a hurricane poses a threat to a specific area within 36 hours and residents of the area should be well into the process of preparation for the hurricane.

All Clear:

All Clear simply means that the hurricane or tropical storm has left the specific area and all the Alerts, Warnings, and Watches are lifted but the residents in that area should exercise extreme caution for downed power lines, debris, fallen trees, flooding etc.

Other Hurricane effects

Tornadoes:

Tornadoes are not normally a tropical phenomenon but are frequently spawned by hurricanes on crossing coastlines and islands. Tornadoes may form especially in the spiral Rainbands of a hurricane as it moves onshore. The changing wind speeds with height acts like a huge twisting mechanism, thus allowing the possibility of tornado formation. Since tornadoes form in conjunction with strong convection, they are more likely to occur near the outer edge of the eyewall cloud or in the outer rainbands.

Lightning and Hail:

Lightning and hail are less frequent occurrences during hurricanes than other severe weather events like thunderstorms. Lightning is more frequent during a typical afternoon thunderstorm because there are more factors present that promote lightning development. The same reason generally holds true concerning hail during a hurricane. There will be some lightning during a hurricane but some of the 'flashes' will actually be electric transformers exploding or power lines sparking; sending an eerie glow in the sky.

Economic Impact:

How many persons died and what was the damage? These are the two most frequently asked questions about tropical cyclones and rightly so. The approximately 80 tropical cyclones that occur throughout the globe each year cause billions of dollars in damage and kill many thousands of persons. However, in addition to the cost, there may be some economic benefits to be derived from tropical cyclones. The direct or indirect costs from a tropical cyclone can be divided into a number of broad categories, some of which include, cost of damage, cost of preparedness, cost of the warning service, cost of relief, loss in business revenue and losses to fisheries and agriculture. Although we tend to focus on the losses due to a tropical cyclone, a complete economic study must also consider the benefits. In many arid regions in the tropics, a large portion of the annual rainfall comes from tropical cyclones. These rains often fill water reservoirs, save crops from drought and the economic agricultural gains more than offset the coastal losses. Another possible economic benefit of a tropical cyclone is the increase in some businesses during the recovery. In fact, outside aid may prompt a local economic boom in the affected community. However, the net economic impact on the country is still negative.

CHAPTER FOUR

The Classification of Hurricanes

The Saffir-Simpson Hurricane Damage Potential Scale is a classification used for most Western Hemisphere tropical cyclones which exceeds the intensities of "tropical depressions" and "tropical storms", and thereby become hurricanes. The scale divides hurricanes into five categories distinguished by the intensities of their sustained winds. Hurricanes are ranked according to strength and by the amount of damage they cause. The weakest hurricane is designated a Category One status with maximum sustained winds from 74 mph to 95 mph and an average storm surge of 4 to 5 feet above sea level. In contrast, a Category Five hurricane has maximum sustained winds of greater than 155 mph and a storm surge of greater than 18 feet. Storm surge depends on many factors such as the shape of the continental shelf just offshore, whether the hurricane makes landfall at high or low tide, and the location of the offshore and onshore winds relative to the eye of the hurricane.

As a result of the difficulty in relating the different and varying factors or characteristics of a hurricane to the destruction potential, the Saffir-Simpson Damage Potential Scale was developed in 1969 and completed in 1971. The scale was introduced to the general public in 1973, and saw widespread use after Neil Frank replaced Simpson at the helm of the National Hurricane Center in 1974. This scale was named for Herbert Saffir a civil engineer in Coral Gables, Florida and Robert Simpson, a meteorologist and the then Director of the National Hurricane Center in Miami, Florida, and has been used for well over 37 years to estimate the relative damage potential of a hurricane due to wind and storm surge. The initial scale was developed by Mr. Herbert Saffir (who at the time was well known as the father of the Miami's building codes) while working on commission from the United Nations to study low-cost housing in hurricane-prone areas. While performing the study, Saffir realized that there was no simple scale for describing the likely effects of a hurricane. Knowing the usefulness of the Richter Magnitude Scale in describing earthquakes, he devised a similar 1-5 scale based on wind speed that showed expected damage to structures. Saffir looked at the scale from an engineering point of view because he was well-versed in Miami's Building Codes. Saffir then gave the scale to the National Hurricane Center, and Simpson added in the likely effects of storm surge and flooding. Simpson became the Director of the National Hurricane Center in 1968 and he was already one of the world's leading authorities on tropical cyclones and a veteran of numerous Air Force and Navy flights into these hurricanes. Simpson later recalled that the National Hurricane Center at the time was having difficulty telling disaster agencies how much damage to expect from particular storms.

Using a mixture of structural engineering and meteorology, they constructed the Saffir-Simpson Damage Potential Scale because both men had first-hand experiences with hurricanes. It does not take into account rainfall or location, which means that a Category 3 hurricane which hits a major city will likely do far more damage than a Category 5 hurricane which hits a rural area. The Saffir-Simpson Scale classifies hurricanes into Categories 1,2,3,4, and 5, depending on the barometric pressure, wind speed, and storm surge and destruction. A Category 1 hurricane, for example, would inflict minimal damage, mainly to shrubbery, trees, foliage, unanchored structures, mobile homes, small craft, and low-lying areas that could become flooded. Whereas, a Category 5 hurricane would cause catastrophic damage, such as blown down trees, power lines, and poles; overturned vehicles; torn down or blown away buildings; complete destruction of mobile or manufactured homes and massive flooding. According to Robert Simpson, there is no reason for a Category 6 on the Saffir-Simpson Scale because it is designed to measure the potential damage of a hurricane to man-made structures. If the speed of the hurricane is above 156 mph, then the damage to a building will be "serious no matter how well it's engineered." However, the result of new technologies in construction leads some to suggest that an increase in the number of categories is necessary. This suggestion was emphasized after the devastating effects of the 2005 Atlantic hurricane season. During that record year Hurricane Emily, Hurricane Katrina, Hurricane Rita, and Hurricane Wilma all became Category 5 hurricanes. A few newspaper columnists and scientists have brought up the idea of introducing a Category 6 and amending the scale to include the risk of flooding but in most cases it is often rebuffed.

The practical usefulness of the Saffir-Simpson Scale is that it relates properties of the hurricane to previously observed damage. Until the Saffir-Simpson Damage Potential Scale was developed, hurricanes were referred to as Great (or Extreme) Hurricanes, Severe Hurricanes, or Minor, Minimal or Major Hurricanes. A Minor Hurricane had Maximum winds of 74 mph and a Minimum Central Pressure of 29.40 inches. A Minimal Hurricane had Maximum winds of between 75 to 100 mph and a Minimum Central Pressure of between 29.03 to 29.39 inches. A Major hurricane had winds between 101 to 135 mph and a Minimal Central Pressure of 28.01 to 29.02 inches. An Extreme or Great Hurricane had winds of 136 mph or over and a Minimum Central Pressure of 28.00 inches or less. However, these terms are no longer used but may appear in historical materials now and then. It is important to note that when dealing with narrative descriptions of historical events, these determinations must be somewhat subjective. For the purposes of this book, these categories will be any storm causing devastating damage through either wind action or storm surge. Some authors over the years have used the word or terminology 'Extreme' very loosely to describe the worst of these events but I will refrain from using that terminology, because the word 'extreme' in my opinion would imply the 'peak' or 'maximum' of a very powerful and destructive storm but for this book I prefer to use the more acceptable and more appropriate word of 'Great' to label these very destructive and powerful storms but I will mention it when it is only necessary. It is important to note that tropical storms are named but are not assigned a Saffir-Simpson category number.

Only a few Atlantic hurricanes have made landfall with winds estimated to have reached the rarefied extreme of 200 mph, at least in gusts. These includes, the Great Labour Day Hurricane of 1935 which passed over the Florida Keys (inspiring the classic Humphrey Bogart movie *Key Largo*); Hurricane Camille, which came ashore at Pass Christian, Mississippi in 1969, and Hurricane Andrew in 1992, which struck the lower Florida peninsula. Some top wind speeds from some of these powerful Atlantic storms will never ever be known because in most cases the instruments were destroyed before they measured the worst of their respective winds. This is because very few anemometers are capable of accurately measuring the winds of a Category 5 Hurricane.

Tropical cyclones are ranked according to their maximum winds using several scales and methods depending on which area of the world they are located. These scales are provided by several bodies, including the World Meteorological Organization, the U.S. Joint Typhoon Warning Center, the National Hurricane Center in Miami, and the Bureau of Meteorology in Australia. The National Hurricane Center uses the Saffir-Simpson Scale for hurricanes in the eastern Pacific and Atlantic Basins. Australia uses a different set of tropical cyclone categories for their region. Many basins have different names of hurricane/typhoon/cyclone strength. The United States National Hurricane Center, the main governing body for hurricanes in the North Atlantic region classifies hurricanes of Category 3 and above as *Major Hurricanes*. Whereas, the U.S. Joint Typhoon Warning Center classifies typhoons with wind speeds of at least 150 mph (67 m/s or 241 km/h, equivalent to a strong Category 4 storm) as *Super Typhoons*. The term 'major hurricane' supplants the previously used term of *Great Hurricane* which was used throughout the 1950's and the 1960's.

The use of different definitions for maximum sustained winds creates additional confusion into the definitions of cyclone categories worldwide. The Saffir-Simpson Hurricane Scale is used only to describe hurricanes forming in the Atlantic Ocean and Northern Pacific Ocean east of the International Date Line. Other areas use their own classification schemes to label these storms, which are called 'cyclones' or 'typhoons' depending on the area they occur around the world. The

Wayne Neely

Australian Bureau of Meteorology uses a 1-5 scale called *Tropical Cyclone Severity Categories*. Unlike the Saffir-Simpson Scale, severity categories are based on the strongest wind gusts and not sustained winds. Severity categories are scaled somewhat lower than the Saffir-Simpson Scale. A Category 1 storm features gusts less than 126 km/h (78 mph), with a severity Category 2 Tropical Cyclone, being roughly equivalent to a Saffir-Simpson Category 1 hurricane, while gusts in a Category 5 Cyclone are at least 280 km/h (174 mph). Whereas, the U.S. Joint Typhoon Warning Center classifies West Pacific typhoons as tropical cyclones with wind speeds greater than 73 mph (118 km/h). Typhoons with wind speeds of at least 150 mph (67 m/s or 241 km/h, equivalent to a strong Category 4 hurricane) are dubbed *Super Typhoons*. In the Southwestern Indian Ocean: (1) a "tropical depression" is a tropical disturbance in which the maximum of the average wind speed is 28 to 33 knots (51 to 62 km/h); (2) a "moderate tropical storm" is a tropical disturbance in which the maximum of the average wind speed is 34 to 47 knots (63 to 88 km/h); (3) a "severe tropical storm" is a tropical disturbance in which the maximum of the average wind speed is 48 to 63 knots (89 to 117 km/h); (4) a "tropical cyclone" is a tropical disturbance in which the maximum of the average wind speed is 64 to 89 knots (118 to 165 km/h); (5) an "intense tropical cyclone" is a tropical disturbance in which the maximum of the average wind speed is 90 to 115 knots (166 to 212 km/h); and (6) a "very intense tropical cyclone" is a tropical disturbance in which the maximum of the average wind speed is greater than 115 knots (greater than 212 km/h).

THE SAFFIR-SIMPSON SCALE

Saffir-Simpson Hurricane Damage-Potential Scale							
Scale Number (Category)	Central Pressure		Winds		Storm Surge		Damage
	Millibar	Inches	Miles per hour	Knots	Feet	Meters	
1	>=980	>=28.94	74-95	64-82	4-5	-1.5	Damage mainly to trees, shrubbery, and unanchored mobile homes. Examples of storms of this intensity include: Hurricane Alice (1954), Danny (1985), Jerry (1989), Ismael (1995), Gaston (2004), and Humberto (2007).
2	965-979	28.50-28.91	96-110	83-95	6-8	-2.0-2.5	Some trees blown down; major damage to exposed mobile homes; some damage to roofs of building. Hurricanes that peaked at Category 2 intensity, and made landfall while still in that category include Carol (1954), Diana (1990), Erin (1995), Hurricane Georges(1998), Hurricane Marty and Hurricane Juan (2003).
3	945-964	17.91-28.47	111-130	96-113	9-12	-2.5-4.0	Foliage removed from trees; large trees blown down; mobile homes destroyed; some structural damage to small building. Examples of storms of this intensity include Hurricane Alma (1966), Alicia (1983), Fran (1996), Isidore (2002), Jeanne (2004), and Lane (2006).
4	920-944	27.17-27.88	131-155	114-135	13-18	-4.0-5.5	All signs blown down; extensive damage to roofs, windows, and doors; complete destruction of mobile homes; flooding inland as far as 10 kilometers (6 miles); major damage to lower floors of structures near shore.

61

Hurricanes of this intensity are extremely dangerous to populated areas. The Galveston Hurricane of 1900, the deadliest natural disaster to hit the United States, would be classified as Category 4 if it occurred today. Other examples of storms at this intensity are Hazel (1954), Betsy (1965),Carmen (1974), Iniki (1992), Luis (1995), Iris (2001), and Charley (2004).

| 5 | <920 | <27.17 | >155 | >135 | >18 | >5.5 | Severe damage to windows and doors; extensive damage to roofs of homes and industrial buildings; small buildings overturned and blown away; major damage to lower floors of all structures less than 4.5 meters (15 feet) above sea level within 500 meters of shore. Storms of this intensity can be extremely damaging. Historical examples that reached the Category 5 status and making landfall as such include the Labour Day Hurricane of 1935, the 1959 Mexico Hurricane, Camille in 1969, Gilbert in 1988, Andrew in 1992 and Dean and Felix of the 2007 Hurricane Season. |

*Courtesy of Department of Meteorology, Nassau, Bahamas.

Note : Classification by central pressure came to an end in the 1990s, and wind speed alone is now used. These estimates of the central pressure that accompany each category are for reference only. Also, these surge values are for reference only. The actual storm surge experienced will depend on offshore bathymetry and onshore terrain and construction.

The Beaufort Wind Scale

This was a scale that was developed by Sir Francis Beaufort in 1805 of the British Navy and was based solely on human observation. The Beaufort Wind Scale is now universally used around the world by seamen and lay persons alike. In 1805-06 Commander Francis Beaufort (Later Admiral Sir Francis Beaufort) devised a descriptive wind scale in an effort to standardize wind reports in ship's logs. As a result of this scale we have hurricane winds starting at 64 knots. His scale divided wind speeds into 14 Forces (later reduced to thirteen) with each Force assigned a number, a common name, and a description of the effects such a wind would have on a sailing ship. And since the worst storm an Atlantic sailor was likely to run into was a hurricane that name was applied to the top Force on the scale. During the 19th Century, with the manufacture of accurate anemometers, actual numerical values were assigned to each Force Level, but it wasn't until 1926 (with revisions in 1939 and 1946) that the International Meteorological Committee (predecessor of the World Meteorological Organization) adopted a universal scale of wind speed values. It was a progressive scale with the range of speed for Forces increasing as you go higher. Thus Force 1 is only 3 knots in range, while the Force 11 is eight knots in range. So Force 12 starts out at 64 knots (74 mph). There is nothing magical in this number, and since hurricane force winds are a rare experience, chances are the committee which decided on this number didn't do so because of any real observations during a hurricane.

Indeed the Smeaton-Rouse wind scale in 1759 pegged hurricane force at 70 knots (80 mph). Just the same, when a tropical cyclone has maximum winds of approximately these speeds we do see the mature structure (eye, eyewall, spiral rainbands) begin to form, so there is some unity with setting hurricane force in this neighbourhood. For example, if whole trees moved and resistance was felt while walking against the wind and the waves produced white foam with streaks on it then the observer would categorize it as a Gale. In the 1800's and early 1900's Bahamian fishermen used this scale almost exclusively to gauge the intensity of a storm. If a tropical storm or hurricane was in the vicinity of the Bahamas many Bahamians especially the older ones would say that 'gale was travelling.' Even in historical records in the Bahamas, many of these storms were simply referred to as 'gales' or 'severe gales' rather than hurricanes or tropical storms. This often resulted in many of these storms going unreported or under-reported because a gale in meteorological terms simply meant that these storms had sustained wind speeds of between 34 to 47 knots (39 to 54 mph) as opposed to 64 knots (74 mph) or greater for a hurricane. Although the traditional definition of a hurricane is Beaufort Force 12 winds ('air filled with foam, sea completely white with driving spray, visibility greatly reduced'), nowadays the Saffir-Simpson Scale is used, especially in this region of the world. It is a scale which is used as a quick means of informing not only meteorologists, but also the public, of the relative intensity of an approaching storm.

THE BEAUFORT WIND SCALE

Force	Wind (Knots)	WMO Classification	Appearance of Wind Effects	
			On the Water	On Land
0	Less than 1	Calm	Sea surface smooth and mirror-like	Calm, smoke rises vertically
1	1-3	Light Air	Scaly ripples, no foam crests	Smoke drift indicates wind direction, still wind vanes
2	4-6	Light Breeze	Small wavelets, crests glassy, no breaking	Wind felt on face, leaves rustle, vanes begin to move
3	7-10	Gentle Breeze	Large wavelets, crests begin to break, scattered whitecaps	Leaves and small twigs constantly moving, light flags extended
4	11-16	Moderate Breeze	Small waves 1-4 ft. becoming longer, numerous whitecaps	Dust, leaves, and loose paper lifted, small tree branches move
5	17-21	Fresh Breeze	Moderate waves 4-8 ft taking longer form, many whitecaps, some spray	Small trees in leaf begin to sway
6	22-27	Strong Breeze	Larger waves 8-13 ft, whitecaps common, more spray	Larger tree branches moving, whistling in wires
7	28-33	Near Gale	Sea heaps up, waves 13-20 ft, white foam streaks off breakers	Whole trees moving, resistance felt walking against wind
8	34-40	Gale	Moderately high (13-20 ft) waves of greater length, edges of crests begin to break into spindrift, foam blown in streaks	Whole trees in motion, resistance felt walking against wind
9	41-47	Strong Gale	High waves (20 ft), sea begins to roll, dense streaks of foam, spray may reduce visibility	Slight structural damage occurs, slate blows off roofs
10	48-55	Storm	Very high waves (20-30 ft) with overhanging crests, sea white with densely blown foam, heavy rolling, lowered visibility	Seldom experienced on land, trees broken or uprooted, "considerable structural damage"
11	56-63	Violent Storm	Exceptionally high (30-45 ft) waves, foam patches cover sea, visibility more reduced	
12	64+	Hurricane	Air filled with foam, waves over 45 ft, sea completely white with driving spray, visibility greatly reduced	

*Information Courtesy of the Department Of Meteorology, Nassau, Bahamas.

In Meteorology as in nature, the elements always try to achieve a perfect balance but thankfully they never do. For example, a hurricane's main objective is a simple one, to take heat from the equator to the poles and likewise, the cold front's objective is similarly to take cold air from the poles to the equator but thankfully none of them ever gets to achieve their objectives so they continue trying in this never ending cycle and the result is life here on Earth as we know it today. The sun is our only source of heat on a global scale. Around 70% of the Earth's surface is covered in water-mostly the oceans. Since water holds heat energy better than the land, our tropical oceans are extremely efficient in storing energy transmitted by the sun. So the heat generated by the sun and stored in the oceans is the first major ingredient for fueling hurricanes. Hurricanes form over tropical waters where the winds are light, the humidity is high in a deep layer, and the surface water temperature is warm, typically 26.5 degrees Celsius or greater over a vast area, often between latitudes 5 degrees to 25 degrees north or south of the equator. Over the tropical and subtropical North Atlantic and North Pacific oceans these conditions prevail in summer and early fall; hence, the hurricane season normally runs from June through November. At this time the water is hot enough to create atmospheric convection that casts moisture 10 miles up into the atmosphere.

These extremely hazardous weather systems occur most commonly across the low-latitude north-west Pacific and its 'downstream' land areas, where on average just over a third of the global total of such storms develop. In an average year there are approximately 80 of these Tropical Cyclones which form over warm tropical oceans with 48 of them becoming hurricanes and 20 of them becoming intense hurricanes. Many residents within this region perceive the North Atlantic Ocean basin a prolific producer of hurricanes because of the worldwide publicity these storms generate. In reality, the North Atlantic is generally only a marginal basin in terms of hurricane activity. Every tropical ocean except the South Atlantic and Southeast Pacific contains hurricanes; several of these tropical oceans produce more hurricanes annually than the North Atlantic. Hurricanes are generally a summer phenomenon, but the length of the hurricane season varies in each basin, as does the peak of activity. The Northeast Pacific averages 17%, the Northwest Pacific averages just over 33%, while the North Atlantic typically sees about 12% of the world's total of tropical cyclones, while the other regions accounts for the remaining 38%(the percentages may vary from year to year and basin to basin but these are just conservative averages) of the world total of hurricanes. Additionally, most basins use a 10-minute average of sustained wind speeds to determine intensity, as recommended by the WMO, but this is not the case in the North Atlantic and Northeastern Pacific regions, where 1-minute averages, almost always higher, are used.

Tropical Cyclone Map

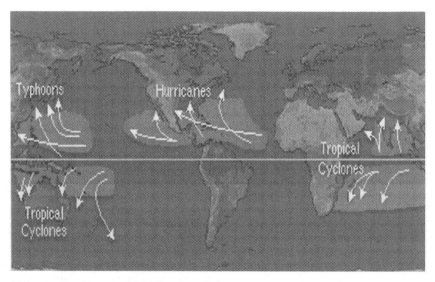

(Courtesy of www.comet.ucar.edu)

- **Northern Atlantic Ocean:** The most-studied of all tropical basins and accounts for approximately 12% of the world's total tropical cyclones. Tropical cyclone formation here varies widely from year to year, ranging from twenty eight to one per year with an average of around ten. The United States Atlantic and Gulf Coasts, Mexico, Central America, the Caribbean Islands, and Bermuda are frequently affected by storms in this basin. Venezuela, the south-east of Canada and Atlantic "Macaronesian" islands are also occasionally affected. Many of the more intense Atlantic storms are Cape Verde-Type hurricanes, which forms off the west coast of Africa near the Cape Verde Islands. On rare occasions, a hurricane can reach the European mainland such as Hurricane Lili, which dissipated over the British Isles in October of 1996, and Tropical Storm Vince in September 2005, which made landfall on the southwestern coast of Spain in the record breaking 2005 Atlantic Hurricane Season. In an average year, about 10 storm forms in this basin with 6 of them becoming hurricanes and of that total 2 of them becoming intense hurricanes. In this basin, the hurricane season runs from June 1 to November 30 with the peak of the season occurring around September 10.

- **Northeastern Pacific Ocean:** This is the second most active basin in the world accounting for approximately 17% of the world's total tropical cyclones, and the most compact (a large number of storms for such a small area of ocean). Storms that form here can affect western Mexico, Hawaii, northern Central America, and on extremely rare occasions, California and Arizona. There is no record of a hurricane ever reaching California; however, to some meteorologists, historical records in 1858 indicate that there was a storm which struck San Diego with winds of over 75 mph. In an average year, about 17 storm forms in this basin with 10 of them becoming hurricanes and of that total 5 of them becoming intense hurricanes. In this basin, the hurricane season runs from May 15 to November 30 with the peak of the season occurring around August 25.

- **Northwestern Pacific Ocean:** Tropical cyclone activity in this region frequently affects China, Japan, Hong Kong, the Philippines, and Taiwan, but also many other countries in Southeast Asia, such as Vietnam, South Korea, and parts of Indonesia, plus numerous Oceanian islands. This is by far the most active basin, accounting for over 33% of all tropical cyclone activity in the world. The coast of China sees the most land falling tropical cyclones worldwide. The Philippines receives an average 18 typhoon landings per year. Rarely does a typhoon or an extratropical storm reach northward to Siberia, Russia. In an average year, about 27 storms forms in this basin with 17 of them becoming hurricanes and of that total 8 of them becoming intense hurricanes. It is interesting to note that in this basin, the hurricane season occurs year-round with the peak of the season occurring around September 1 and the minimum occurring in February.

- **Northern Indian Ocean:** This basin is sub-divided into two areas, the Bay of Bengal and the Arabian Sea, with the Bay of Bengal dominating (5 to 6 times more activity). This basin's season has an interesting and rare double peak season; one in April and May before the onset of the monsoons, and another in October and November just after the monsoons. Tropical cyclones which form in this basin has historically cost the most lives — most notably, the November, 1970 Bhola Cyclone killed approximately 300,000 to 500,000 persons mainly in Bangladesh and coastal India from drowning. Nations affected by this basin include India, Bangladesh, Sri Lanka, Thailand, Myanmar, and Pakistan. Rarely, a tropical cyclone formed in this basin will affect the Arabian Peninsula. This basin accounts for about 12% of the worlds' total of tropical cyclones. In an average year about 5 storms forms in this basin with 2 of them becoming hurricanes and of that total 1 becoming an intense hurricane. In the North Indian basin, storms are most common from April to December 30, with peaks in May 15 and November 10.

- **Southwestern Pacific Ocean:** Tropical activity in this region largely affects Australia and Oceania. On rare occasions, tropical storms reach the vicinity of Brisbane, Australia and into New Zealand, usually during or after extratropical transition. This basin accounts for about 11% of the worlds' total of tropical cyclones. In an average year about 10 storms forms in this basin with 5 of them becoming hurricanes and of that total 2 of them becoming intense hurricanes. In this basin, the hurricane season runs from October 15 to May 1 with the peak of the season occurring around March 1.

- **Southeastern Indian Ocean:** Tropical activity in this region affects Australia and Indonesia. According to the Australian Bureau of Meteorology, the most frequently hit portion of Australia is between Exmouth and Broome in Western Australia. This basin accounts for about 7% of the worlds' total of tropical cyclones. In an average year about 7 storms forms in this basin with 3 of them becoming hurricanes and of that total 1 becoming an intense hurricane. In this basin, the hurricane season runs from October 15 to May 1 with the peak of the season occurring January 15 and February 25.

- **Southwestern Indian Ocean:** This basin is often the least understood, due to a lack of historical data. Cyclones forming here impact Madagascar, Mozambique, Mauritius, Reunion, Comoros, Tanzania, and Kenya. This basin accounts for about the remaining 8% of the worlds' total of tropical cyclones. In an average year about 10 storms forms in this basin with 5 of them becoming hurricanes and of that total 2 of them becoming intense hurricanes. In this basin, the hurricane season runs from October 15 to May 15 with the peak of the season occurring January 15 and February 20.

A hurricane is a circular, cyclonic system with a diameter anywhere from 100 to 500 miles extending upwards to heights of 40,000 to 50,000 feet. At the base of the hurricane, air is sucked in by the very low pressure at the center and then spirals inward. Once within the hurricane structure, air rises rapidly to the top and spirals outward. It is this rapid upward movement of great quantities of moisture rich air that produces the enormous amounts of rain during a hurricane. A hurricane consists of huge swirl of clouds rotating around a calm center-the eye-where warm air is sucked down. Clouds, mainly cumulonimbus clouds are arranged in bands around the eye, the tallest forming the wall of the eye. The eyewall as it is commonly called is the area of highest surface winds in the tropical cyclone. It is composed of many strong updrafts and downdrafts. The mechanisms by which the eyewall and the eye are formed are not very well understood but it is generally thought that the eye feature is a fundamental component of all rotating fluids.

Hurricanes have very strong pressure gradients with isobars that decrease in value toward the center of the very low pressure. The strong pressure gradients are the main reason behind the powerful winds of the hurricane. In addition, the resulting latent heat of condensation that is released provides the power to drive the storm. High pressure air in the upper atmosphere (above 30,000 feet/9,000m) over the storm's center also removes heat from the rising air, further driving the air cycle and the hurricane's growth. As high pressure air is sucked into the low-pressure center of the storm, wind speeds increase. At the center of the hurricane is the eye of the storm, which is an area of calm, usually warm and humid, but rainless air. Spiral rain bands and these bands of heavy convective showers that spiral inward toward the storm's center surround hurricanes. Cumulus and Cumulonimbus clouds ascend and lightning develop. Although a great deal of time, money and effort has been spent on studying the development, growth, maturity and tracks of hurricanes, much is still not known about these mysterious but powerful storms. For example, it is still not possible to predict the exact track of a hurricane with pinpoint accuracy, even though it can be tracked with weather radars and studied through reconnaissance aircrafts, computer models and weather satellites. Furthermore, meteorologists can list factors that are favorable for development of a hurricane or list pre-conditions that are necessary for the formation of a hurricane but they can't say with a degree of certainty or pin-point accuracy that in a certain situation or scenario that a hurricane will definitely develop and travel along a particular path. However numerical weather predictions models are becoming more accurate and precise in trying to predict the movement and strength of these storms and meteorologists from all around the world have come to rely on the accuracy of these models to help predict the movement and strength of these storms thereby improving the hurricane forecast of these dangerous storms.

CHAPTER FIVE

Conditions necessary for Hurricanes to form and dissipate

Although many tropical disturbances occur each year, only a select few ever develop into full-fledged hurricanes. This is because hurricanes need a very specific environment and the ideal set of ingredients to build into these powerful storms. As stated earlier, hurricanes are most numerous and strongest in late summer for most ocean basins. This is because the three favorable conditions which are, warm waters, weak wind shear and cyclonic disturbances are optimum in late summer, which seems paradoxical because the longest day is in June. However, the days are still longer than the nights until fall; therefore the water is still accumulating heat into late summer. Even though not everything is known about their formation, it is known that certain necessary ingredients or criteria are required before a weak tropical disturbance will develop into a full-fledged hurricane. A hurricane does not form instantaneously, but reaches this status in an incremental process. Hurricane formation occurs in two distinct phases. The first phase is called the *genesis stage*, and includes tropical disturbances and tropical depressions. The second phase includes the tropical storms and hurricanes, and is called the *intensification stage*. These phases are separated because many disturbances and depressions never reach tropical storm intensity, and eventually dissipate. The formation of tropical cyclones is the topic of extensive ongoing research and is still not fully understood. However, here are some general factors that are necessary to make tropical cyclone formation possible, although tropical cyclones may occasionally form without meeting these conditions.

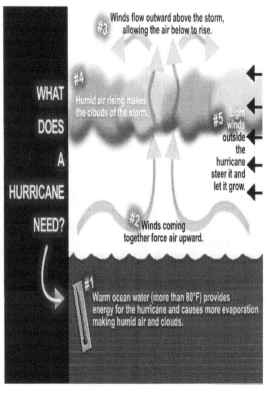

(Courtesy of comet.ucar.edu)

Among the factors that can lead to a hurricane development is a warm ocean surface temperature of 26.5 degrees Celsius or greater to a depth of about 150 feet. Although warm water is significant, it is nearly as important that the warm water be at least 150 feet deep, because hurricanes generate huge oceanic waves that mix the water to great depths. For example, Hurricanes Katrina and Rita strengthened dramatically when they crossed the Loop Current in the Gulf of Mexico. Ocean probes showed that the Loop Current's warmth extended to a depth of over 300 feet, increasing the supply of heat to the storms. As a result of this factor, hurricanes also play an important role in our food chain. As they spread death and destruction along their paths, they also stir up the sea enough to turn up much needed nutrient rich fresh food for plankton, which in turn feed fish and ultimately, people. If the warm water only covers a thin film at the top, the hurricane will bring colder water to the surface and cut off the storm's warm water energy supply, thereby weakening the system. Infact, sometimes a hurricane will kill itself when it becomes stationary for an extended period of time. Should a hurricane stop moving for several days, it can mix the ocean so much that all the warm water is replaced by cold water, and the hurricane will eventually dissipate. An example of this was Hurricane Roxanne in 1995 when it became stationary in the Bay of Campeche.

It was in 1948 that the world famous researcher in meteorology in Finland, Erik Palmen first demonstrated that hurricanes do not form over waters colder than 26.5 degrees Celsius. Inaddition, he also showed that warm water is an essential requirement for hurricanes to form and intensify. Waters of this temperature cause the warm, moist and overlying atmosphere to be unstable enough to sustain convection and thunderstorms. These conditions are needed to provide the hurricane with the continuous supply of energy that the system needs to survive and are probably the reasons why hurricanes occur most often in late summer and early fall when the air masses have their maximum humidity rather than early June to mid-July. Similarly, in the Southern Hemisphere, the peak season occurs when the sea is warmest, in January and February when the air masses have their maximum humidity and sea surface temperatures are at their peak.

Hurricanes can be thought of as heat engines, as this warm, moist air from the ocean surface begins to rise rapidly and as this warm air rises; its water vapour condenses to form storm clouds and droplets of rain. The condensation releases heat called latent heat of condensation. This latent heat warms the cool air aloft, thereby causing it to rise. This rising air is replaced by more warm, humid air from the ocean below. This cycle continues, drawing warmer, moist humid air into the developing storm and continuously moving heat from the surface to the atmosphere. This exchange of heat from the surface creates a pattern of wind that circulates around the center. This circulation is similar to that of water going down a drain. At this point in the development of the hurricane there is now a chain reaction in progress, or what meteorologists call a *Feedback Mechanism*.

Another factor is that converging winds must move in different directions and run into each other. Converging winds at the surface collide and push warm, moist air upward. This rising air reinforces the air that is already rising from the surface, so that the circulation and wind speeds of the storm increase. In the meantime, strong winds blowing at uniform speeds at higher altitudes (up to 30,000 ft/ 9,000 m or greater) help remove the rising hot air from the storm's center, maintaining a continual movement of warm air from the surface and keeping the storm organized. If the high-altitude winds do not blow at the same speed at all levels-if wind shear is present-the storm loses organization and weakens. When wind shear is high, the convection in a cyclone or disturbance will be disrupted, blowing the system apart.

Another key parameter for hurricane formation is the presence of the Coriolis force, which must be great enough to support the rapid spiraling of the hurricane. The earth's rotation sets up an apparent force called the Coriolis force which pulls the winds to the right of motion in the Northern Hemisphere (and to the left in the Southern Hemisphere). So when a low pressure starts to form north or south of the Equator, the surface winds will flow inward trying to fill in the low and will be deflected to the right and a counter-clockwise rotation will be initiated in the Northern Hemisphere. Hurricanes in the Northern Hemisphere rotate counterclockwise (west to east) and move through the ocean clockwise (east to west). In the Southern Hemisphere, hurricanes rotate clockwise (east to west) and move counterclockwise (west to east). These motions, known as the Coriolis force, are caused by the Earth's rotation. As stated earlier, air flowing toward or away from the Equator invariably follows a curved path that swings it to the right of motion in the Northern Hemisphere and to the left of motion in the Southern Hemisphere. The reason for this was discovered in 1835 by a mathematician and mechanical engineer Gustave-Gaspard de Coriolis. It occurs because the Earth is rotating counterclockwise on it axis, so as air moves across the surface itself is also moving beneath it but at a different speed. The magnitude of the Coriolis force depends on the latitude, and the speed of the moving air. The Coriolis force is greatest at the poles and weakest at the Equator. Because of this factor, hurricanes neither develop nor survive in the Equatorial zone between approximately 5 degrees north or south of the Equator. The minimum distance is 310 miles or about 5 degrees north and south of the Equator. Below 5 degrees north or south of the Equator, the force of the Earth's rotation (Coriolis force) is too weak to allow the winds to begin to rotate. This allows the Coriolis force to deflect winds blowing towards the low pressure center, causing a circulation. One rare exception to the lack of tropical cyclones near the Equator was Typhoon Vamei which formed near Singapore on December 27, 2001. Since tropical cyclone observations started in 1886 in the North Atlantic and 1945 in the western North Pacific, the previous recorded lowest latitude for a tropical cyclone was 3.3°N for Typhoon Sarah in 1956. With its circulation center at 1.5°N Typhoon Vamei's circulation was on both sides of the Equator. U.S. Naval ships reported maximum sustained surface winds of 87 mph and winds gusts of up to 120 mph.

Another factor that is needed is a pre-existing disturbance such as an easterly wave or a monsoon trough and in fact; they will not develop without the driving force of such a disturbance. A substantial amount of large scale spin must be made available from these pre-existing disturbances to start the initial process of a hurricane development. With the warm oceans during the summer months, all we really need is something to come along and take advantage of the situation. Often times, Africa is the source of the 'spark' that gets the fire going. Every few days, a tropical wave migrates westward off the coast of Africa-near the Cape Verde Islands. Nearly 100 of these concentrated areas of lower pressure traverse the Atlantic each hurricane season. Only a small portion of them, perhaps 10 to 15 a year, ever become anything more than a large area of thunderstorms over the oceans. The majority of the western hemisphere's worst hurricanes can be traced back to a tropical wave that originated over Africa. Most Atlantic Ocean hurricanes originate near the Cape Verde Islands just off Africa's west coast, where the trade winds of the northern and southern hemispheres meet and cause tropical disturbances. This is not to say that every tropical wave that develops will become a historic hurricane, but these so called 'Cape Verde' storms always need to be watched. Over the long term, these

Cape Verde storms account for about 85 percent of the Atlantic's major hurricanes.

Another factor that influences the formation of these powerful storms is light winds in the upper atmosphere (low vertical shear). One key ingredient is the lack of strong upper level winds blowing in the opposite direction that a fledgling tropical cyclone is moving, in other words, low vertical shear. Hurricane formation also necessitates relatively calm winds throughout the atmosphere. Too much wind shear can quickly tear a hurricane apart. A tropical storm and especially a hurricane need to be able to stack up its thunderstorms neatly around the center or eye of the storm. If strong winds blow the tops of the thunderstorms then there is little chance for the system to strengthen because its breathing mechanism is disrupted when the strong upper level winds blow the tops of these thunderstorms inhibiting their growth. Strong winds tend to disrupt the organized pattern of convection and disperse the heat, which is necessary for the growth of the storm. In fact, many potential major hurricanes have met their demise because of strong winds (shear) imposing on the system. Most of the time, the shear or strong upper level winds will approach the storm from the southwest or west. So, a tropical storm or hurricane moving westward and head-on into these strong winds and will easily weaken or dissipate because of the shearing on the system. Because of this and other factors, most of these storms die out within hours or days of their birth. Only about one out of ten grows into a hurricane. This situation of strong winds in the upper atmosphere typically occurs over the tropical Atlantic during a major El Niño event. As a result, during El Niño there are usually fewer Atlantic hurricanes than normal. However, the warmer waters of El Niño in the Northern tropical Pacific favor the development of hurricanes in that region. During the cold water episode in the tropical Pacific (known as La Niña), winds in the upper atmosphere over the tropical Atlantic usually weaken and become easterly-a condition that favours hurricane development.

Just as African thunderstorm complexes are the initiating entities for tropical waves, fronts and other extra-tropical systems can initiate tropical disturbances as well. If one of these systems is going to trigger tropical cyclone development, it usually happens early or late in the hurricane season, when these northern weather systems can move much closer within the tropical latitudes. For example, when a front moves south and stalls in the Gulf of Mexico, it normally brings cool, dry air that initially inhibits any tropical cyclone development; however, the front can then become the triggering disturbance if the weather pattern in the overall atmosphere is conducive to it. In addition, on rare occasions, an upper-level extratropical low pressure system that moves out over the warm ocean can be the trigger mechanism for these storms to form. The low can generate thunderstorms. The air that rises in those thunderstorm cells is warm and humid, which in turn warms the surrounding atmosphere. Sometimes, over time, a tropical cyclone will form; an example of this was Hurricane Katrina in 2005 which formed from an upper level low just east of the Bahamas.

Hurricanes are 'steered' by the prevailing wind currents that surround the storm from the surface to 50,000 feet or more. The storms move in the direction of these currents and with their average speed. The movement of a hurricane affects the speed of the winds that circulate about the center. On one side of the storm, where the circulating winds and the entire storm are moving in the same direction, the wind speed is increased by the forward movement of the storm. On the opposite side of the storm, the circulating wind speed is decreased by the forward motion. In the Northern Hemisphere, the right side of a hurricane, looking in the direction in which it is moving, has the higher wind speeds and thus is the more dangerous part of the storm. The average tropical cyclone moves from east to west in the tropical trade winds that blow near the equator. When a storm starts to move northward, it exchanges easterly winds for the westerly winds that dominate the temperate region. When the steering winds are strong, it is easier to predict where a hurricane will go but when the steering winds are weak, the storm seems to take a mind of its own, following an erratic path that makes forecasting its movement very difficult.

The major steering winds which influences most Atlantic hurricanes is an area of high pressure known as the Bermuda High. This high pressure dome is over the eastern Atlantic Ocean in the winter, but shifts westward during the summer months. The clockwise rotation of air associated with high pressure zones is the driving force that causes many hurricanes to deviate from their east-to-west movement and start northward. Sometimes this is favorable where this keeps the hurricane offshore over the open oceans, and at other times, hurricanes south of the U.S. are steered northward directly towards the coastline. Weather patterns that carry a hurricane are a bit like a highway. The Bermuda High, a settled high-pressure area that swells and contracts seasonally, dominates wind patterns over the north Atlantic and determines the tracks of Atlantic hurricanes as they move west. In winter, when temperatures are low, the high is small; but July through September, when water temperatures are much warmer, it expands over the entire center of the North Atlantic. This area of high pressure functions like a barrier wall that low-pressure tropical cyclones cannot penetrate. So they skirt west in the Atlantic along its southern edge and travel around its western edge to the Caribbean or the waters just north of it. Then, as they approach the coast of the United States, they begin to be influenced by the weather systems that move across the country and out to sea. They turn toward the north. Whether they will ease to the northwest, or curve north, or continue curling northeast until they are guided into the North Atlantic's cooler waters is the crucial question that hurricane forecasters must answer hours or often days in advance of the approaching storm. This information is critical because better forecast of hurricane tracks and intensity could reduce deaths and property damage by enabling officials to issue more timely and accurate warnings and evacuation orders. For example, the impact of the 2005 Atlantic hurricane season for the region was widespread and ruinous with at least 2,280 deaths and record damages of over $128 billion USD.

A Tropical Cyclone will progress through a series of stages from birth to dissipation. First, it begins as a tropical disturbance which is a large area of organized thunderstorms that maintains its' identity for more than 24 hours. If the area of thunderstorms organizes so that a definite rotation develops and winds become strong enough, the system is upgraded to a tropical depression. At this point, a low pressure center exists (there is at least one closed isobar and the system is then given an assigned number). If the winds continue to increase to 34 knots, the system becomes a tropical storm and is given an assigned name. The system now has several closed isobars at the surface. The storm becomes more organized and the circulation around the center of the storm intensifies. As surface pressure continues to drop, the storm becomes a hurricane when wind speed reaches 64 knots. An eye develops corresponding to the lowest atmospheric pressure near the center of the storm with spiral rain bands rotating around it. The major factors that cause the development of storms in the Atlantic Ocean are, ocean temperature, atmospheric pressure, and the Gulf Stream and wind currents. The first stage in a storm development begins in a long, narrow region of low pressure that occurs in ocean winds. These areas are called *The Trade Winds*. This area of low pressure eventually grows into a tropical depression.

When a storm passes over cooler waters it will begin to dissipate as its' main energy source, the warm ocean is no longer there. When a hurricane moves over colder waters, expansional cooling dominates, which stabilizes the atmosphere; the thunderstorms that feeds the hurricane disintegrate; and the hurricane weakens. When a hurricane moves over land, the weakening occurs even faster because not only has the surface heat flux been lost but so has the moisture source for cloud formation. Land also has more friction than water, which weakens landfalling hurricanes, but this influence is minimal compared to the loss of heat and moisture flux. In contrast to their terrific wind speeds, these storms themselves move very slowly, averaging 10 to 12 miles per hour and infact, they on rare occasions may even remain stationary for a day or so. The slower they pass over a country or area, the longer they have to inflict damage there. The tracks of these storms are often very unpredictable however; most of these storms originating over the eastern Atlantic travel in a westerly direction into the Caribbean and then curve northwest to northwards. Those developing over the other two centers of origin-the southern Caribbean and the Gulf of Mexico usually travel northwards from the onset.

Hurricanes don't usually last very long over land for two main reasons. First their source of moisture (hence their energy source) is cut-off and their 'breathing' mechanism is disrupted. Secondly, it is thought that friction with the land surface produces a drag on the whole system. What this means is that friction will slow down the movement of the storm, disrupt the low level inflow into the hurricane, and weaken the deep convection causing the central pressure to rise. A hurricane will begin to dissipate when the conditions for tropical cyclone formation are taken away. A tropical cyclone can weaken or cease to have tropical characteristics in several ways. First, if the system moves over land, thus depriving it of the warm water it needs to power itself, and quickly loses strength. Most strong storms lose their strength very quickly after landfall and become just disorganized areas of low pressure within a day or two. There is, however, a chance they could regenerate if they manage to get back over open warm waters. If a storm remains over a mountain for even a short time, it can rapidly lose its structure. However, many storm fatalities occur in mountainous terrain, as the dying storm unleashes torrential rainfall which can lead to deadly flash floods and mudslides.

Second, if it remains in the same area of ocean for too long, drawing heat off of the ocean surface until it becomes too cool to support the storm. Without warm surface water, the storm cannot survive. Third, if the system experiences strong upper level wind shear thereby causing the convection to lose direction and the heat engine to break down. In the upper atmosphere, there must be a high-level anticyclone to disperse the rising air and thereby drawing more air from below. The anticyclone may weaken, or drift away, or the hurricane may move from beneath it. Fourth, the system can be weak enough to be consumed by another area of low pressure, disrupting it and joining to become a large area of non-cyclonic thunderstorms. Finally, if the system enters colder waters it will greatly affect the intensity and characteristics of the storm. This does not necessarily mean the death of the storm, but the storm will lose its tropical characteristics and derive its primary energy from a different source other than latent heat of condensation but through baroclinic processes. These storms are often referred to as *Extratropical Cyclones.* Tropical cyclones often transform into extratropical cyclones at the end of their tropical existence, usually between 30° and 40° latitude, where there is sufficient forcing from upper-level troughs or shortwaves riding the Westerlies for the process of extratropical transition to begin. The low pressure system eventually loses its warm core and becomes a cold-core system. Even after a tropical cyclone is said to be extratropical or dissipated, it can still have tropical storm force (or occasionally hurricane force) winds and drop several inches of rainfall. When a tropical cyclone reaches higher latitudes or passes over land, it may merge with weather fronts or develop into a frontal cyclone, as stated earlier are also called extratropical cyclone. In the Atlantic Ocean, such tropical-derived cyclones of higher latitudes can be violent and may occasionally remain at hurricane-force wind speeds when they reach Europe as European windstorms, such as the extratropical remnants of Hurricane Iris in 1995.

The North Atlantic hurricane season occurs during the months of June 1st through November 30th, with late August and September generally having the greatest number of storms and the peak of the hurricane season occurs on the 10th of September. In other parts of the world, such as the western Pacific, hurricanes can occur almost year round. Infact, a Pacific typhoon, named Cobra, just off the coast of Luzon in the Philippines, inflicted great damage on the United States Navy during the final year of World War II. In just a matter of hours during the month of December of 1944, it claimed 3 destroyers, 146 aircrafts, and the lives of 790 sailors. The total number of hurricanes or tropical storms shows great variation from year to year. In fact, certain past multi-decadal periods have significantly greater number of hurricanes or stronger hurricane cycles than others.

The direction of movement relative to the coastline has a large bearing on its added destructive forces, with the perpendicular landfall being the most dangerous situation. This is because the wind field in a hurricane is typically asymmetric, the strongest winds generally being within the right-front quadrant of the storm as viewed in the direction of movement and with the forward speed added to the wind speed. The right-front quadrant is the side of the wind field that produces the strongest storm surge, which is the most destructive part of the hurricane. A storm surge, also called a hurricane surge, is the abnormal rise in sea level accompanying a tropical cyclone. The height of the storm surge is the difference between the observed level of the sea surface and its level in the absence of the storm. In other words, the storm surge is estimated by subtracting the normal or astronomical tide from the observed or estimated storm tide. Surge heights vary considerably and result from a combination of direct winds and atmospheric pressure. Additional factors are, water transported by waves, swells, rainfall, and shoreline layout or configuration, bottom topography, and tide height at the time the storm hits the coast. An example of an extreme storm surge occurred during the passage of Hurricane Katrina in late August of 2005. It had a storm surge of over 30 feet in Louisiana in the United States. In a hurricane, the most damaging effects are caused by the storm surge, however the strong winds, rainfall, battering waves and flooding also plays a major role in the destruction process of a hurricane.

CHAPTER SIX

The Sponging Industry and The Hurricanes of 1926

Sketches of the various stages within the Sponging Industry (from the harvesting of the sponges to the shipping of the sponges) here in the Bahamas (Courtesy of the Department of Archives Nassau, Bahamas).

Blockade Running in the Bahamas during the American Civil War was extremely profitable and supplemented income made by the fairly lucrative Wrecking and Salvaging Industry. As well travelled routes passed through or near to the Bahamas, its waters, lurking with many dangers, became an ideal area for salvaging shipwrecks. Thus, an only slightly productive archipelago acquired another means of support well suited to a people long accustomed to roving and predatory ways. The occupation of salvaging was known as 'wrecking'; however, two other terms were also once in common use, namely 'raking' and 'wracking.' To 'go a raking' meant to search with diligence and care while to 'go a wracking' derived its meaning from 'wrack,' a foundered ship. The passage through the Bahamas was termed the most dangerous area of any country along the Atlantic coast.

Over 500 years since it was discovered by Christopher Columbus in 1492, the Bahamian reefs have claimed thousands of ships and lives. In the 1850's, the heyday of the wreckers, ships were piling up on the Bahamian reefs at the rate of nearly one a week. Salvaging these wrecks was highly competitive, hazardous gamble of lives, limbs, and vessels of the wreckers against an elusive gain. In the age of sail, the Bahamas became the most favored passage for shipping traffic between ports in the western Caribbean and the Gulf of Mexico and ports along the Atlantic east coast and in Europe. Nassau was centrally located among the islands for wrecking and salvaging and had easy access to the several frequently traversed channels through and bordering the Bahamas. Because of the swift flowing currents, unpredictable counter currents, calms in summer, hurricanes in fall, gales in winter, and inaccurate navigational charts, the passage through the Bahamas made this popular shipping route one of the most dangerous shipping routes in this region and ideally suited for the wrecking and salvaging industry. However, by the 1880s, such opportunistic maritime activities were on the verge of decline. At the end of the 19th Century things were definitely changing, the shipping industry had become more streamlined with a switch from sail to steam power, fewer ports of call, and new and improved navigational charts.

The sea itself was by no means unproductive, yet little of its abundance could be exported with ease. The exceptions were turtle shells, ambergris, and an occasional pearl. On land, the sisal industry developed in the late 1880's and 1890's also became an important industry in the Bahamas. Industrialists established sisal companies such as the Munroe Fibre Company, Sisal Fibre Company and the Bahamas Fibre Company on Andros, Grand Bahama, Abaco and a few other islands. The first plants of the sisal tree from which rope was made were introduced by the Colonial Secretary C.R. Nesbitt in 1845. It reached its peak in the late 1800's and the early 1900's where well over 400 tons of sisal was exported annually. Unfortunately, the acquisition of the Philippine Islands by the United States led to the decline of the Bahamian sisal industry. The Philippines had privileged access to the American market and the Bahamas was unable to compete. The large Bahamian estates, many of them badly located on unsuitable and nutrient lacking soils with an insufficient labour force, fell into bankruptcy and the mills closed. Produced uneconomically on smallholdings and beaten crudely by hand in salt water, the quality and price of the Bahamian Fibre declined even further. The government ordinances supervising the production and grading the sisal became a dead letter and the Bahamian product became far inferior to those grown in vast quantities in the Philippines, India and East Africa. By the 1920s, the sisal industry in the Bahamas was dead. Worldwide, by the late 1930's it came to an end with the introduction of synthetic nylon which was much cheaper to produce and more versatile than the natural sisal plant.

In December 1919, *The Volstead Act*, was introduced in the United States as a wartime measure and was passed by the United States Congress as the Eighteenth Amendment of the Constitution. This ill-fated and ill-advised law, which forbade a large proportion of otherwise innocent and law abiding American Citizens into a life of crime, because by this law it was illegal to manufacture, sell or import intoxicating liquors. For the Bahamas it was a blessing in disguised. 'Bootlegging' between 1920 and 1933 became a rich and prosperous industry, in the swashbuckling tradition of privateering, wrecking and running the blockade. The Bahamas, with its ideal location, being in such a close proximately to the United States, with the nearest land area of only less than fifty miles from the American coast, was an obvious and natural base for smuggling of liquor into the alcohol thirsty United States. Initially, however, the island economy lacked the necessary complex organization for such a venture, and it was by no means certain that the authorities have would allow or turn a compliant eye to such a dubious export trade. Exports for 1920 and 1921 did not exceed by much the steady average of about £30,000 for the previous decade. It was not until the end of 1921 that it became obvious that the Bahamas Government would not actively support the United States Excise Service.

More than twenty giant liquor concerns sprang up in Nassau almost overnight to cater to this illegal trade and speedy motor-boats began to sneak from Grand Bahama and Bimini across the Gulf Stream to the Florida coast, and infact, some chartered schooners even made longer trips to as far north as 'Rum Row' off New York, Boston and Philadelphia. Inaddition, in some cases planes were used, taking off from Bimini and landing in some secluded lake deep into the Everglades of Florida to off load their valuable goods. Re-exports of liquor in 1922 were valued at £1,612,122, an increase of tenfold over the figures for 1921. The total for 1923 was £1,591,538 and the average for the ten years between 1922 and 1932 was well over half a million pounds. The hard-pressed for cash Bahamian Government was one of the happiest profiteers from the Prohibition era. This was because the Bahamas Customs Act of 1919 had laid comparatively heavy duties upon imported liquor and, with the enormous increase in the trade, revenue rose proportionately. For example, Customs revenue sky-rocketed from £103,492 in 1919 to £313,949 in 1921 and £640,798 in 1923, and this was only a small portion of the wealth that flooded into Nassau.

As a result of this trade, many new Bahamian infrastructures were built or upgraded, Civil Servants got a much needed raise, many new and expensive cars were arriving into the capital on a weekly basis, new and modernized large expensive houses and hotels were being built at an alarming rate and for the first time Nassau was gaining the appearance of a modern city, while losing little of its 'old colonial charm.' This prosperous era however, would not last forever and it vanished almost as swiftly as it had arrived. The world-wide slump (also known as 'the Great Depression') brought little new investments into the Bahamas during this time and by the early to mid-nineteen thirties this bootlegging era came to an end. When these three hurricanes struck, they decimated these warehouses used to store these barrels of liquor. Infact, a longtime Nassau resident, Mr. H. Johnson, later reported that as much as 90% of these rum warehouses were blown away in the *Nassau Hurricane of 1926*, and the few remaining warehouses which survived this storm were simply blown away in the second hurricane. A factor which he said was attributed to God's displeasure of the illegal alcoholic trade in the Bahamas at the time. *"As soon as they were built back up, another hurricane struck each year from the 1926 hurricane season all the way through to the 1936 hurricane season and destroyed those warehouses again, putting their owners in far greater debt than they had been the year before"* he said.

Many Bahamian men accustomed to making their living on boats or on land turned their attention from sisal production more fully to marine resource extraction, in particular the sea sponge industry. In 1926, farming, fishing, sponging, and to a much lesser extent bootlegging were the four main ways most Bahamians supported their families. Throughout the 17th and 18th centuries, products from the sea such as, conch shells, turtle shells, and turtle meat had been exported from the Bahamas but on a much lesser scale, however, it was sponging that was the first industry which was profitable enough to employ thousands of men for nearly a century. From 1841 to 1910 exports grew exponentially, reaching a peak of 1.5 million metric tons. The sponging industry began as early as 1841 when a Frenchman named M. Gustave Renouard was ship wrecked here in the Bahamas. He exported parcels of prized Bahamian sponges to Paris, where the varieties from 'wool' to 'velvet' found in the Bahamas was highly favoured over sponges from the Mediterranean(prior to this time, sponges were imported from the Mediterranean). The export trade was greatly expanded by Mr. Edward Brown, Renouard's son-in-law, and the Great Bahama Bank was opened up to full scale development. This large extensive area offshore from the island of Andros was called 'The Mud' and was about 140 miles long and 10 to 40 miles wide and was one of the greatest sponge beds in the world. The seabed was shallow and the water very clear enabling the sponge fishermen to easily harvest the sponges from the seabed with little effort or diving equipment as compared to other areas of the world. This trade eventually encompassed, Jamaica, Honduras, Nicaragua, and Mexico, however, the Bahamas, Cuba, and Florida were always the largest producers.

Workers at a sponge house in Nassau cleaning and clipping sponges (Courtesy of Jonathon Ramsey Balmain Antiques)

Before the Second World War, well over 47 million pounds of live sponges were harvested annually from our waters and employed thousands of people and hundreds of ships here in the Bahamas. Although marine sponges have been a highly sought after product since ancient times, industrialization created a growing worldwide demand for them in cleaning, ceramics, shoe-finishing, and printing industries in addition to household, bathing, and medical uses, which generated a lucrative international trade. As Bahamian sponges became highly favored on the world market, further beds were opened on the Little Bahama Bank, off southern Eleuthera and in Acklins. A Sponge Exchange was opened in Nassau and many Greeks familiar with the trade emigrated from Greece, bringing with them their families, language, religion and customs, which are still proudly maintained in the Bahamas today. Infact, the Vouvalis Company brought in the first Greek sponge experts in 1887. Vouvalis established his sponge warehouse on West Bay Street between the now Mayfair Hotel and the now defunct Ocean Spray Restaurant and Hotel. He then sent Aristide

Daminanos and his brother George here to manage his business. The Damianos brothers would eventually sent up their own business at the top of Fredrick Street steps. In the 1920s Christodoulos Esfakis established an operation on Market Street and many other Greeks sponge merchants opened similar operations in or near the Downtown area. James Mosko was brought in to rebuild the Vouvalis operation after the *Nassau Hurricane of 1926* devastated his sponge warehouse and his son would eventually established Mosko's Construction Company. Over time the Greeks were more or less assimilated, and the second, third and fourth generations still now form a close-knit community of more than 300 professionals and business owners scattered throughout the Bahamas.

In 1901, at the peak of the Bahamian sponge industry, there were 265 schooners of up to 43 tons burden, 322 sloops of up to 16 tons and 2,808 open boats engaged in sponging. It was 5,967 men and boys, or roughly one-third of the available labour force, were employed in this trade. The sponge fishermen were all Bahamians; it was illegal for non-Bahamians to engage directly in harvesting the sponge. Before a vessel went out on a sponge fishing trip, the 'outfitter' as he was called, furnished the consumable goods and services to the sponge fishermen. This was done entirely on a credit basis and he was not reimbursed until the catch was marketed at the end of the voyage. The goods were booked at cost, plus a considerable margin of profit. These 'personal advances' to members of the crew, often including food for their families, were recovered at high rates of interest, making it almost impossible for the sponge fishermen to make any economic profit. Often he was left in debt seldom breaking even. Very rarely did a fisherman made even three hundred dollars a year. The outfitters, however, felt justified in their high rates, as they themselves took considerable risks. Their vessels were not insured and there were risks of bad weather such as, hurricanes which affected the size of the catch, mismanagement and unscrupulous behavior on the part of the crew, theft from kraals, and damage to the catch during transit to Nassau.

Workers clipping sponges at a sponge warehouse in Nassau, Bahamas (Courtesy of the Department of Archives, Nassau, Bahamas).

The sponging trips usually lasted from five to eight weeks. Each sponging schooner or sloop carried about five dinghies which were used for gathering the sponge. The value of the catch was almost wholly dependent upon the skill of the fishermen and the fickled luck of the Bahamian weather. At the sponge beds, the water was very clear and shallow only between eight to twenty four feet deep making it very easy to harvest the sponges. Once the sponges were harvested they would be placed in large storage and cleaning containments called 'kraals' filled with salt water which allowed the animal matter to die because the sponge is really the skeleton of a soft coral. The sponge 'kraal', was an enclosed pen, fenced in by sticks of wood or mangrove to allow a free circulation of the ebb and tidal flow of the sea water. Here, the sponges were soaked and washed for four to six days by the action of the sea water. The sponge vessels visited the kraal once a week to land the sponge load. The sponges were then taken out and beaten with sticks until the decayed outer coverings had been entirely removed. After the sponges were beaten and gelatinous tissue removed, they were scraped to remove excess coral, sand or rock. After the dead animal was washed out and they would then be clipped, graded and strung in the boat rigging to dry.

They then took the sponges to Nassau where the sponges were sold by auction to the Greeks merchants who were agents for houses in New York, London and Paris. Once at the exchange, men and women, usually women sat on boxes clipping the sponge using sheep-shearing shears. During the clipping of the sponges the women often smoked their clay tobacco pipes and sang spirituals and other religious hymns to keep themselves occupied. The roots were cut off, and the sponges trimmed, retaining the symmetry of the sponge as much as possible. Once trimmed, and the pieces of rock removed, the sponges were thrown into large native straw baskets. A full basket was removed and handed over to the 'sorters' who trimmed the sponges further if necessary, and examined them for elasticity, size and texture. They were then placed in pens, packaged and prepared for shipping.

Workers clipping sponges and preparing the sponges for export at a sponge warehouse in Nassau, Bahamas (Courtesy of the Department of Archives, Nassau, Bahamas).

Until the disastrous visitation of a microscopic fungus which devastated up to about 90 percent of all West Atlantic sponges and all the Bahamian 'velvet' variety in November and December of 1938, sponge continued to be the major item in the Bahamian economy. In December 1938, spongers instead of pulling up intact sponges, hooks came to the surface with only slivers and strings and the rest of the sponge skeleton at the bottom of the seafloor had disintegrated due to this deadly fungus. Within two months from the time it was first observed, the disease (fatal only to sponge) had reached epidemic proportions and had wiped out ninety-nine percent of the sponge; as a result, thousands of Bahamians lost their livelihood because of this disaster. The sponge disease appeared in Florida about three months after it had struck the beds in the Bahamas. It was believed to have been transmitted to the Florida sponge beds by means of the ocean currents. In addition to the fungus which destroyed the sponge beds, hurricanes, the introduction of synthetic sponges and over sponging also led to a great decline in the trade. Sea sponge is a very slow growing sea animal and whenever the sponges were harvested; the entire sponge was removed from the sea bottom thereby not allowing re-growth by the sponge. In addition, the sponges in the area of the Mud was a finite resource so gradually, the sponges in the late 1920's and early 1930's were already starting to see a drastic decline in the industry even before the fungus attacked the sponges. As a result of this decline, the demand for sponge at this time was high, and so consequently the price, due to the scarcity of it. Up to 1925 it must have seemed that sponge-fishing would endure forever and get better and better. At that time, the total income earned by sponge fishermen soared to over £200,000, and the local song, *'Sponger Money Never Done,'* commemorated both the durability and prosperity of the sponge trade.

The series of severe hurricanes, which began in 1926, did much damage to the sponge beds, but apart from this, there developed unmistakable evidence of over sponging. The three hurricanes in 1926(plus a tropical storm) and a series of hurricanes in the late 1920's and 1930's devastated the sponge beds. In addition, these hurricanes especially, the three powerful hurricanes in 1926, one in 1929 and a series of powerful hurricanes in the 1930's (1933 had four hurricanes and one tropical storm which hit the Bahamas) destroyed the sponging infrastructure such as the warehouses and the sponging schooners and sloops. For example, H. & F. Pritchard were among the most important Bahamian sponge merchants, and in 1899 a powerful hurricane struck the Bahamas and totally destroyed both their ships and the sponges. Another hurricane struck the Bahamas in 1883 totally wiping out the sponge beds in Eleuthera. After the three hurricanes of 1926, the sponge industry was crippled and sponge cultivation diminished considerably in spite of efforts on the part of sponge businessmen Mr. H.C. Christie, father of the late Sir Harold Christie, to encourage artificial sponge cultivation.

Although sponge planting produced encouraging results, output still diminished considerably, largely due to over-sponging of the beds, and the practice of hooking the younger, and not-quite matured sponges. This abuse led to the Agricultural and Marine Products Board Sponge Amendment Rules of 1937 which forbade the fishing of sponge under a certain size and imposed a closed season. In 1929, a powerful and deadly hurricane known as *'The Great Bahamas Hurricane of 1929'* devastated the sponging infrastructures in Nassau and wiped out many of the sponging schooners on some of the Family Islands, especially on the islands of Andros, Eleuthera and Abaco, further crippling the industry. Infact, from 1926 to 1940 at least two storms a year devastated the Bahamas and the sponge beds (except for 1930 when there was none and 1931 when there was only one). So these storms changed the economy of the Bahamas and it can be argued that hurricanes played a minor if not a major role in the decline in the sponging industry.

The late great George Symonette in the front of his piano

The optimism of Bahamian sponge fishermen about the sustained growth of sponging was reflected in the local song, ***"Sponger Money Never Done."*** A popular version sung by the late great Bahamian folklore artist George Symonette. George Symonette made this song famous on an album called *'George Symonette, Bahamian Troubadour: "Calypso" and the Native Bahamian Rhythms.'* On this album, it featured the popular songs called *'Delia Gone,' 'Sponger Money'* and *'Peas N Rice.'* His other popular Bahamian songs were, *'Don't touch me tomato,' 'Nassau Samba (when you come to little Nassau),' 'No Lazy Man (Did you see Uncle Lou when he fall in the well),' 'Jones Oh Jones,'* and *'See how it flies (Run ma mama come see da crow).'* Mention any of these popular Bahamian folk songs by George Symonette and most Bahamians will not only immediately recognize them but will perhaps give you a few words from each of them or if you are lucky enough, they may even sing you a chorus. However his most popular song was *"Sponger Money*

Never Done" based on life and money made in the Sponging Industry during its' heyday. As the song goes, in those days it seemed as if the sponger money really never done. His unique style no doubt helped earn him the much deserved title as *"King of Goombay."* George was a star attraction in Nassau where he delighted both locals and tourists with his easy going personality and sharp wit. He was one of the original performers in the region to capture the native sound of the Bahamas which continues to play on stereos all over the world today.

SPONGER MONEY NEVER DONE

Go gal go, go gal go, gal ya gat sponger money,
sponger money never done ya gat sponger money,
sponger money is a lotta fun ya gat sponger money,
sing gal sing, sing gal sing ya gat sponger money,

Laugh gal laugh, laugh gal laugh ya gat sponger money
Ya gat Bay Street money, Bay Street money is a lot of fun
ya gat Bay Street money, Bay Street money is a lot of fun
ya gat Bay Street money
sing gal sing, sing gal sing ya gat sponger money,

Laugh gal laugh, laugh gal laugh ya gat sponger money
Ya gat straw work money, straw work money is a lot of fun
ya gat straw work money, straw work money is a lot of fun
ya gat straw work money
sing gal sing, sing gal sing ya gat sponger money,

Laugh gal laugh, laugh gal laugh ya gat sponger money
Ya gat tomato money, tomato money is a lot of fun
ya gat tomato money, tomato money is a lot of fun
ya gat Tomato money
sing gal sing, sing gal sing ya gat sponger money,

Laugh gal laugh, laugh gal laugh ya gat sponger money
Ya gat tourist money, tourist money is a lot of fun
ya gat tourist money, tourist money is a lot of fun
ya gat tourist money
sing gal sing, sing gal sing ya gat sponger money,

Laugh gal laugh, laugh gal laugh ya gat sponger money
sailor money never done ya gat sailor money, sailor
money is a lot of fun ya gat sailor money,
sing gal sing, sing gal sing ya gat sponger money,

Go gal go, go gal go, gal ya gat sponger money,
sponger money never done ya gat sponger money,
sponger money is a lot of fun ya gat sponger money,
sponger money never done ya gat sponger money,
sponger money is a lot of fun ya gat sponger money,

When the first signs of disease appeared in 1938, the sponge population was already severely stressed from over-sponging and only a few reserve populations remained. This disease ultimately reduced the remaining commercial sponge populations by up to 99%. Over sponging, the introduction of synthetic sponges, hurricanes and sponge disease caused a drastic decline in the sponging industry in the 1930s. By the 1940s, the economic situation in the Bahamas was again so desperate that the British (the Bahamas was still a colony of England at the time) and Bahamian officials began in earnest to develop export and subsistence fisheries to support the local population. In 1935, the Bahamas export in sponges ranked third in quantity but seventh in value. Sponge output had been diminishing for a little while due to over-sponging of the beds. For example, the total weight of the sponge exported in 1940 was 70,848lbs, and the total value was 13,986 ($41,958) as compared to 164,000 ($492,000) in 1917. This shows the tremendous decline in the total sponge exports brought about by over sponging and the disease of 1938. The low output was also attributed to a poorer quality of sponge being fished from the beds. Probably with diminishing output, the sponge fishermen were not conscientious of the quality of the sponges they removed.

The sponging industry received a devastating blow from these three hurricanes in 1926. As a result from the first two hurricanes to hit the Bahamas, a fleet of approximately 135 vessels were destroyed and had these hurricanes not hit these islands they would have been for the greater part at sea fishing or employed in the sponging industry. It was estimated that in the first hurricane at least seventy five percent of the vessels throughout the Bahamas were destroyed and perhaps at least fifty percent of the remaining vessels destroyed in the second hurricane. The entire sponging industry fleet in 1926 represented an actual value of well over £25,000. In addition to the losses of the sponging vessels and schooners owned by the brokers, they also had to absorb the loss of outfitting the fishermen and schooners, including stores and advances to the crewmen and their families during the lying up period. About 1,600 men were left unemployed as a result of the destroyed sponging vessels and many remained unemployed for well over a year after the storm, further exacerbating the economic hardships that these residents throughout the Bahamas faced. In addition, these men had families to support so these storms affected them in a negative way as well. To get some idea of the value of the sponge industry to the Bahamas, was gathered from the fact that the sales on the sponge exchange from October 1925 to July 1926 before the first hurricane struck amounted to over £100,000. This money was vital because it circulated throughout the country and kept the industry and the Bahamian economy going and sustained the majority of Bahamian families. As a result, many persons especially on the Family Islands found it very difficult to make ends meet and many Bahamians went to bed hungry with little or no food for many months to follow.

Today in the Bahamas, the sponge industry has almost come to a complete halt with the more commercially viable industries of Tourism, Agriculture, Sports and Commercial fishing, and Banking and Finance providing sustainable economic growth for the Bahamian Economy. However, it is important to note that today sponging is still harvested and exported from the Bahamas but on a much lesser scale than during its heyday, such as in Mangrove Cay and Red Bays, Andros. Some of it is sold locally in the tourism market mainly for souvenir sales and the rest is exported. Aside from its cultural fascination, the history of the Bahamas sponge industry has important lessons for the future of other valuable marine resources like conch, lobster and grouper. That is that these resources are not limitless and requires careful management or we risk losing them just like we did with the sponging industry. The era of sponge fishing lasted less than a century, but it left its mark on the culture and economy of the Bahamas and the ecology of the reefs that will never ever be forgotten.

CHAPTER SEVEN

Meteorological Perspectives of the three Hurricanes of 1926 as they moved through the Bahamas.

There were three major hurricanes and one tropical storm to affect the Bahamas in 1926. This was an extremely active year for hurricanes making landfall in the Bahamas and don't be surprised by this high total because, the Bahamas is ranked as 2nd, 3rd and 4th cities, islands or countries for the most active areas of being hit by hurricanes and tropical storms in the North Atlantic. The Bahamas on average gets brushed or hit by a hurricane once every three years, and gets hit by a major hurricane once every twelve years. There are three Bahamian Islands ranked in the top ten effects from tropical systems of all cities, islands and countries in the North Atlantic Basin and they include, Andros, Abaco and Grand Bahama.

The first on the list of the most active area to get hit or brushed by a tropical storm or hurricane is Grand Cayman, which is affected once every 2.21 years and since 1871 it was brushed or hit by a tropical storm or hurricane 62 times. The average years between direct hurricane hits are once every 6.52 years. Second, is Andros here in the Bahamas, which is affected once every 2.40 years and since 1871, it was brushed or hit by a tropical storm or hurricane 57 times. The average years between direct hurricane hits are once every 8.06 years. Third, is Abaco here in the Bahamas, which is affected once every 2.45 years and since 1871 it was brushed or hit by a tropical storm or hurricane 56 times. The average years between direct hurricane hits are once every 8.57 years. Fourth, is Grand Bahama here in the Bahamas which is affected every 2.49 years and since 1871 it was brushed or hit by a tropical storm or hurricane 55 times. The average years between direct hurricane hits are once every 6.52 years.

Fifth, is Cape Hatteras, North Carolina which is affected every 2.49 years and since 1871 it was brushed or hit by a tropical storm or hurricane 55 times. Sixth, is Delray Beach, Florida which is affected every 2.54 years and since 1871 it was brushed or hit by a tropical storm or hurricane 54 times. Seventh, is Cancun, Mexico which is affected every 2.54 years and since 1871 it was brushed or hit by a tropical storm or hurricane 54 times. Eighth, is Hollywood, Florida which is affected every 2.58 years and since 1871 it was brushed or hit by a tropical storm or hurricane 53 times. Ninth, is Deerfield Beach, Florida which is affected every 2.58 years and since 1871 it was brushed or hit by a tropical storm or hurricane 53 times. Finally, tenth is Bermuda which is affected every 2.58 years and since 1871 it was brushed or hit by a tropical storm or hurricane 53 times. Just out of interest, Nassau, the capital city here in the Bahamas is ranked 39th on the list with this island being affected every 2.98 years and it was brushed or hit by a tropical storm or hurricane 46 times since 1871. The average years between direct hurricane hits are once every 11.42 years.

The 1926 hurricane season was one of the most active hurricane seasons on record in the Bahamas, third only to the 1933 hurricane season which saw an astounding 4 hurricanes and one tropical storm in that year and the 1837 hurricane season which saw an amazing 6 hurricanes. In 1926 there were three powerful hurricanes and a tropical storm to affect the Bahamas. The 1926 Atlantic hurricane season officially began on June 1, 1926, and lasted until November 30, 1926. These dates conventionally provide the boundary periods of each year when most hurricanes form in the North Atlantic Basin. The 1926 season was slightly above average in activity, but was a very

Wayne Neely

eventful one. This season produced 11 tropical storms, of which 6 became major hurricanes. Notable storms of this year included *the Great Nassau Hurricane, the Great Miami Hurricane* and *the Havana-Bermuda Hurricane.*

Several sponging schooners and native sloops in Nassau Harbour-some sunken and others totally destroyed in the Nassau Hurricane of 1926(Courtesy of Charles. J. Whelbell Collection-The Department of Archives, Nassau, Bahamas)

The first storm of the season was a Category 4 hurricane which made landfall over the Bahamas and then continued onto make a direct hit near Melbourne, Florida. The next was a Category 3 storm which grazed Bermuda and struck Nova Scotia as an extra tropical cyclone. The third struck Louisiana as a Category 2 storm. Another Category 3 storm made a loop around the Azores. It struck Miami dead on as a Category 4 hurricane. The storm surge tore through the city, wiping away thousands of homes and businesses. Over 373 people were killed in Florida alone and several dozen more were killed when the hurricane skimmed the Gulf Coasts of the Florida Panhandle, Alabama, and Mississippi. *The Great Miami Hurricane* as it was known(also called

100

'*The Big Blow*')was one of only three hurricanes to ever come so close to perfect storm status. The phrase 'perfect storm' refers to the simultaneous occurrence of events which, taken individually, would be far less powerful than the result of their rare chance combination. Such occurrences are rare by their very nature, so that even a slight change in any one event contributing to the perfect storm would lessen its overall impact. The term is also used to describe a hypothetical hurricane which happens to hit at a region's most vulnerable area, resulting in the worst possible damage by a hurricane of its magnitude. It hit Fort Lauderdale, Dania, Hollywood, Hallandale and Miami. The death toll range was estimated to be from 325 to perhaps as many as 800 but the official Red Cross total was 373 persons who perished in this storm.

No storm in previous history had done as much property damage to the state of Florida. It ranks as by far as one of the costliest hurricanes in Florida's history, causing over $100 million in damage in 1926 dollars. If adjusted for today's inflation and increased population density, *The Great Miami Hurricane* would dwarf Hurricane Andrew in cost with a damage total of over $98 billion. The unnamed hurricane or Hurricane #10 of the 20th and 21st of October 1926 was the third hurricane that had passed over the Bahamas within three months and not a single island of the group of islands had escaped one or more of these visitations.

The Great Nassau Hurricane of 1926.

Track Of the Nassau Hurricane of 1926

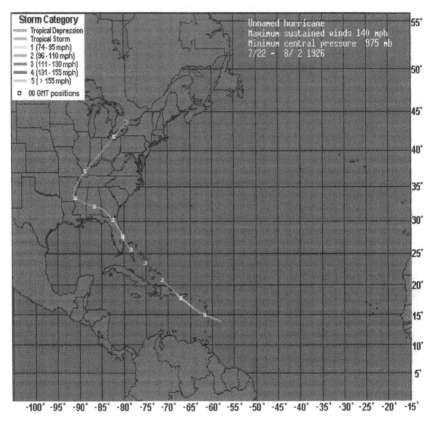

This map shows the track of the Nassau Hurricane of 1926 as it moved through the Leeward Islands, Puerto Rico, Dominican Republic, the Bahamas and the USA (Information courtesy Of The Weather Underground Inc.)

Nassau Hurricane of 1926	
Category 4 Hurricane	
Formed	July 22, 1926
Dissipated	August 2, 1926
Highest winds	140mph
Lowest pressure	≤ 975 mbar (hPa; 28.8 inHg)
Fatalities	~500 direct
Damage	$7.85 million (1926 USD) $91 million (Today's USD)
Areas affected	Lesser Antilles, Puerto Rico, Hispaniola, Bahamas, Florida, and Southeastern United States.

This hurricane inflicted widespread devastation and loss of life here in the Bahamas and is one of the most deadly hurricanes to ever cross these islands. Most of those persons died at sea during the storm with no knowledge of an approaching storm. It is estimated that this hurricane alone caused well over £2,000,000 in damages in the Bahamas.

A completely demolished church with the altar broken in half by *The Nassau Hurricane of 1926* **(From the private collection of Patricia Beardsley Roker used with permission)**

This was the first storm of the season and was a powerful Category 4 hurricane that formed near the Lesser Antilles on July 22 and crossed through the Bahamas on July 26. It weakened as it headed northwestward, brushing the east-central Florida coast as a Category 2 hurricane, and made landfall near Cocoa Beach, Florida on July 27th. It continued across the United States, and became extratropical on August 1 and later dissipated on August 2. The storm caused massive widespread damage in the Bahamas, as well as heavy rainfall over the southeastern United States. The storm's lowest recorded pressure was 975 mbar.

It is frequently referred to as *the Great Nassau Hurricane of 1926,* also known as the *Bahamas-Florida Hurricane of July 1926, Hurricane San Liborio, and the Gale of 1926* (mostly by persons on the Family Islands) or quite simply *Hurricane # 1 of 1926.* It was a destructive and powerful Category 4 hurricane which affected the Bahamas at its peak intensity. Although it weakened considerably before it made its Florida landfall, it was reported as one of the most severe storms on record to ever affect Nassau in the Bahamas in several years until *the Great Lake Okeechobee Hurricane of 1928* and *the Great Bahamas Hurricane of 1929*, which occurred just two and three years later respectively. The storm also delivered flooding rains and loss of crops to the southeastern United States and Florida.

The system was first spotted east of the Lesser Antilles as a tropical disturbance on July 22. Moving northwest, the tropical storm passed near Dominica with moderate intensity, then passed just south of Puerto Rico on July 23 with a gradual increase in intensity. San Juan, Puerto Rico, recorded maximum winds of around 66 mph and a low barometric pressure of 1005 mbar as the storm's center passed near the extreme southwest corner of Puerto Rico. The storm continued northwest and tracked over Hispaniola while strengthening to hurricane status. The storm continued strengthening, and by the time it reached the Central Bahamas, it was at full Category 4 intensity with 140 mph winds. On July 26, while still moving northwest, the storm's eye passed directly over Nassau, where winds were unofficially estimated at 135 mph and heavy damage was reported on all of the major islands of the Bahamas. Moving slowly, the storm weakened while sliding up the Florida coast, making final landfall near Melbourne, Florida, on July 27 as a Category 2 hurricane. In Florida, the storm's lowest barometric pressure of 975 mbar was recorded and observed. The storm weakened rapidly as it moved inland, weakening to a tropical storm and eventually a depression as it moved across Georgia and Alabama while dumping torrential rainfall, resulting in serious flooding. It continued across the southeastern United States while losing tropical characteristics, gradually beginning to re-curve northeastward over Arkansas, Missouri, and the Ohio Valley, becoming extratropical on August 1. It finally dissipated the following day as it moved northeastward over Lake Ontario.

Prior to the record-breaking 2005 Atlantic hurricane season, this was the most intense hurricane ever recorded in July for quite sometime (with 140 mph winds) until Hurricane Emily of the 2005 hurricane season, a Category 5 hurricane which had top sustained winds of 160 mph and a pressure of 929 millibars, surpassed the intensity of the July 1926 hurricane. Hurricane Dennis, also from 2005, was also still more intense in barometric pressure and wind strength than *the Nassau Hurricane of July 1926*. It is also important to note here that Hurricane

Audrey was also more intense and occurred even earlier in the season in June.

Steel telephone poles bent like paper in Nassau after *The Nassau Hurricane of 1926*(From the private collection of Patricia Beardsley Roker used with permission)

In total this storm was responsible for well over 500 persons in Puerto Rico, the Dominican Republic, Bahamas, and Florida. The storm initially caused little damage until it passed near Puerto Rico, where heavy crop damage, most notably to the coffee plantations in the west-central region of the island, occurred. Heavy rainfall of around 6.18 inches occurred on the island, while the average rainfall reported for July was 6.50 inches. Around 25 lives were lost when heavy floods resulted from rapid rise of rivers. Total losses in Puerto Rico were estimated at $2.35 million dollars. While, in Hispaniola, estimated damage amounted to around $3 million in eastern Santo Domingo as the storm center passed over the eastern half of the island.

Here in the Bahamas, damage reports and casualties are not often clear, however, the storm was reported to be destructive around Nassau, where "some roofs were torn off entirely" and that the storm was "more fearful and devastating than any most people can remember", according to an eyewitness account posted in the July 1926 issue of *the Monthly Weather Review.* Approximately 268 persons lost their lives in this storm here in the Bahamas. Trees, power poles, and various debris littered streets, and many people were left homeless and had to leave their houses in the peak of the storm stumbling pitifully through many wrecked houses to seek shelter elsewhere. The few automobiles at the time in Nassau were also reported damaged by the storm, and widespread flooding was reported. The hurricane also caused heavy damage nearby on Acklins, Long Island, Abaco, Grand Bahama, Eleuthera and Andros, as well as in the Exumas.

A Church with its roof completely blown off in *The Nassau Hurricane of 1926* (Courtesy of Charles. J. Whelbell Collection-The Department of Archives, Nassau, Bahamas)

The storm was also reported to have caused massive damage around the point of landfall in Melbourne, Florida, where uprooted citrus trees and roofs blown off were reported. An observer on Merritt Island reported a heavy storm surge along the Indian River which damaged or destroyed homes, docks, and boats. Points further south along the Florida coast, such as Miami, received only a brush from the storm, resulting in rains and some light wind damage. Flooding was also experienced at points such as Palm Beach. Damage estimates in Florida exceeded $2.5 million.

The Great Miami Hurricane of 1926.

The Track of The Great Miami Hurricane of 1926

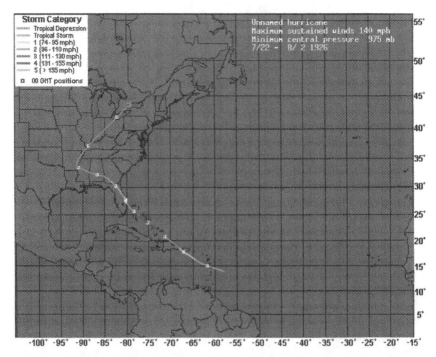

This map shows the track of the Great Miami Hurricane of 1926 as it moved through the Bahamas and the USA (Information courtesy Of The Weather Underground Inc.)

The Great Miami Hurricane of 1926
Category 4 Hurricane

Formed	September 6, 1926
Dissipated	September 22, 1926
Highest winds	150mph
Lowest pressure	≤ 935 mbar (hPa)
Fatalities	~349 direct
Damage	$105 million (1926 USD)
Areas affected	The Bahamas, Florida, Mississippi, and Louisiana.

The 1926 Miami Hurricane (or Great Miami Hurricane or the Big Blow) was an intense hurricane that devastated the Bahamas and Miami, Florida in September of 1926. It was it is referred to as the *Great Miami Hurricane of 1926* because of the massive damage it inflicted on the city of Miami, Florida in the United States. This storm also caused significant damage in the Florida Panhandle, the U.S. state of Alabama, and the Bahamas. The storm's enormous regional economic impact helped end the Florida land boom of the 1920's and pushed the region on an early start into the Great Depression. The Great Depression (also known in the United Kingdom as the Great Slump) was a dramatic, worldwide economic downturn beginning in some countries as early as 1928. The beginning of the Great Depression in the United States is associated with the stock market crash on October 29, 1929, known as Black Tuesday. The depression had devastating effects in both the industrialized countries and those which exported raw materials. International trade declined sharply, as did personal incomes, tax revenues, prices, and profits. Cities all around the world were hit hard, especially those dependent on heavy industry. Construction was virtually halted in many countries. Farming and rural areas suffered as crop prices fell by 40 to 60 percent. Facing plummeting demand with few alternate sources of jobs, areas dependent on primary sector industries such as farming, mining and logging suffered the most. At the time, Hoover was the US President.

The Pelicaus Sponge Warehouse in the background-totally destroyed in the 1926 Miami Hurricane and workers in the foreground gathering the natural sea sponges after the hurricane had scattered them throughout the yard in Downtown, Nassau, Bahamas. (Courtesy of Charles. J. Whelbell Collection-The Department of Archives, Nassau, Bahamas)

This classic Cape Verde-Type hurricane formed on September 6. It was first spotted as a tropical wave located 1,000 miles east of the Lesser Antilles on 11th September 1926. Initially it began moving west-northwest while traversing the tropical Atlantic, the storm later passed near St. Kitts on September 14. By September 17, it was battering the Bahamas, impacting the Turks and Caicos Islands with winds estimated at 150 mph, making it a powerful Category 4 hurricane. Then, in the early morning hours of September 18, it made landfall just south of Miami between Coral Gables and South Miami as a devastating Category 4 hurricane on the Saffir-Simpson Hurricane Scale. This hurricane produced the highest sustained winds ever recorded in the United States at the time, and barometric pressure fell to 26.61 inches as the eye moved over Miami. The storm crossed the Florida Peninsula south of Lake Okeechobee, entered the Gulf of Mexico, and made another landfall near Mobile, Alabama as a Category 3 hurricane on September 20. It then moved westward along coastal Alabama and Mississippi, eventually dissipating on September 22 after moving inland over Louisiana.

The hurricane continued northwestward across the Gulf Mexico and approached Pensacola on the 20th September, 1926. The storm became near stationary just to the south of Pensacola later that day and grazed the central Gulf Coast with 24 hours of heavy rainfall, hurricane force winds, and storm surge. The hurricane weakened as it moved inland over Louisiana later on the 21st nearly every pier, warehouse, and vessel on Pensacola were destroyed. The *Great Miami Hurricane of 1926* ended the economic boom in South Florida and would be a $90 million disaster had it occurred in recent times. It had not been a good year for South Florida because a wild real-estate boom had collapsed and millionaires at the end of 1925 had become poor folks by the middle of 1926. Most of the 200,000 people living in the storm's projected path were new to Florida, lured there by the easy money of the Florida's land boom. Having never seen a hurricane, they had little knowledge of a storm's destructive force and it ended up costing many of them their lives. With a highly transient population across southeastern Florida during the 1920s, the death toll is uncertain since more than 800 persons were reported missing in the aftermath of the hurricane. There were varying totals of how many persons perished in this storm but a Red Cross list reported 373 deaths, 6,381 injuries and 47,000 homeless as a result of this hurricane.

The inside view of Trinity Church badly damaged during the Nassau Hurricane of 1926. Founded in 1868, this church stands at the corner of Frederick Street and Trinity Place. The first five grades of Queen's College (now located on Village Road) were conducted on the ground floor of Trinity Church itself-kindergarten, transition, Form 1, Form 2 and Form 3. After that, students crossed Frederick Street to the upper school of Queen's College, whose primary building looked like a large chapel and was located on Charlotte Street. (Courtesy of Charles. J.Whelbell Collection-The Department of Archives)

At the time, Miami's Hurricane was considered the country's greatest natural disaster since the San Francisco earthquake and fire of 1906. Today this Category 4 storm ranks among 20th Century worst U.S. hurricanes and as the 12th strongest and the 12th deadliest hurricane of the North Atlantic region. In Florida, winds at the surface were reported around 125 mph and the pressure measured at 935 mbar (hPa) (though all such data is suspect). During the hurricane's second half, winds however, reached a terrifying 128 mph. Most of the coastal inhabitants had not evacuated, partly because of short warning (a hurricane warning was issued just a few hours before landfall) and partly because the "young" city's population knew little about the danger a major hurricane posed. A 15 foot storm surge inundated the Coconut Grove area, causing massive property damage and numerous fatalities.

Many people were unaware of the anatomy (especially with what to expect with the passage of the eye) of the hurricane because as the eye of the hurricane crossed over Miami Beach and downtown Miami, many people believed the storm had passed. The last major hurricane to hit Florida was in 1910 when the population was indeed much smaller than in 1926. Some tried to leave the barrier islands, only to be swept off of the bridges by the rear eyewall. They were suddenly trapped and exposed to the eastern half of the hurricane shortly thereafter. Most of the causalities succumbed after the lull. "The lull lasted 35 minutes, and during that time the streets of the city became crowded with people," wrote Richard Gray, the local weather chief. "As a result, many lives were lost during the second phase of the storm." Inland, Lake Okeechobee experienced a high storm surge which broke a portion of the dikes, flooding the town of Moore Haven and killing many. This was just a prelude to the deadly 1928 Okeechobee Hurricane, which would cause a massive number of fatalities estimated at 2,500 around the lake. Coastal regions between Mobile and Pensacola, Florida also suffered heavy damage from wind, rain, and storm surge, but this paled beside the news of the destruction in Miami. According to the Red Cross there were 373 fatalities. Other estimates vary, since there were a large number of people listed as "missing." Between 25,000 and 50,000 people were left homeless, mostly in the Miami area.

The damage from the storm was immense; few buildings in Miami or Miami Beach were left intact. The toll for the storm was $100 million in 1926 dollars and it is estimated that if an identical storm would hit today, with modern development and prices, the storm would have caused over $98 billion in damage. After the hurricane, the Great Depression started in South Florida, slowing recovery. In response to the widespread destruction of buildings on Miami Beach, John J. Farrey was appointed Chief Building, Plumbing and Electrical Inspector. He initiated and enforced the first building code in the United States, which more than 5000 US cities have since duplicated.

The University of Miami, located in Coral Gables, had been founded in 1925 and opened its doors for the first time just days after the hurricane passed. The hurricane had destroyed several buildings on campus and the University did not have the money to rebuild or to continue construction that was underway at the time. To make money and obtain building resources, the University decided to harvest coral from the campus, thus creating Lake Osceola. The coral was either sold or used as building material to complete construction around campus. The University's mascot was named the *Hurricanes* in memory of this catastrophe in 1926. The University's mascot is represented by Sebastian, who is an ibis. The ibis is a small white bird that can be seen around South Florida and especially on the UM campus. An ibis was selected to represent the Miami Hurricanes because of the folklore in which it represents, is typically the last bird to leave before a hurricane strikes and the first to return once it's gone.

Hurricane #10 of 1926.

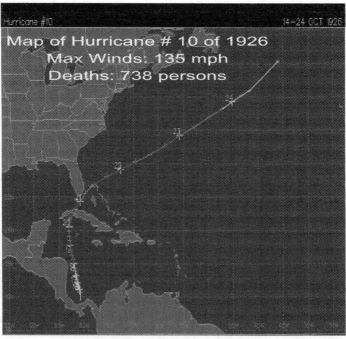

This map shows the track of Hurricane #10 of 1926 as it moved through Western Cuba, the Bahamas, the USA and Bermuda (Information Courtesy Of Unisys's Weather.)

On October 14th 1926, a tropical storm developed in the southwest Caribbean Sea. It moved northward, becoming a major hurricane on the 20th before crossing Cuba, Northern Bahamas and Southeast Florida. It headed northeastward, and strengthened into a Category 4 before hitting Bermuda on October 22. It became extratropical on the 23rd. The hurricane's impact was great as it caused severe damage in Cuba and 650 deaths. The hurricane then moved over the islands of Grand Bahama and northern Abaco in the Bahamas. The hurricane then passed directly over Bermuda where it sank two British warships drowning 110 sailors. Overall the hurricane left 738 people dead and over $100 million dollars (1926 USD) in damage.

CHAPTER EIGHT

The Impact of these Three Hurricanes of 1926 on the Various Islands Affected

Each hurricane was responsible for, destroying many lives, wrecking thousands of houses, sinking and destroying numerous fishing vessels on many of the Family Islands to such an extent that many of these islands devastated by these storms took years to recover. Financially, the loss was enormous because it was estimated that well over a million pounds was needed to bring the Bahamas back to some form of stability after the first hurricane and twice that amount for the second hurricane. Inaddition, these 'native' houses as they were called throughout the Family Islands were sub-standard houses, comprising of just a straw or wooden roof and the walls were made of dry limestone rocks, sometimes coral and built without the benefit of any type of cement. As a result, they were no match for the ferocity of winds in these storms, so they were often the first victims of the storm.

Under these desperate circumstances, the Bahamian Government was faced with the tremendous problem of feeding, clothing and sheltering a large proportion of the population throughout the hurricane ravaged islands for many months and even years to come. Furthermore, the Government had to spend record sums of money in relief and reconstruction work. On the majority of the islands, most of the houses, farms and infrastructure were destroyed in the first hurricane. After the first hurricane many persons rushed to rebuild their homes, boats, and replant their farms destroyed by the *Nassau Hurricane of 1926*. This would prove to be an unwise decision because the second storm came along and destroyed them once again putting them into far greater debt than they had been by the first hurricane. By the time the third hurricane had struck, there wasn't really much for it to destroy because the other two hurricanes had done such a tremendous job of displacing the residents and destroying most of the infrastructure, homes, farms and ships on each of the islands. Most residents simply waited until the end of the hurricane season to re-start any rebuilding efforts because of the fear of being hit by another major hurricane.

Men repairing damaged electrical wires in the foreground and the home of Mr. Uriah Saunders and his wife Rebecca Roberts Saunders on the left and Trinity Methodist Church on the right on Fredrick Street both badly damaged in the background during the Nassau Hurricane of 1926 (Courtesy of Charles. J. Whelbell Collection-The Department of Archives)

Abaco

After the first hurricane, all of the wharves and seawalls were destroyed and those houses within reach of the wharves were simply washed away. Much damage was done to the fruit bearing trees such as pears, mangoes, sapodillas, grapefruits and oranges, in most of the settlements but major damage was reported in the settlement of Marsh Harbour where no trees were left standing. At Hopetown, there was widespread devastation as many houses were destroyed. It was estimated that in the settlement of Marsh Harbour alone suffered a loss of well over two thousand pounds. Also in this settlement, the schoolhouse and many of the dwelling homes were blown down and two Wesleyan churches and one native Baptist church were destroyed. The three mast schooner, owned by Messer's Jas. P. Sands Co. of Nassau, parted one of the anchors; refuge was found at the point near Marsh Harbour, but the motor tender and small boat were broken up. Most of the three mast schooners near Marsh Harbour were totally destroyed. Three fishing smacks, *Forward, Venture* and *Iona* from Cherokee Sound were totally destroyed and five of the crew members drowned in the waters off Nicholls's Town, Andros. The three mast schooner *Beecham*, contracted to transport lumber from Norma's Castle to Cuba, was wrecked on the west side of Great Abaco.

All throughout most of the settlements in Abaco, water was said to be well over four and a half feet deep and many trees were uprooted and quite a number of them fell across the main roads which made them impassable for many days. Many of the homes, toilets and kitchens were either badly damaged or totally wiped out by the storm. In the settlement of Cherokee Sound 7 men lost their lives besides from the ones lost at sea in this settlement. In Marsh Harbour there was one loss of life, which was a 5 year old boy who lost his life when he came out of his home and saw a large hole filled with water in the school yard, and probably thinking the water was not deep, through childish ignorance plunged into it, unknown to anyone. He was missed at home and a search revealed him dead at the bottom of the hole. A great deal of effort was done by the public school teacher and others to resuscitate him but to no avail.

After the Hurricane #10 of October 21st and 22nd the Governor visited Abaco by sea plane and by boat and found that the island was completely devastated by this hurricane and it didn't help the situation that two other previous hurricanes had also devastated the island. He found out that in every settlement the wharves and seawalls were destroyed and those houses which were within reach of the waves were washed away. On this island, there were hundreds of houses which were destroyed leaving thousands homeless by this storm. After the storm, there were very few houses which remained standing and for weeks and months it was said that those few remaining houses which were not destroyed supported each on average of 30 to 40 persons in them until their houses were repaired or rebuilt. Hundreds of chickens, a large number of cats, dogs and hogs were also killed in the storm, many decayed and the stench of these dead animals could be smelled for many miles for many days and even weeks after the storm had passed. In addition, thousands of fish were carried inland for many miles by the storm surge and they also added to the unbearable stench in this settlement.

Much of the fishing and shipping transport vessels including several large schooners were destroyed. At Guana Cay, a few houses were destroyed but the damage was relatively light compared to that of the other settlements. One large motor boat was swept away never to be seen again, while another was simply destroyed and the only road in this settlement was washed away. At Green Turtle Cay, the Government dock and the main road were washed away and many homes were destroyed. At Man-O-War, considerable damage was sustained in this settlement especially to the fruit trees such as, oranges and grapefruits which were wiped out and one house was destroyed and 10 others were blown of their foundations. This settlement shipped annually to Nassau citrus fruits to the value of £2,000, and this hurricane wiped out their main source of income-citrus for years to come. The Commissioner of Abaco would later declare in his report that in this settlement, *"There is absolutely nothing left. What had once been a pretty little town covered with fruit trees and nice homes is today nothing but a wilderness and a swamp."*

At Marsh Harbour, the destruction was almost complete and no other settlement suffered more damage than this settlement because all but two houses which stood on high ground were completely destroyed. The storm surge at Marsh Harbour, rose to about twenty feet above the high water level, many of the houses could not endure the battering waves and were carried inland for distances of nearly a mile. Three persons Mrs. Dells Weatherford, Lydia Bethell and an infant child Eleanor Van Ryn daughter of August Van Ryn drowned in this settlement. Most persons said that had the worst part of the storm had occurred in the night rather than the daylight the casualties would have been significantly greater. At Hopetown, there was widespread devastation as many houses were destroyed when the storm surge swept over the settlement. In this settlement, sixty houses were partly damaged and one third of the houses were totally destroyed and the roof from the light-keeper's home was blown off. During the storm, this island had sustained winds of over 150 miles per hour. The estimated damage to Government and private properties were about £2,000. The water rose as high as 8 feet in this settlement and the sea rushed in as far as the Methodist Mission House a quarter of a mile inland from the sea front. A building was carried 1,000 feet and deposited upside down in the front of the cemetery.

The streets were blocked in several places and many houses floated into the streets from their original sites. Only two boats remained untouched after the storm in this settlement and Dr. Dolly's yacht, well known in Nassau, received great damage. The two wireless towers and the Government dock were completely destroyed. The public school house was blown down and it would end up costing the Government £200 to repair it. The three-masted schooner *Abaco* dragged her moorings and was blown up on the land in a place where ordinarily the tide would never come. Another fishing boat *Abaco-Bahamas*, which sailed from Hope Town to Marsh Harbour during the storm was similarly blown up on the rocks and was completely destroyed.

At Marsh Harbour, the experiences of the Acting Commissioner Mr. Roberts and his wife, both over sixty years of age, were interesting but not exceptional. The winds during the first part of the storm had been blowing off the land and done little damage. During the calm which fell soon after daylight, while the center of the storm was passing, the acting Commissioner left his house to secure his boat *The Vigilant* which was lying in the creek about 400 yards away, and having succeeded in doing this he started to return home assuming that the hurricane had passed. Most persons at the time really didn't fully understand the anatomy of a hurricane especially the fundamentals of the eye feature of the storm. Before he could reach his house, however, the wind began to blow once again more furiously than before but from the opposite direction. Mr. Roberts crept for safety behind a Sapodilla Tree, up which he was forced to climb as the sea swept over the land and the water rose higher and higher; finally he took refuge among the top branches where he clung onto the branches for his dear life for several hours. It was not until late in the afternoon, after some of the flood waters had subsided, that his cries for help was heard and he was rescued by the aid of a tall ladder from his dangerous and undignified position. In the meantime, Mrs. Roberts, who had remained at home, was driven upstairs by the rising water. The house (a wooden one) was soon swept off its' foundations and carried inland, gradually sinking, while Mrs. Roberts made a vain attempt to get through the attic window onto the roof. Her danger was seen by people in another house which was also floating away and a young Spanish Wells woman by the name of Marion Higgs, with great gallantry, swam from one house to the other and succeeded in pulling Mrs. Roberts onto the roof of the house where both remained until the storm subsided.

Most of the inhabitants of Marsh Harbour lost everything they possessed, houses, boats and fruit orchards being completely destroyed, while many people who had before the storm been comparatively well-to-do owned nothing afterwards and rendered penniless with only the clothes on their backs. The finest building in Abaco containing the public library, post office and courthouse, a new building of over forty feet long was blown 1000 feet away into a swamp from its original site and destroyed. The cemeteries in Marsh Harbour and in other settlements were destroyed and the coffins and bodies were washed out of the graves. The large 9 bedroom house of the wireless operator was carried about half a mile inland. Mr. Goodwin Roberts's large house was carried three quarters of a mile away and he lost his child during the storm. Mrs. Lydia Bethell drowned in the storm but her body was never found until three days later in a swamp a quarter of a mile away from where she went missing. Abaco shipbuilder Mr. John Lowe's house was destroyed along with all of his tools.

At Guana Cay the damage was moderate and all of the sugar cane crop and the sugar mills were destroyed. A few houses were completely destroyed and the others badly damaged in this settlement and quite a few of them were blown of their pillars. The Bahamas Cuba Lumber Mill at Norman's Castle was only partially damaged and the total damage to this mill and surrounding houses were estimated at £10,000. At Cherokee Sound, the waves from the east met those from the west. It rose about six feet and considerable damage was done. A few houses were completely destroyed and a considerable number were partially destroyed and blown off their pillars. The Methodist Church which stood near the street was completely destroyed and the Government dock was partly destroyed. Most of the persons on Abaco were fishermen or farmers so the loss of their only means of livelihood devastated this island, leaving many penniless for months or even years to follow. After this storm, the generosity of many persons throughout the Bahamas and outside the country eased the hardship of the inhabitants of Abaco by donating funds, building materials, food and clothing to the hurricane stricken residents to supplement the relief given by the Government. In addition, in order to persuade the inhabitants to rebuild their houses in a safer position, a grant of land on higher ground was offered to the residents to rebuild on.

Andros

During the first hurricane, the Commissioner's Office at Staniard Creek was blown down. All of the bridges were totally destroyed and most of the dwelling homes in most of the settlements were destroyed. Part of the Methodist Church roof was blown off; the roof of the Social Union Society Hall was blown off. The Good Samaritan Lodge Hall and other buildings were also destroyed. The Sisal crop of well over fifteen hundred pounds was totally wiped out. About 95% of the coconut trees estimated to be in the hundreds were blown down. Throughout most of the settlements the standing water was said to be well over five feet deep. About 89 houses, many of them stone buildings were destroyed at Mastic Point. One eye witness Percy Wemyss said that the settlement of Staniard Creek was totally devastated and that if anyone who saw this settlement a few days before the storm hit as compared with a few days after the storm, they would not have been able to recognize it as the same settlement. In the settlement of Staniard Creek alone it was said that more than 25 houses and several churches were totally destroyed.

In Nicholls's Town, 27 houses were totally destroyed and many others badly damaged and rendered uninhabitable. At Lowe Sound, only ten buildings were left standing and three of them were badly damaged. At Conch Sound, only nine buildings were left standing and the rest were blown down or washed away. The roof of the Commissioner's Office was blown off and the prison's roof was badly damaged. The teacher's residence at Nicholls's Town was completely blown down and nearly all of the furniture inside was destroyed. After the storm passed over the settlement of Nicholls's Town, 97 homeless persons had to seek shelter in the public schoolroom. Nearly all of the streets were blocked with portions of shattered houses, walls, boats, fallen coconut trees and all sorts of rubbish and miscellaneous items. Damage to government property alone was estimated at well over 10,000 pounds.

At Fresh Creek, the bridge connecting the eastern and western Ridges was blown down. During the hurricane, a surge of water from the beach came ashore and met the floodwaters from the Creek on the East Ridge with that of the West Ridge. There were 48 buildings completely destroyed and 35 badly damaged and 500 coconut trees blown down. The schooner *Imperial* was found wrecked off Red Bays on the western shore of Andros and the crew of 7 persons were lost with the vessel and several other vessels in the vicinity of North Andros with many persons onboard were reported missing and never found. At Red Bays, the sea washed up to the houses and swept them away taking several lives in the process. Most of the sponges in the kraals which were kept on the west coast of Andros were swept out to sea. The surge was so terrible that those boats lying on the outside of the Creek, with the exception of the Bishop's Yacht *Lavonia*, were unable to make harbour, but she forced her way into the Creek with great difficulty. The sponging schooners *Mary B, Sea Breeze* and *Anne* the latter two owned by W.J. Amaly a sponge merchant, were totally destroyed with five of the crew members perishing. At least three men drowned in the storm from Fresh Creek.

In the settlement of Long Bay Cays, South Andros a number of vessels were destroyed while others were sunk or stranded. Inaddition, in this settlement of Long Bay Cays, the main road located along the sea shore was obliterated for many miles, and where the road still remained, it was choked with debris, fallen trees and shrubs, together with heaps of seaweed and other marine growth making it impassable in many places. The large drainage canal which was constructed in 1925 for the purpose of draining about two miles of coastal swamp was wrecked, the sea making a clear breech over it, tearing away the sea ridge to a width of 30 or 40 feet, and filling the canal with hundreds of tons of sand. It was estimated that it would cost well over £50 to put the drainage canal back in operation and £150 to repair the damaged road.

After the second hurricane, the conditions throughout Andros was said to be in a deplorable state. In Nicholls's Town, only one boat was available to bring the Commissioner's Report to Nassau as the district was almost totally wrecked. The hurricane was accompanied by very consistent torrential rainfall beginning at 5:30pm on the 17th and lasting for over twelve hours. Over thirty persons lost their lives and hundreds more rendered homeless after this hurricane. Every settlement had suffered severely and towards the northern end of the island only a small percentage of the houses in each settlement remained standing and even the ones that remained standing were also badly damaged. The damages to homes at Nicholls's Town, Conch Sound and Lowe Sound were as follows: 39 totally destroyed and 60 badly damaged. At Nicholls's Town, one gable end from the Commissioner's Office was blown away (the top was blown off in the first hurricane), the schoolroom walls were cracked in several places and the roads were blocked in several places. The Baptist Church at Nicholls's Town was badly damaged and the one at Conch Sound was totally destroyed. At Mastic Point, the roof of the Commissioner's Office was blown down, the teacher's residency was totally destroyed and the schoolroom was slightly damaged. Inaddition, there were 60 houses totally destroyed and 99 houses badly damaged in this settlement. The Methodist, Baptist and Episcopal Churches at Mastic Point were totally destroyed.

The public graveyards at Fresh Creek and Calabash Bay were washed away and the coffins with dead bodies had to be reburied in new burial grounds. In the settlement of Little Harbour, Mangrove Cay there were 70 houses totally destroyed and many others badly damaged. One child was crushed to death by a falling house and several other persons were injured. Nearly all of the boats in Mangrove Cay were destroyed or badly damaged and six men were reportedly drowned in their sponging vessels. The entire landmass, except the hills at Mangrove Cay was covered in water for days and most of the coconut trees were snapped off and blown down by the wind. At Victoria Point, there were 68 dwelling houses and 3 Baptist Churches which were totally destroyed. In South Andros, very few houses remained standing and the public schoolhouse and teacher's residency were blown away. Many fishing and sponging vessels were destroyed or badly damaged including *The Repeat* which was sunk at Pure Gold but fortunately would later be repaired. *The Repeat* would eventually be completely destroyed in the *Great Bahamas Hurricane of 1929*. In South Andros, there was a fishing vessel with six of the seven crew members perishing in the storm. One child was also killed when a house fell on him.

Many of the persons who received building materials to aid them to replace their homes damaged by the *Great Nassau Hurricane* of 26th July had only begun to rebuild and this hurricane swept away their materials leaving them in a worse condition than they were in after the first hurricane. The people in many of the settlements throughout the island were living to a great extent in the open and sleeping at night either in damaged churches or on the ground in the ruins of their homes. Most of the sponging vessels on which the people depended on for their livelihood were totally wrecked. Much needed relief supplies were dispatched from Nassau, the following day after the hurricane. The inhabitants didn't suffer from food but from the difficulty of obtaining fresh water, because most of the wells were contaminated by salt water due to the abnormally high storm surge.

At the time of the hurricane, the Commissioner for the entire island of Andros was Mr. Elgin Forsyth and his tenure lasted from 1922 to 1946. He was responsible for distributing the food, clothing and building materials to the residents after each of these hurricanes. Mr. Forsyth, a resident of Mangrove Cay was born August 28, 1877 at Rum Cay and he moved with the family to Wood Cay, Andros in 1880, however, in 1886, the family migrated to Florida. His family moved back to Nassau when he was 14 years old, where his father, L.E. Forsyth, worked as a land surveyor. However his father will be remembered for being in charge of the 20,000 acre Chamberlain Sisal Plantation near Mastic Point Andros. In 1892 his father gave up surveying and became a Resident Justice for the Andros district. Elgin's three main duties as a Commissioner were first, to take care of the sponger fishermen and their needs (there were several thousand men during this time engaged in the sponging trade). Secondly, he had to report on the state of affairs on the island of Andros to the Governor in Nassau. Third, to make a comprehensive report on the conditions in Andros after a major hurricane had passed.

St. Ann's Church in Nassau with the spire and roof totally blown away. (From the private collection of Patricia Beardsley Roker used with permission)

San Salvador

During the first storm, slight damage was reported to this island as compared to the other southern islands. There were a few blown down trees throughout the island. There were two Episcopal and more than seven Baptists churches destroyed. *The Brontes*, a mail schooner of 42 tons, had set sail from Nassau on Friday for its regular trip to San

Salvador and Rum Cay. Including the crew, there were 30 persons on board, among them Rum Cay's Commissioner Mr. T.A. Greenslade's wife, four other members of his family, and the wife and children of H.A. Varence, the schoolmaster at Roker's Point, Exuma. At the time of *The Brontes* departure, the hurricane was quite some distance away-only approaching Hispaniola. The captain of *The Brontes*, W.P. Styles, was a much admired figure in the maritime life of the colony. Renowned for his reliability as a mailboat captain and exceptional skill as a sailor, he was in the words of Sir Etienne Dupuch, a *"very, very valuable mariner."* *The Brontes*, then, was a ship that had many lives because a year before the hurricane, it had sunk between Graham's Harbour and Riding Rocks(Cockburn Town), San Salvador, taking its then captain, a man named Burrows, to his grave.

By the time *The Brontes* got to south Eleuthera near Powell's Point they started to experience some deteriorating weather conditions of the storm. So they decided to wait out the storm at Powell's Point but the weather conditions deteriorated so fast that they decided to outrun the storm-a move that they would soon live to regret. The problem, however, was not one of direction but of timing. As fate would have it, Styles had waited too late, as a result he was not able to outrun the storm but rather the direction of movement of his ship took them directly into the heart of the storm. A pastor at Wemyss Bight, just south of Powell's Point, would later report seeing *The Brontes 'scudding past the settlement, apparently steering for the Exuma Cays.'* Two hours later the weather had deteriorated so badly that he *'didn't think the Captain would be able to see to go through the Cays.'* At some point on that Sunday night, *The Brontes*, probably after broaching, would be smashed to pieces somewhere in the Exuma Cays, hurling its 30 passengers and crew into the unforgiving sea. Sadly, there would be no survivors. Pieces of the wreckage would later turn up at Beacon Cay in the Exumas. A few days later a search party from Cat Island would make a gruesome discovery at Highbourne Cay (Norman's Cay according to another account). Two women, one of them the wife of Commissioner Greenslade, lay dead on the beach. Describing the scene in gratuitously morbid detail, Arthur's Town Commissioner Duncombe would note that bodies were: *"swollen, one having her head bound up in the usual manner for keeping out the draught and the other having sand all through her hair; the former was more swollen than the latter and her face was bursting open, the skin mostly peeled of.*" Fearing contagion, the search party buried the bodies right away. Another body or two would turn up in the ensuing days but for the rest of *The Brontes'* passengers, captain and crew, would forever be lost to the merciless waters of the Atlantic.

Exuma

On Exuma, there were many stories of persons sailing to and from different Family Islands who were caught in the storm but were forced to stop on the Exuma mainland or one of its Cays to escape the storm. Some were lucky and were rescued while others were not so fortunate because they would later be found dead on some of the deserted cays in Exuma chain of islands, most likely from starvation or the over exposure to the weather elements. The schooner *Ladysmith* (Captain Solomon Smith) on its route from Exuma to Nassau, rescued 27 survivors of the schooners *Graceful* and *Columbia* who were picked up at Highbourne Cay in the Exumas. The schooner *Graceful* left Nassau at six o'clock on Saturday morning just before the storm for Watlings Island with ten persons onboard. She was struck by the storm just off Highbourne Cay and the captain anchored just offshore there to escape the storm. Soon the boat began to drag her anchors so dangerously that the captain decided to put the crew ashore. They saved a small quantity of provisions, but sadly, they were ruined by water. They took shelter under a piece of torn sail and remained in this precarious situation for three days until they were rescued.

The *Invincible*, a small schooner was lost in the storm but fortunately the five persons onboard were able to swim ashore. The boat was a total wreck and the sheep, sisal and fruits onboard were all lost, as well as about £60 in cash. The *Sarah Jane* was lost with six onboard perishing. Another sloop, name unknown, was reported sunk near Cat Island with twenty persons onboard perishing. The sloop *Doris* and its captain Gustave Rolle rescued 22 persons on Brigantine Cay and brought them to Nassau. Inaddition, two other sloops were wrecked on Brigantine Cay, the *Ella Jane* of Rolleville and the *C.E.M.I* from Ragged Island. The sloop *Sidney* on its way from Long Island was caught in the storm and was wrecked just offshore forcing the occupants to swim ashore. An unknown sloop from Acklins sunk in the storm with one person drowning as he tried to make it ashore to one of the Exuma Cays during the storm.

At George Town, the Anglican Church was left standing with little damage but the Rectory was swept away. Also about 90 percent of all the houses were destroyed on the island itself. Inaddition, there were 4 Baptist and 2 Episcopal churches destroyed at George Town alone. On the island about 500 houses were destroyed, while another 300 were partially destroyed and well over 1,000 persons were rendered homeless. Infact, at Georgetown alone, more than half of the houses were destroyed forcing many of the residents to take refuge in the schoolhouse, jail and in any other building left standing. They were forced to remain in these few remaining structures for weeks after the storm. The bridge over the canal at Farmer's Cay had been swept away along with many of the roads. Sheep and cattle lay dead everywhere and all of the unharvested crops and every fruit tree on the island was destroyed. The two vessels employed temporarily to convey mails and several other vessels which were anchored in the harbour were badly damaged when they sunk during the storm. After the storm, there were no vessels which remain unaffected or undamaged to take news of the devastation in Exuma to Nassau.

The Churches at Williamstown and the Forest were completely destroyed and a great deal of damage was done to the church at Hart's. On the island itself, there were six to seven Baptist churches which were destroyed. Among the more notable church structures to fall in this hurricane was St. Andrews Anglican Church at Georgetown. It was located above a hill overlooking the most picturesque harbour in the Bahamas. The church rectory had also been wrecked, adding Father Devard, an English priest, to the list of homeless persons. He would later move into the Commissioner's Residency which together with the schoolhouse, library, jail and administrative office, would soon be overflowing with others of the homeless for a long time to come. Many hundreds of others, however, would be left with nowhere to live except under the open skies or amidst the remains of their destroyed homes. The Commissioner's Residency, refuge to so many, and had itself suffered serious damage, losing its porch and four of its out-buildings one of which had been intended for use as a wireless station.

At the peak of the storm, the Commissioner George Clarke of the island went outside during the storm to catch the French doors which had become separated from the porch by the gusty winds. In doing so, he slipped and fell and was tossed against the Poinciana tree, hitting his side. Soon it would become swollen and infected. Little could Clarke have known it then but that injury, soon to be exacerbated by his tireless exertions and the horrific nightmares for Exuma that still lay ahead, would eventually send him to an early grave. George H. Clarke, who was only 52 years old at the time, had less than 3 months to live after the storm. Well over 10 vessels in George Town alone were destroyed during the storm and the entire corn crop and other field crops of the entire island were destroyed in the storm. Survivors reported shipwrecked persons from Acklins and other islands were stranded and starving in the Exuma Cays and were said to be in very bad condition. Most of the deaths in Exuma occurred from the turtling crew of *The Ready*, a schooner belonging to George Smith, who himself would be included among the dead.

During the second hurricane a large number of houses were destroyed in various settlements throughout the island and in some settlements no buildings were left standing and the sisal fields were also badly damaged. A number of fishing vessels including the Sloop *Invoice* and several houses were destroyed at Staniel Cay leaving over 40 person's homeless. In the settlement of Black Point there were over 300 persons rendered homeless, 23 houses, 1 church and 1 shop were destroyed leaving only 3 houses standing, and people had to find refuge under the damaged roof of the houses for weeks after the storm. Five sloops were totally destroyed, while many more were badly damaged and the storm surge rose several feet high and came inland and destroyed all of the field crops. At Farmer's Cay, which had a normal population of over 250 persons but during the storm only 70 persons were located here because the others were pre-occupied at Andros and Eleuthera on sponging trips. There were 16 houses and 1 Baptist church destroyed and 9 badly damaged. At George Town, very few buildings remained standing and the Commissioner's Office and resident were badly damaged. St Andrew's Church was badly damaged along with the main roads and recreation grounds. Some buildings at William's Town and Little Exuma were destroyed.

A study in topsy-turvydom after the Nassau Hurricane of 1926 lifted this house from it's' foundation and flipped it over in a settlement in Andros. (From the private collection of Patricia Beardsley Roker used with permission).

Bimini

At Bimini, the new Anglican Church lost its roof and a number of houses were destroyed. The public school room and the Methodist Church were completely destroyed. The majority of the crops were wiped out by the hurricane. The Episcopal Church roof was completely blown off. The wireless station and the lighthouse at Bailey Town north Bimini were completely destroyed. Following the hurricane, the Imperial Lighthouse Service decided not to rebuild the lighthouse at the current location but instead it erected a new lighthouse at North Rock, which is about 2 miles north of Cayce Point. Six vessels were wrecked at Gun Cay and two sank at Bimini. The *U.S.S. Bay Spring*, with Captain Thomas James and a crew of 25 Navy men brought much needed 1000 tons of food, water and building materials courtesy of the United States Government's Bureau of Navigation to the residents of Bimini after this storm.

On September 17, 1926, at 4pm the Radio Operator at North Bimini received a telegram from Nassau which read, *"Storm coming, prepare quickly."* News of this impending storm passed quickly by word of mouth throughout the settlements of Alice Town, Bailey Town and Porgy Bay for what would be called the worst hurricane in Bimini's history to date. After the second hurricane it was estimated that sixty percent of the houses on the island were destroyed and the hotel was also badly damaged and all communications were cut off. Wooden houses in low-lying areas floated off their ground pins and floundered like ships. Many persons abandoned their homes in the low-lying areas and ran to seek shelter in houses on higher ground. The school teachers' residence was destroyed and the public school building severely damaged, forcing the suspension of classes for many months. Mt. Zion Baptist Church, Wesley Methodist Church, Our Lady's and St. Stephen's Anglican Church were all severely damaged and most of their church records were destroyed.

There were approximately twenty five deaths and six persons badly injured. All the vessels in the harbour with one exception were destroyed and all of the provisions lost. The vessels *The William H. Albury* and *Monarch*, chartered by Messer's, Finley and Kemp were completely destroyed and their much needed provisions lost. Mr. Kemp, who was on the schooner *William H. Albury*, took refuge at Cat Cay which lies opposite Gun Cay and was taken in at one of Mr. Strong's houses. Mr. Bruce and Bertie Bethell, who were on the three masted schooner *Purceller* which had been partially wrecked in the July hurricane, had to abandon their boat and make for the shores of Cat Cay where they spent a terrible night clinging onto the rocks and hanging onto the bushes to save themselves. Unfortunately, the *Purceller* was totally destroyed in this storm. During this storm, *The Finisterre* was sent to Bimini Harbour for safety but was lost with most of her cargo. The schooner *Laura Louise* as well as the mail schooner *Defence* sunk and were smashed to pieces and the schooner *The Tryon* was blown out of the harbour. Mr. Bethell's warehouse and dwelling house were destroyed. Mr. Saunders, who with his family lived there, was found alive, but sadly, his wife, sister and daughter were all found dead in the wreckage.

Bishop Randal Saunders, whose boat was the only one that survived the hurricane, simply because it sank instead of being wrecked or washed away, played a major role following this hurricane. He was able to repair his boat very quickly after the storm and sailed it to Miami, Florida to gather much needed emergency supplies of food, water and clothing to relieve the hurricane stricken inhabitants on this island. Then for nearly three months he substituted his boat for mail, passengers and freight services between Nassau and Bimini, because the original mail boat was destroyed in the hurricane.

All of the farms on the south side of Bimini were destroyed. Salt water from the storm surge contaminated the fresh water wells. It was estimated that as much as six to seven feet of water flooded the streets in some areas of North Bimini. As the days went by, drinking water became increasingly a problem as the island residents became more thirsty and impatient for relief supplies to come from Nassau and the United States. As a result, many persons ended up drinking the contaminated salty water from the brackish wells and were stricken with typhoid fever and sixteen of them died from the disease. Eventually they obtained safe drinking water from South Bimini and this fresh water well was attributed with saving the lives of many of the inhabitants of Bimini. The well was called *'Brother Peter's Well'* named after an early settler to South Bimini called Peter Russell. Mr. Russell, an ex-slave, carved the well with only a hammer and chisel into the solid limestone rock. He used this well to irrigate his field crops and sugarcane, located adjacent to the well. After this hurricane, they hired Bradford Saunders and Henry Hanna to construct a historical stone monument around the well in early October of 1926. The vessel S.S. *'West Ekonk'* supplied the starving residents with a limited amount of emergency supplies. Approximately 4,000 gallons of distilled water and necessary medical supplies, foodstuff and clothing were furnished by the local doctor, Dr. Little and the United States Navy and Coast Guard.

After the third hurricane, approximately seven persons were killed and most of the remaining houses which survived the previous two hurricanes were destroyed and the entire island was said to be devastated by this storm. Great suffering occurred because the storm surge from the hurricane contaminated the fresh water wells with salt water. Some vessels from Nassau were dispatched to the island with an abundant supply of fresh water, food, clothing and building materials.

As soon as the residents of Bimini were able to begin to recover from the three hurricanes, a major rebuilding program was launched, particularly in the area of housing and public works. It began during the month of October 1926 after the second hurricane and continued into the following year. The Bahamas Government carried out repairs on the courthouse, Commissioner's Office, jail, and quarters for the Radio Operator and three concrete water tanks which were heavily damaged by these hurricanes. Eight houses destroyed in this storm were built at the expense of the Government for the destitute widows who lost their husbands in this storm.

The Berry Islands

There was major damage reported in the Berry Islands where there were only a few houses which were left standing and not a single boat escaped complete destruction. Food, clothing, water and building supplies were dispatched to this island by the Central Government in Nassau, the American Red Cross and the British Embassy in Washington to alleviate starvation. In the second hurricane, at Bullock's Harbour, the farms were totally destroyed, the sisal crop was totally ruined, all of the houses left standing from the previous storm were blown away and many of the inhabitants were in great distress. There was not a single morsel of food on the island for sale for quite some time after the storm.

Nassau

After the *Great Miami Hurricane of 1926*, His Excellency, Sir Harry Cordeaux the Governor of the Bahamas toured the hurricane ravaged areas of the Bahamas on the British warship *HMS Valerian*. After rendering assistance to the Bahamas Government after the hurricanes of July and September, 1926 it was lost near Bermuda. A Special Committee was appointed by the Governor to oversee hurricane relief in the islands, to raise funds for the people affected by the hurricane and to gather information as to the extent of the damage of the hurricane on the domestic and economic life of the Colony. The Hurricane Relief Committee consisted of the Hon. G.H. Gamblin, Mr. W.C.B Johnson, and His Lordship the Bishop, Rev. W.H. Richards and Mr. W.H.H. Maura. This Committee reported widespread damage throughout Nassau with significant damage to many of the houses and businesses and many fallen trees across the major thoroughfares of Nassau. The number of buildings destroyed in Nassau was well over 4,300 buildings. The number of persons left destitute, with no shelter but that afforded them by neighbours, was well into the thousands in Nassau and neighbouring districts alone. The damage done to buildings in Nassau and suburbs was roughly £82,762. The damage to government property alone in Nassau was well over £150,000. The damage to shipping was severe and far exceeded well over £250,000.

A private dwelling home along with a three car garage totally destroyed in the Nassau Hurricane of 1926. One of the three cars in the foreground was damaged beyond repair and the other two sustained minor damages when the sides and roof of the home collapsed onto them during the storm (Courtesy of Charles. J. Whelbell Collection-The Department of Archives).

Major damages were reported to many of the churches in Nassau such as, St. Matthew's, St. Ann's, Salem, St. Mark's, Zion Baptist and Trinity Church. Immediately after the storm, the Trustees and Finance Committee of Trinity Church got together and arranged for the immediate repair of the roof and the building(unfortunately, it was again badly damaged in the second storm). Almost the entire roof of Salem Baptist Church was blown off. The pastor of Salem Baptist Church at the time was Rev. D. Wilshere who estimated that it would cost well over £3000 to rebuild the church. Zion Baptist Church and its Mission House were destroyed and would end up costing over £500 to repair. St. Ann's Church on the top of Fox Hill was unroofed and the building badly damaged and would end up costing well over £2000 to repair. St. Matthew's Church had some broken windows and part of the eastern wall torn down. Wesley Chapel, Grant's Town had the roof completely blown off and the church and its interior badly damaged. St. John's Church had the roof completely torn away and the eastern and western walls were blown down, it was later repaired at a cost of over £7000. St. Mark's Church needed over £7000 to repair the roof and the building and Gambier Church, almost totally destroyed also needed a similar amount to repair.

Adelaide Village in the southwest district of Nassau was devastated- all of the dwelling homes with one exception and the churches in this settlement were all totally destroyed. Food, clothing and building supplies were supplied to them to ease their hardships. Until help arrived, 38 of the residents were forced to live of a few green mangoes fallen of the trees during the storm. It was reported that only one habitable house was left standing and many persons were forced to live in this house and under the fallen roofs of their homes. At the Eastern Parade on East Bay Street was totally blocked by fallen trees and access to Shirley Street was blocked off by fallen trees. The Fort Montagu Hotel suffered significantly because the roof was practically stripped of its red Spanish tiles and the front part of the roof was torn off and many of the glass panes and windows were blown out and the interior badly damaged by flood waters. The Fort Montagu Hotel stood in several feet of water for days after the storm and all of the trees on the property were blown down and would end up costing over £1,000 to fix and repair the damages. The damage to the New Colonial Hotel was well over £500. Significant damage was reported to the Royal Victoria Hotel and Gardens and would cost over £4,000 to fix and repair the damages.

There was widespread devastation in the settlements of Fox Hill and Grant's Town because most of the dwelling homes were totally destroyed rendering many of these residents homeless. The trees and wreckage of many of the houses littered the streets for days after the storm. To add to the hardship there was flood waters of four feet and higher in many of the streets. The following buildings suffered significant damages, St. Matthews Church, *'Miramar'* home of Mr. G. K.K. Brace. *'Breezy Ridge'* home of Capt. Corbett, R.N., Outbuildings on Knowles Dairy Farm, Mr. R.W.D. Albury's house on West Bay Street, Mr. Sumner's house and Dr. Hess's house in Cable Beach which had his roof completely blown off and his house completely destroyed. The Keepers dwelling on the Eastern Lighthouse was blown away. The roof of the Hon. P.W. Ambrister and the Verandah on East Bay was blown off. Mr. Theo. M. Knowles' new house opposite St. Anne's Rectory had his roof completely blown off and the garage was turned upside down during the hurricane. The Bahama Islands Import and Export Company's liquor warehouses (better known as Murphy's Buildings) on the north side of Bay Street were completely wrecked. Two of Mr. C.E. Bethell's warehouses on the south side of Bay Street had their roofs entirely blown off. The roof was partially lifted off the Girls' Eastern School, leaving only four walls.

Mr. Cedric Farrington's new house on East Shirley Street, opposite the Fort Montagu Hotel, was demolished; the family who lived in a bungalow in the rear had to take refuge in a Ford Sedan during the storm. Mr. R.T. Symonette ship house and home on Paradise Island were totally destroyed costing well over £2,500 to repair. Mr. T.G. Johnson's Restaurant on the Waterloo Slope property near the hotel, was destroyed. Great havoc occurred at Salt Cay but the bungalows there were not damaged. The New Piccadilly Restaurant was badly damaged and its stock almost totally ruined. The Star, also owned by Capt. Isaac had its stock completely ruined. Capt. Isaacs had to leave the building (residence upstairs) and take refuge with Ned Isaacs and his estimated loss was about £500. The roof of the West Indian Oil Company roof was blown off. Emma Whylley roof and house were torn down leaving five people destitute and would end up costing £80 to fix. Miss A. Armbrister house and outbuilding were destroyed costing £200 to fix. Mr. R.H. Curry roof, porch and outbuildings were destroyed costing £800 to repair. Alfred Maycock house was destroyed costing £150 to repair. Tiliacos, Christofilis and Christodoulakis sponge warehouses were destroyed costing £300, £250 and £700 to repair respectively.

Commissioner Thompson's house and kitchen were badly damaged. Jane Davis and Eliza Saunders houses in Grant's Town were totally destroyed and the occupants left destitute and it would end up costing £30 and £150 to repair respectively. The home of the Hon. W.K. Moore on West Hill Street was badly damaged. *'Ocean View,'* home of Mr. R.M. Lightbourn, was badly damaged along with his verandah and part of his roof. Dr. Hess home on Nassau Street had his roof completely blown off and destroyed. Mr. Jas. H.Rhodes and Co, large sponge rooms on West Bay Street split in two and was destroyed and the car belonging to Mr. Mike Nicholas (who was in Greece on vacation at the time) was destroyed when the building collapsed on it. Mrs. John Bosfield home on Delancy Street was completely destroyed. The sponge room on Curry's Wharf was completely destroyed and the sponge warehouse owned by Mr. P.C. Smith was destroyed but the sponges inside were saved. The home of Mr. Alfred Holmes reported significant roof and other damages. *'The Farm's'* eastern and northern verandahs were blown away and the sisters inside were forced to seek refuge in St. Agnes rectory during the storm. The storerooms of Mr. C.E. Bethell were blown away. Mr. Thaddeus Johnson restaurant was destroyed and would end up costing £500 to repair.

Mr. W.E.G. Pritchard building was destroyed costing £400 to repair. Mr. and Mrs. Kingsbury Moore had a fearful experience in their home adjacent to their dairy farm near Chapman's Estate. The roof was torn off and they sought shelter in the various outbuildings during the storm but slowly but surely all of the shelters where they sought refuge were eventually blown down forcing them back into the raging winds and torrential rainfall of the storm. Their cattle stampeded in the sheds, which they had to break open to release the frightened animals, eventually, Mr. and Mrs. Moore found refuge in a garage at Westward Villas. The Workshop-Board of Trade was damaged beyond repair and many windows were blown away and the sashes were smashed in the main building and a very valuable dinghy was destroyed. A portion of the roofs of Mr. Wheatley's Turtle's and Mr. Edwin Mosley's homes were destroyed. All of the bath houses and bathing piers from Ramsay's to the Parade were washed away. The home of Mr. W.E. Fountain was badly damaged. Charles. E. Bethell warehouse roof was blown off and would cost over £800 to fix. Mr. G. Maillis had two of his out buildings destroyed at a cost of over £300.

Salem Baptist Church with its roof partially destroyed in the Nassau Hurricane of 1926. Its roof was also damaged in a similar fashion three years later in the Great Bahamas Hurricane of 1929 (Courtesy of Charles. J. Whelbell Collection-The Department of Archives).

When the storm was raging on Sunday night and part of Monday, a large iron safe and other valuable goods were stolen from Mr. Geo Farrington's Liquor Store on Market Street. Fortunately, the culprits were caught in the act by Mr. William Armbrister during the peak of the storm trying to lift the heavy safe across the street. The two men, Leonard Tucker and Lawrence Pennyman were caught, arrested and charged in connection with this theft. They were eventually tried in the Supreme Court and were found guilty and both men were sentenced to three years imprisonment. The electrical and telephone wires in the eastern and western suburbs were completely destroyed and it was estimated that it would take over a month before they can be repaired. The acting Chief Justice Mr. H.F. Cox postponed the session of the Supreme Court for over a week until the standing water in the Supreme Court building could be removed.

The *Columbia, Mathoke* and *Home Comfort* were sunk and destroyed in the Nassau Harbour. Infact, of the forty-nine boats in the harbour channel, forty-two were blown out of the channel and totally destroyed. The *Old Vim* and several other boats were completely destroyed and smashed against the rocks over on Hog Island (Paradise Island). The *Eula M* skipper and owner Capt. Robert Archer came into the harbour on Sunday afternoon with lumber for the Bahamas Cuban Company from Norman's Castle, Abaco; she could not make safe anchorage and was abandoned near the bar. She was smashed to pieces on the rocks below Fort Charlotte during the storm. The sloop *Handy* owned by Mr. Rolly Cleare, of Fresh Creek, Andros, left on Friday morning for Nassau. Running into bad weather, he sailed to the south side of Nassau and anchored near Adelaide. Two of the crew, Milton Thompson and Daniel Solomon, were sent ashore for provisions. When they returned to the south side where the sloop was located, they discovered that the sloop was gone with Milton Ambrister and his wife Ann, who they left onboard. Parts of the missing vessel and some clothing would later show up on the Adelaide Beach but the two persons onboard were never heard from again.

A seaplane was sent from Miami by the Associated Press and the Miami Daily News to Nassau to cover the aftermath of the storm but somehow the plane got lost and ran out of gas and was forced to land on Billy Island, near Andros but fortunately another seaplane in the vicinity provided them with some gas for them to resume their flight. This other plane had come to search for the staff and crew of the yacht *Seminole*, which was hired to take the staff of the American Museum of Natural History in New York to Nassau and Andros for research work. According to the pilot, the reason why the plane missed her original course was that the islands were totally unrecognizable by air because they were all flooded making them appear as if they were simply dotted with lakes with only a few land masses sticking above the flood waters. They were still uncertain of their bearings, until they sighted the familiar sponging vessel *Resolute* just West of Morgan's Bluff, Andros.

Grand Bahama

The majority of the boats on this island were completely destroyed and the ones remaining were badly damaged. The majority of the damage done on this island was to the dwelling homes and the field crops. A Baptist Church was also blown down and completely destroyed. The Police Dock was swept away and Ambrister, Crawford and Maury docks were completely destroyed. The Schooner *Dauntless* was lost with at least nine persons onboard perishing. The bridge at Hawks Bill Creek was destroyed. This island sustained winds of well over 120 miles per hour. On this island, two doctors were dispatched by the American Red Cross to assist the residents after the storm. Some residents rejected to these doctors being sent to Grand Bahama because they believed they were sent with ulterior motives in mind, so a few persons pelted them with stones and others simply refused to be seen by them.

Long Cay

Between 400 to 500 buildings including dwelling houses, churches, kitchen, barns and shops were destroyed in the first hurricane. The remaining 12 houses left standing after the first hurricane were destroyed in the second hurricane.

Ragged Island

The public school house was blown down and as much as 50,000 bushels of salt was washed away by the storm surge.

Rum Cay

Most residents on Rum Cay never received any warnings that a storm of such great intensity was heading directly towards this island, so they never made any preparations for this storm and that would be a mistake they would soon live to regret. All of the salt ponds were completely flooded and all of the 130,000 bushels of salt accumulated from the previous months were completely destroyed. The damage to the salt pond was estimated at £1000 and conditions were so bad on this island that one resident even offered to fix the salt pond for half of the estimated price if he along with his labourers were allowed to be paid in flour and corn seeds-the offer was refused. This was devastating for the island because the majority of persons on this island were employed in raking of the salt for local consumption and for export. The island's entire field crops were completely destroyed. There was widespread devastation throughout the island as 1 church (Episcopal) destroyed, 2 chapels (Baptists) destroyed and 2 severely damaged, 1 police office and prison unroofed, 1 schoolhouse destroyed, 2 wharves destroyed, 22 dwellings destroyed and 18 severely damaged and twelve kitchens were totally destroyed and eight kitchens badly damaged. Approximately 317 coconut trees fell down, 27 sheep and 417 chickens drowned.

St. John Baptist Church collapsed and destroyed (its roof flying off and penetrating a woman's house on the other side of the road) and one person was reportedly drowned. After *The Great Miami Hurricane of 1926* on September 17, the Governor left Nassau on the *HMS Valerian* on the morning of the 8th October and returned to Nassau on the morning of the 16th October. Between those dates he visited San Salvador (Watlings), Rum Cay, Fortune Island (Long Cay), Inagua, Mayaguana, Long Island, Exuma and Cat Island. He attempted to visit Acklins by a local boat from Long Cay but was unfortunately, hindered by a series of accidents so he had to abandon his attempts. On all of the islands he visited, except Inagua and San Salvador, he reported that the damage done by *The Great Miami Hurricane* of the 17th September was very much greater than that done by the first hurricane. At Rum Cay, the salt pond, which provided a means of livelihood for the greater part of the population, was severely damaged and was only restored at great expense.

Cat Island

Cat Island was the island of the greatest fatalities of *The Nassau Hurricane of 1926*. The Commissioner of the island Nathaniel Dorsett would claim in his annual report for 1926 that *'74 persons were drowned from the Bight District alone.'* At Arthur's Town nine houses were completely destroyed and twelve badly damaged. At Devil's Point 27 houses were blown down including two churches and one Society Hall. Several boats from Cat Island were lost at sea and sadly were never heard from again. The sloop *Surprise* was totally wrecked at Alligator Bay near Roker's but all were saved. The sloop *Saucy Sea Bird* of Mason's Bay, Acklins was wrecked at the Bight, but fortunately the crew of five was saved.

The Rev. James Smith of Port Howe, Cat Island built the vessel *The Mountain King* which was used as a freight and passenger vessel between Cat Island and New Providence. This vessel was caught by the *Nassau Hurricane of 1926* between Bird Cay and Little San Salvador (later Disney's Half Moon Cay) on the return trip to Cat Island, Captain Elliston Bain wanted to put the vessel into the shallow waters and let the passengers wait out the hurricane on either of the two named cays. The mate, Napoleon Rolle of Devil's Point, Cat Island who was also a captain, strongly disagreed stating that the vessel would be badly damaged and somehow he managed to convince Captain Bain to continue the journey to Cat Island against his better judgment. Captain Bain was said to have stated that if they continued, by the next day, "*They would all surely die!*" Some 25 miles from Orange Creek and Arthur's Town, Cat Island, *The Mountain King* sunk in the rough seas and raging winds of the hurricane and all 26 souls (14 women, 7 men and 5 children) on board with one exception was lost. The mate Napoleon Rolle was as fate would have it was the sole survivor of this boat when he swam to Bird Cay during the storm. There he would be taken care of by the 5 shipwrecked crew of another Cat Island vessel *Hero*. While searching the island in the aftermath of the storm, they came across a rickety 20 ft. boat and used it to make their way back to Cat Island, landing at Orange Creek with the 'miracle boy' onboard in early August. Napoleon was said to for the rest of his life regretted not listening to Captain Bain's advice. Many persons in this community became overnight paupers, widows and orphans due to this incident. The bodies of Sally Davis and Claudius Simmons were two of the few bodies ever found from *The Mountain King* and they were eventually buried in a special burial service.

During the second hurricane, a large number of houses were destroyed in various settlements throughout the island and in some settlements no buildings were left standing. The very valuable and productive sisal fields were badly damaged. The Commissioner's Office at the Bight was badly damaged, several schoolhouses were blown down and all schools were closed as the buildings were found to be unsafe for occupancy. At the Bight, at least one life was lost and two boats loaded with supplies were lost.

Long Island

Many houses were destroyed, all of the public roads were blocked and the bridge was badly damaged. There were 4 churches (2 Baptist and 2 Episcopal), 1 schoolhouse, 5 stores, 230 dwelling houses, 5 schooners, 2 sloops and 16 boats which were totally destroyed from this hurricane. The majority of the damage from the hurricane was done to the southern end of Long Island where very few houses were left standing. During the hurricane, 62 persons found shelter in the jailhouse and 23 in the police officer's residence and sadly, they had to remain living there for a few weeks because their homes were destroyed in the hurricane. On one of the most flourishing estates at the north end was destroyed, all of the buildings were blown down except one kitchen which was left standing and 47 persons had to take refuge there for several weeks because their houses were destroyed. One man, Sidney Burrows, was drowned on the south shore. The cotton fields, which had been destroyed or severely damaged by the first hurricane was replanted immediately afterwards but sadly they were destroyed again in the second hurricane.

Several vessels including the sloops *Lilla* and *Speedwell* and a few other smaller boats were also lost. Eight vessels of various sizes that were away on voyages; six were entirely lost and two badly damaged. The fishing vessels *Albertine* and *Iona* from Clarence Town were washed ashore during the first hurricane. Four men and three women were lost on these boats. The sloops *Rose Bell, Serene* and *Sacramore* were sunk and driven ashore at Deadman's Cay and the *Eclipse* and two Acklins vessels were lost but fortunately no lives were lost. A Long Island man with his young bride, a child and a crew of nine from the sloop *Celeste* were reported drowned near Farmer's Cay in the Exumas. Three young boys aboard the vessel, however, would have better luck by hanging onto a piece of wreckage, they made it safely ashore. The light stations at North End and Simms were blown away. A bridge at Simms' forming part of the road was badly damaged from the storm surge. Many of the Clarence Town public buildings suffered some damage and most of the private properties throughout the island suffered significant damages.

During the second hurricane a large number of houses were destroyed in various settlements throughout the island and in some settlements no buildings were left standing and the sisal fields were badly damaged. Approximately twenty five persons throughout the island died during this hurricane and hundreds more rendered homeless. In the settlement of Simms, only 1 building was left standing and water flowed inland for about two to three miles and in some places the fields were submerged and many sheep, goats, chickens, turkey buzzards and cattle drowned. Many sections of the main road was destroyed or washed away. The Methodist, Anglican and Baptists Churches at Simms were totally destroyed. The mail schooner *'Columbia'* was washed ashore along the beach. In the settlement of Clarence Town 42 houses were destroyed, at Victoria Village 21 houses were destroyed, at Scrub Hill to Gaythorn's 129 houses were destroyed, in the southern District 31 houses, 2 schools, 1 church and 1 chapel destroyed. The Commissioner's residence and kitchen, the teacher's resident and jail were badly damaged. The wharf at Clarence Town was washed away and the light at the harbour was destroyed. One of the radio towers was blown down and shattered to pieces. At the settlement of Dunmore South End, only 1 house was left standing after the storm. All of the fields were wiped away and to make matters worse all of the foodstuffs in the various stores and homes were destroyed.

After the third hurricane, over eleven persons were killed and just about every house which survived the first and second hurricanes were destroyed.

Acklins

In the *Nassau Hurricane of 1926* well over 427 houses were destroyed in Acklins and many persons from different settlements throughout the island drowned from the storm surge. The majority of the island residents were left homeless and starving after this hurricane. In Snug Corner all but one of the 92 houses in the settlement were flattened, at Hard Hill some 90 houses were blown down, and at Spring Point 53 houses were destroyed including the church and the school house. In the settlement of Thompson's 3 houses were destroyed. In the settlement of Anderson's 19 houses were destroyed and in Pine Field and Jew Fish settlements 22 and 9 respectively were destroyed. In the settlement of Relief 17 houses were destroyed and six persons drowned. In the settlements of Chester's and Pastell's 22 and 13 houses were destroyed respectively. In the settlement of Delectable Bay 43 buildings were destroyed and a building collapsed and crushed the female occupant to death. In the settlements of Pompey Bay, Aston Cay and Binnicle Hill, 48, 26 and 26 houses were respectively destroyed. Many losses also occurred at sea when Moses Hanna and his two crew members comprising of two young boys were lost at sea.

According to Sir Clifford Darling, the former Governor General of the Bahamas recalled that this was the most powerful and frightening hurricane he has ever experienced. During the hurricane, he recalled how nine families in the settlement of Chester's, including his own, were trapped in their homes between the waterfront on the north and the overflowing waters of a tidal creek on the south. As the houses started to collapse with the storm surge water rising within these houses during the hurricane, a quick decision was made to flee to the hilltop some 60 to 80 feet above the beach. Young Sir Clifford, who was only four years old at the time, was placed in a canvas sack along with his sister with only their heads sticking out, slung over his brother's back. In total, 45 persons in all assembled themselves into a human chain and together they made that fateful journey to the safety of the hilltop and rode out the rest of the storm on top of that hill. When the storm abated and they went back home, they were surprised to find that the storm blew the roof off their house. His brother turned the roof right-side up and took a hand saw and cut a hole in that roof resting a few yards away from the damaged house and they lived in the cramped up confines of that roof for a few weeks after the storm, until his father returned home from *'the Contract'* to repair the damaged house. Unfortunately, four of his uncles were on a fishing vessel and were on the way back from San Salvador to Acklins, but sadly they were lost in the storm.

After the second hurricane, there was widespread devastation and much more lives were lost in this storm than in the first hurricane. At Acklins many of the settlements were totally destroyed and well over 52 lives were lost. Over 300 buildings and virtually all of the local vessels were destroyed on this island. At Ashton Cay to Delectable 25 houses were destroyed, Spring Point 6 houses destroyed, the Church of England and schoolhouse were destroyed, at Mason's Bay 71 houses and shops were destroyed and 10 persons died, at Chester's 50 houses were destroyed, at Pastel 20 houses destroyed and at Lovely Bay 30 houses and one school house destroyed. The were 7 persons who drowned at Lovely Bay, 8 at Brown's, Ashton Cay 5, Thompson Creek 3, and 19 returning from wrecks at San Salvador. After the hurricane, many persons suffered from severe cases of diarrhea due to drinking contaminated ground water and quite a few of them died from drinking this contaminated water. Foodstuff from Nassau was dispatched within 48 hours after the hurricane to relieve the starving population on Acklins.

Crooked Island

After the first hurricane, this island suffered widespread devastation. The Broon settlement lost 4 houses, True Blue 10 houses, Bullock's Hill 12 houses, Thompson's 7 houses, Major's Cay 30 houses, including the walls of the new schoolhouse, MacKay's 9 houses, Colonel Hill 63 houses, Moss Town, Fair Field and Richmond 39 houses respectively and Church Grove 20 houses and one church.

After the second hurricane many of the settlements were totally destroyed and many lives lost. At Colonel Hill there were 30 houses and shops destroyed. The Government office at Church Grove was destroyed and only three houses in this settlement were left standing. At Clearfield 15 buildings were destroyed. In total, some 200 buildings and virtually all of the local vessels were destroyed on this island. Foodstuff from Nassau was dispatched within 48 hours after the hurricane to relieve the starving population on Crooked Island.

Mayaguana

Some lives were lost and the people were in great distress and starving with very little food and all of their fresh water wells were contaminated by sea water from the hurricane surge. A 34 year old man, Daniel Brown, died when he tried to secure his boat into a safe harbour. The Governor on his visit to the island of Mayaguana after the second hurricane supplied the residents with food, clothing and a medical doctor and he speculated that it would be some time before a sufficient supply of fresh water could be restored to the island. Island wide devastation from Pirate's Well to Betsy's Bay was reported.

The Abaco sloop *Magdalene D* captained by Herbert Archer but owned by Mr. W.J. Amaly a sponge merchant and the mailboat *None Such* owned by Fred Black were destroyed. Archer had also been on his way to San Salvador with a 6-man crew to take Bahamas Customs Officer, Joseph Sands, to the *S.S. Kembala*, a 9000 ton British steamer, bound from Norfolk to New Zealand, which had struck a reef and taken in 14 feet of water. As for Captain Archer and the sloop of the *Magdalene D*, the vessel would founder in the Exuma Cays, drowning five of its crew members in the process. As for Archer, mate George Hudson and Customs Officer Sands, they would be 'dashed on the rocks' of an uninhabited cay. Sands would sustain several gashes in his head and Archer would be injured as well. For three days they would remain on that cay undiscovered and starving. Their desperation growing, the three men decided to swim to a nearby cay. Much weakened by his injuries, however, Sands lost contact with Archer and Hudson during the crossing and by the time night fell he was nowhere to be seen, nor would he ever be seen again. Reaching another cay and discovering that it was no more helpful than the one they had just deserted, Archer and Hudson built a raft from floating debris and set out once again. They would be adrift for another eight hours before being spotted by a search party and taken to Nassau to recover from their ordeal. Weeks after, Archer would still be suffering from the effects of exposure and complaining of 'severe pain in his feet.' These afflictions notwithstanding, he could well have counted himself the luckiest man on earth.

Eleuthera

During the first hurricane, the damages were slight as compared to the other islands; several houses were destroyed and numerous coconuts and other fruit bearing trees were blown down throughout the island. There were 14 churches and two school houses which were destroyed on this island. There were 240 dwelling houses totally destroyed, 56 badly damaged and 831 persons rendered homeless. There were 8 vessels and boats destroyed and another 16 badly damaged. The majority of the farm crops throughout the island were destroyed with the exception of the pineapple crop which only sustained 50% crop damage. Most roads were destroyed and rendered impassible and the major causeways were all washed away. In some of the settlements, more houses were destroyed than were left standing. Throughout all of the settlements, there was standing water between two to four feet in depth but fortunately it drained away quickly in most places.

On Harbour Island, the damage consisted of, 1 Episcopal Church destroyed, 1 police office and prison partially destroyed, 2 schoolhouses destroyed, 26 dwelling homes totally destroyed and 21 dwelling homes badly damaged, 4 schooners lost, 12 schooners badly damaged. At Spanish Wells and the Current, one Episcopal Church and 4 Wesleyan Chapels were destroyed in each settlement. Four women and five men drowned in the settlement of James Cistern. A child of three drowned in a water hole in the school yard having apparently gone there to play without realizing the depth. Two persons got injured when an old house collapsed on them. The fishing schooner *Imperial* was lost at Rock Sound with 7 people onboard. The schooner *Imperial* left Tarpum Bay for Rock Sound for safe harbour, reached Sound Point and anchored, later parted moorings and went adrift and was never heard from again taking those seven lives with it. William McCartney of Tarpum Bay who was one of the leading merchants and tomato exporters of Eleuthera, together with his son, Charles, and a crew of five had set out at noon on Sunday to take McCartney's schooner, *Imperial* to safe harbour but got only as far as Rock Sound due to the deteriorating weather conditions. It would prove to be a fatal decision because three days later, a search party was assembled and would find bits and pieces of the *Imperial* scattered between Rock Sound and Green Castle. McCartney, his son, and the entire crew, had all perished.

A fishing vessel owned by Inspector Albury was destroyed. Another schooner with fourteen or fifteen females and an unknown number of children onboard, as well as the crew, dragged her anchors, and was driven out to sea and was never heard from again. The sloop *Lily G* arrived at the settlement of Deep Creek just before the storm but parted her moorings and was never heard from again. Nine houses fell, 6 at Green Castle, 2 at Wemyss' Bight and 1 at Tarpum Bay. At Spanish Wells, a newly built boat was lost during the hurricane and a search party was dispatched to find and salvage her from on the Great Bahama Bank. The light at Powell's Point was destroyed. Several small houses at Governor's Harbour and up shore were blown down and destroyed. Mr. W.T. Cleare, the Commissioner for Governor's Harbour, reported that four women and five men left that Sunday morning for Nassau and was never heard from again. Two persons got injured when an old house collapsed. A body was spotted floating in the waters on the western side of the island on the night of the hurricane but by the time lanterns, a boat and a search team could be assembled, it had disappeared never to be seen again. The boat *The Molly O* was travelling through the Northwest Channel on her way to Gun Cay also saw a body afloat on the water. The vessel *Isles of June* was dispatched from Nassau to Governor's Harbour by the Governor a few days after the storm had passed with 500 bags of flour and much needed hurricane relief supplies.

After the hurricane (the third hurricane) of October 21st and 22nd there was major damage reported and practically every wharf was destroyed and all of the roads and causeways near the sea were swept away. It was reported that water was up to six feet deep and up to the window sills in many of the settlements. The vessel *Endion* was badly damaged at Harbour Island. The Eastern Cemetery was completely washed away, causing the coffins to be floated away like little boats to a distance of over 1,000 feet from the cemetery. The damage to Government property at Governor's Harbour alone was estimated at £10,000. In the outlying settlements of Palmetto Point and Tarpum Bay, the wharves were completely destroyed and the one at Rock Sound was partially destroyed. The main road and bridge leading to Tarpum Bay for a length of about ½ mile was entirely under water to depth of over 18 feet in the storm surge. Twelve homes on Cupid Cay were washed away and the prison and engine room were used as temporary shelters for the homeless. The causeway on the mainland was practically washed away. The water in Colebrookville was deep enough to carry small boats. The sea came in so rapidly that some people, including the wireless operators had to flee for their lives in a depth of water of over four feet. A large proportion of the tomato fields were washed away and the farmers had to sow fresh seeds setting them back 4 to 6 weeks. At James's Cistern some portions of the main street was washed away and a few homes were blown away and destroyed.

CHAPTER NINE

The Work of the Government after these Three Hurricanes in 1926 to Stabilize the Economy of the Bahamas

After the hurricanes, the Governor of the Bahamas, Sir Harry Cordeaux was able to explain the Government's plans for reconstruction to the Family Island Commissioners and the people, and to settle any doubtful questions as to the amount of relief to be given in special cases. At every settlement, His Majesty's King George V message of sympathy was received with gratitude and loyalty. Immediately after the second hurricane, the Governor dispatched relief boats filled with a small amount of relief supplies and fresh water to each island. Two boats were sent to Andros, one to Bimini and the Berry Islands, *The Halcyon* left for Exuma, Long Island and Long Cay. *The Graceful* was sent to Rum Cay and San Salvador. Inaddition, the Governor travelled to each island after each hurricane on the British Naval ship *HMS Valerian* to find out the extent of the damages which occurred on each island and to assure the residents that their needs will be met by the Government. After his tour throughout the Family Islands, he was satisfied that the preliminary reports of the widespread devastation and damages done in these islands had not been exaggerated and that he promised them that he will do everything in his power to assist them to the best of the Bahamas Government's ability.

On the Governor's return to Nassau after the first and second hurricanes, he immediately summoned a meeting of the Executive Council to consider what measures should be taken to deal with the situation at hand. The first emergency measures taken were to supply the people with food, clothing, seeds and a small quantity of building materials. This council approved of the following measures:-

1) Notices were posted up in all the Family Islands warning the residents not to proceed to Nassau, where work was scarce and housing accommodations were difficult to obtain, and assuring them of the government's assistance if they remained in their respective settlements in the various islands.

2) To make good the loss of vessels, the government arranged for at least two sloops to be built in each district by local builders at the public's expense, these vessels when completed were sold at cost price to local persons who were required to pay for them in easy installments.

3) A loan on easy terms was made to any person whose vessel was damaged in the hurricane and who was prepared to repair it immediately.

4) Instead of confining relief works to the construction of roads and other public utilities, the Family Island Commissioners were directed to employ people in the construction of kilns and the burning of lime(the lime to be given away to those who were prepared to rebuild their homes) and to employ others to clear and prepare the fields for planting.

5) In order to leave the people time to rebuild and repair their own homes damaged during the storms, relief work was given on three days a week only, except in special cases.

6) Seeds for planting were distributed freely in all districts.

7) Wooden homes of a standard size were constructed for distribution throughout the islands; the lumber was being

sawed to given dimensions by the Bahamas Cuban Company at their mills at Abaco, and it was a simple matter for the homes to be erected without employing skilled labour.

8) The Deputy Civil Engineer was instructed to proceed on a tour through those islands which have suffered to advise the Commissioners on the reconstruction of roads, wharves and public buildings, and, if desired, to advise the people on the rebuilding of their homes and churches.

9) Competent and practical spongers were sent at the Government's expense to the sponging grounds to report on the condition of the sponge beds (which, it is feared, have suffered severely) so as to save vessels from making useless trips to the sponging grounds.

10) To assist the owners of fishing and sponging vessels, a grant of £13,000 to be loaned by the Government in sums of £100 in respect to any boat lost or badly damaged in these storms and the loan was to be paid off after 5 years to help stimulate the local Nassau and Family Island economies.

Family Island Commissioners were instructed by the Governor to begin work on the damaged and destroyed roads and government buildings to generate employment within the various communities throughout the islands. The clearing and preparing of the fields at public expense was an unusual step but the Governor considered it to be justified in the peculiar set of circumstances that existed after these hurricanes. The first hurricane, of the 26th July, destroyed a growing crop in most of the islands; a second crop was immediately planted and was doing well when it was destroyed by the second hurricane of the 17th September, 1926 and the small farmers who made up the bulk of the population were so disadvantaged by this second disaster that they were abandoning their fields and seeking employment elsewhere. If matters were left to adjust themselves naturally the Governor doubted whether any crops would be planted for another year and the population would be dependent on imported food, which, would besides increasing the cost of living, add greatly to the already difficult problem of transportation.

In addition to the government schemes for relief and reconstruction, private organizations were assisting the people by the distribution of food, clothing and water, while private subscriptions were received by the Hurricane Relief Committee, a semi-official body appointed by the Governor after the first hurricane, which gave financial aid to persons in need after careful inquiry into each case. The contribution of £1,000 from Crown Funds, approval of which was conveyed to the Governor by the King of England via a telegram on the 04th October, was gratefully accepted by the Hurricane Relief Committee, and was much appreciated by the public.

The fact that the Governor's application for naval assistance from England by the use of the *HMS Valerian* had been granted was a great relief to the Governor because he was able to proceed to all of the hurricane stricken islands to render assistance to them when and where possible by the use of this ship. Unfortunately, after it was finished this task, it was lost en-route to Bermuda. With the loss of 88 of the crew of 115, it became one of the greatest peacetime losses for a British warship. According to the Governor, provisions were made after careful enquiry, for the expenditure of £50,000 in relation to the hurricane of the 26th July, and more than double this amount was needed in relation to the second hurricane. It was speculated that the reserve funds of the Colony were sufficiently large enough to meet these heavy expenditures.

A warehouse near downtown, Nassau completely destroyed in the Nassau Hurricane of 1926(Courtesy of Charles. J. Whelbell Collection-The Department of Archives).

In the aftermath of these hurricanes hitting the Bahamas, it became apparently clear that well-constructed buildings with shutters had suffered significantly less damage from winds than the lesser constructed buildings. Buildings with well-constructed frames, and those made of steel, concrete, brick, or stone were somewhat less immune to winds than the wooden structure houses, and the use of shutters prevented damage to windows and the interior of the buildings. These storms began the much needed debate for the introduction of building codes here in the Bahamas to combat the destruction caused by these powerful storms. One of the lasting results of these three storms in 1926 and the Great Bahamas Hurricane of 1929 three years later, was the introduction of building codes and building codes legislation throughout the Bahamas. As a result of the great damages incurred from these storms in the late 1920's, the Bahamas became the first country in the Caribbean to enact these mandatory building codes into law. These new laws focused on housing regulations throughout the Bahamas, which required that all houses built after these storms were built to stricter standards so as to withstand hurricane force winds of at least 74 mph. This new result was made apparently clear when the later storms of similar intensity, such as Hurricane Donna and Hurricane Betsy, caused substantially less damage than the hurricanes of the late 1920s.

Better and more detailed evacuation plans were also worked out because of experiences with this storm. Inaddition, the decline of the sponge industry led the government to begin to support agriculture and tourism to support the colony. Britain, the United States and other countries sent emergency aid after these storms, including, cash, dry goods and building supplies. The cost was tremendous. In addition to unplanned government spending, wages were lost, commerce was disrupted, sponge beds were devastated, tourism dropped and farms were destroyed. The impact of a storm can be measures in various ways, including loss of life, income and property, recovery time, and the impact it has on society as a whole. The impact of these hurricanes in 1926 scored high on every scale. Even the psychological impact of these storms, which is often difficult to measure, was easy to perceive. Those who survived these storms can recall the impact they had on their lives to this day. In particular, these storms left many persons dead and countless others homeless.

CHAPTER TEN

The lost of the British Warship HMS Valerian in the Hurricane after it left the Bahamas

A) A rare photo of taken of the British Warship *HMS Valerian* rendering much needed assistance to the Colony of the Bahamas after two of these devastating hurricanes in 1926, but sadly it was lost en-route to Bermuda by Hurricane #10 of 1926, which also struck and devastated the islands of the Bahamas.

B) An artist sketch of the HMS Valerian as it was nearing the stormy waters off the coast of Bermuda(Courtesy of gpvillain).

The British Warship '*HMS Valerian*' was built by Charles Rennoldson and Company and was built under the Emergency War Program; this British warship was launched on the 21st February, 1916. A Flower Class Sloop of 1250 tons, these Class Sloops were specifically built as Minesweepers and were constructed with triple spaced hulls at the bow to give extra protection when mine hunting. Those ships which survived the War were converted to the Convoy protection sloops until the late 1920's. A frequent visitor to the Caribbean in the 1920's the *HMS Valerian* sank when it was hit by a powerful hurricane leaving the Bahamas en-route to Bermuda on 22nd October, 1926. With the loss of 88 of the crew of 115, it became one of the greatest peacetime losses for a British warship. Inaddition, it was also a great loss for many of the British Colonies of the Caribbean who were often heavily serviced by this ship, especially to render assistance after a major hurricane had passed. The 1926 hurricane season was a devastating one that ultimately claimed well over 1,400 lives and caused billions of dollars in damages mainly to the Bahamas and Florida. However, considering all the damages and destruction caused by these storms in 1926, the lost of the *HMS Valerian* made front page news on most of the major newspapers around the world, and stories of the devastation in Florida and the Bahamas having to settle for the second, third and fourth pages in the same newspapers.

From the end of the *American War of Independence* 'til 1953, the Somers Isles (or Bermuda) occupied a position of some prominence in the structure of British Imperial defence. This was especially true in the ability of the British Royal Navy to project its might across the Atlantic and in the Caribbean. Approximately 800 miles from Halifax, Nova Scotia, and 1,100 miles from Miami, Florida (and the Bahamas), the Colony of Bermuda was ideally situated and it allowed not only control of the Eastward Sea lanes to Europe, but also the dominance of the Eastern seaboard of North America and the Caribbean. This was to be one of the primary causes of the War of 1812. By then, the Royal Navy had largely relocated from its early facilities in Saint George's to Ireland at the opposite end of the colony. This island had been purchased by the Admiralty with the specific intent of creating a full naval dockyard; a base and headquarters for the North America and West Indies fleet, allowing full repairs to be carried out on naval ships without necessitating their return to Britain.

Late in the summer of 1926, two hurricanes brought great damage to the British Colony of the Bahamas. The Governor of the Bahamas, Sir Harry Cordeaux sent an urgent appeal to the King of England George V, requesting his assistance in providing a British warship to take him and a few Government representatives to the various islands which were greatly devastated by these two storms. Inaddition, to take much needed hurricane relief supplies such as, building materials, fresh water, food and clothing to the starving residents. As the naval headquarters for the Americas, the HM Dockyard at Ireland Island dispatched a sloop, a minor vessel from its fleet to render what aid it could (a duty which, today, would fall on the *West Indies Guard Ship*, a frigate that the Navy rotates through deployments to protect British West Indian Waters, and that with the Dockyard long closed, only stops in Bermuda on its way to and from its deployment). The ship sent to the Bahamas' aid was the *HMS Valerian*. An Arabis type of the Flower Class built during the Great War, she was under the command of Commander W.A. Usher, with a full complement of 115 men. On the 18th October, 1926, having rendered what assistance it could, it then left Nassau to return to her base in Bermuda. Due to a shortage of coal in the Bahamas, the boat began the voyage with little more than what it needed to complete the 1,100 mile journey. This left the boat relatively light in the water with a detrimental effect on its stability.

A day after she began her voyage, the *HMS Valerian* received reports from the US weather service that a tropical storm was forming to the South of Puerto Rico. This storm initially moved north and seemed no threat, but soon began curving to the northeast to follow the *HMS Valerian* home. Since the weather reports indicated that the "eye" would pass some 300 miles north of the island, Commander Usher never really gave it much thought. Besides, no major hurricane had hit Bermuda in October for well over 100 years - a dangerous precedent on which to rely because it meant that Bermuda was well overdue for a major hurricane to hit this island. Despite the late date, the storm quickly grew far more powerful than the weather forecasters had predicted. The *HMS Valerian*, unaware of the true strength or speed of the storm still raced for home, not wanting to be caught at sea in so light a condition and lacking the coal to fight the weather for long if she were to ever to encounter this storm at sea.

She very nearly made it. By 8am on the morning of the 28 October she radioed the Bermuda Dockyard to say that she was situated about eight miles from Gibbs Hill Lighthouse, to the South West of Bermuda. At that time, Commander Usher would report, there was no sign of the approach of a large storm, and even though the wind howled about them and waves came with tremendous force over on her deck, still he anticipated no difficulty making Timlin's Narrows-the channel, located a handful of miles to the east of Bermuda, which provided the sole access through the isles' enclosing reefs. Commander Usher anticipated no difficulty in entering the Narrows, having done so many times before under similar conditions. Inside the reefs, the vessel would be protected from the worst the sea had to offer. But this was not to be because; this would be his last report from this ship.

Only when the few survivors were plucked from the waters near Bermuda and only by the following day would the extent of this tragedy be known, because the *HMS Valerian* was finally succumbing to the powerful winds and rough seas of the storm. At 10:00am the following day, 19 men were picked from the water by the cruiser *HMS Capetown* which had ridden the storm out safely at sea. The *HMS Capetown* had actually begun a search for the *HMS Valerian* the previous day, but had been called away by the SOS of the steamer the *Eastway*, which also reported being in a desperate plight with her bunkers awash. While the *HMS Valerian* went down less than five miles from the safety of the Royal Naval Base in Bermuda, another ship the *Eastway* sunk near Bermuda in the same storm, taking 22 crew members with her. The dead from the *HMS Valerian* numbered 4 officers, and 84 men. A commemorative plaque for those who lost their lives first hung in the Dockyard RN Chapel in Bermuda but was moved and is now held at Commissioner's House at the Bermuda Maritime Museum. This storm would become one of the most powerful hurricanes in Bermuda's history.

A survivor of the *HMS Valerian*, one of only 19, would recall the events of that day on the front page of The Royal Gazette and Colonist Daily. But the events surrounding the loss of the *Eastway*, and the rescue were never published-until much later. As a survivor would later testify before a court martial he said: *"Indeed, at that time, I felt assured of reaching harbour in safety as there was no immediate indication of a violent storm, also there was a complete absence of swells that sometimes denotes the approach of a storm."* However, this was no ordinary storm and a half-hour later the weather changed so drastically that Commander Usher himself realized he could no longer proceed through the Narrows. He turned the ship around and headed straight into the storm. Gale force winds were lashing the ship at more than 100 mph with a driving rain and flying spray obliterating everything from view.

By noon the centre of the storm was reached and the clearing came, but with it mountainous seas that seemed to approach the ship from all sides, shooting the vessel onto a crest and dragging it down into the trough until it seemed she would snap in two. Once the centre of the storm had passed over, the wind picked up from the Northwest and again tossed the ship from crest to trough as if it were no more than a bath toy. At 1 p.m. a series of squalls struck the ship on the port side with such force that it was thrown on its' beam ends and heeled 70 degrees over to starboard in a stomach-churning movement. It was at this moment that the mainmast and wireless equipment were carried away in the storm and preventing the possibility of sending out another SOS to Bermuda or any other passing ships. Above the howling wind, Commander Usher heard the engines stop and word reached him that the *HMS Valerian* had run aground. Before he could catch his breath, the enormous vessel keeled over about 60 degrees and started going down fast. Word spread "all hands on deck" and with only enough time to cut away one raft, the crew had less than one minute to abandon ship before the ocean claimed the *HMS Valerian*.

Hanging onto the bridge, Commander Usher was swept away by waves, bumped his head and finally came up alongside a raft to which he and 28 of his men clung. In his account before the court later, Commander Usher recalled the events that followed: *"Unfortunately, the bottom of the raft got kicked out and this entailed much greater effort in holding on. The experience of clinging to this raft for 21 hours, with only a problematical chance of being picked up was indeed trying enough for the hardest. Luckily the water was warm, but the northwest wind felt bitterly cold to those parts which were exposed. Sunset came and as it grew dark we looked for Gibbs Hill Light, or some other light, as we had no idea of our position, but nothing was seen, not even the glare. The 12 hours of night, with waves breaking over us, was an experience never to be forgotten and many gave up during that time. They got slowly exhausted and filled up with water and then slipped away. The raft was slowly losing its buoyancy and as everyone wanted, as far as possible, to sit on the edge, it capsized about every 20 minutes, which was exhausting; we all swallowed water in the process and the effort of climbing back again. Twelve held out until the end, when HMS Capetown was most thankfully sighted at about 10am the following day."* By the time the *HMS Capetown* picked up the survivors, the buoyancy of the raft was such that it would not have supported anyone for another hour. The *Capetown*, which had ridden the storm out safely at sea, had actually begun a search for the *HMS Valerian* the previous day, but had been called way by the SOS of the steamer, the *SS Eastway*, which was about 70 miles south of Bermuda and in serious trouble.

The *SS Eastway* left Norfolk, Virginia for Brazil on October 18, 1926 with 7,500 tons of cargo and 1,760 tons of bunker coal. She was commanded by Captain J.H Vanstone and carried a crew of 35. On October 21, the ship received a wireless warning that a hurricane was approaching, but on the course she was steaming, it was assumed that she would encounter only its outer fringes. This assumption proved a fatal miscalculation as by the 22nd, she was being swept by extremely rough seas which smashed one of her port lifeboats, washed away much of deck gear and ripped off her hatch covers. She also developed a slight list which increased as the day wore on. Captain Vanstone personally supervised the efforts of his crew to place fresh covers over the hatches, and it was while engaged in this work without a lifeline that he was washed overboard and drowned. At 5:38 pm the *Eastway* sent an SOS: *"Urgent bunkers awash and hatches broken urgent no life belts."* This message was picked up by the steamship *Luciline* which returned the following message: *"According to your position I am only 30 miles away am standing toward you at full speed suggest you send up rockets on chance I may see them."* An hour and a half later, the *Eastway* turned on her beam ends and sank with 22 crew members, including all the officers, except the third officer, referred to in various documents only as "Mr. Davey." The crew had earlier unhooked the falls of the starboard lifeboat and cut the lashings so the boat floated clear when the vessel sank. Twelve men, who were swimming in the vicinity, managed to scramble into her and could only watch in horror and shock as the steamer sank with 22 of their friends and fellow crew members still on board. It was thought that those below were unable to come up when the vessel turned onto her beam ends, while those on the bridge were unable to get off because of the heavy seas and the ships' 15 degree list. The *Luciline* arrived on the spot at about 10 pm and searched the area until noon the following day when she came upon the survivors who had drifted all night. They were brought to Bermuda and transferred to the tug, *Powerful* at daybreak on October 24, 1926.

During a formal investigation in the United Kingdom in April of the following year, it was revealed that the *Eastway* was overloaded by 141-tons when she left Virginia. This decision cost the crew their lives, and the registered manager, Watkin James Williams, was found "blame-worthy" and culpable, and ordered to pay £1,000 towards the costs of the inquiry. On the other hand, a court-martial on the survivors of *HMS Valerian* was conducted, but later this court acquitted all of the survivors of the *HMS Valerian* of all blame. They examined 15 or 16 witnesses, including ten of those who were saved from the shipwreck, others being technical witnesses. While it was described as a court-martial, it was really an inquiry. A court-martial was held because it was, pursuant to the practice of the British Naval Laws in such cases, to inquire into the cause of the wreck, loss and destruction of the *HMS Valerian*.

CHAPTER ELEVEN

Newspaper and Personal Accounts of These Three Hurricanes of 1926

In July of 1926 a group of scientists from the American Museum of Natural History in New York were on a scientific field trip to Nassau and Andros studying Marine life, birds, insects, amphibians, reptiles and mammals of the Bahamas. While they were on this trip they encountered *the Nassau Hurricane of 1926*. Below is their fascinating account of this storm as told by Chief Scientist Roy Waldo Miner and the scientist who was responsible for studying Lower Invertebrates on this trip.

On Saturday, July 24, our glass began to go down. A swell was working its way in from the Tongue of the Ocean. The wind was swinging north of east. That night the moon was at its full and seemed very large in the heavens, across which light-flecked clouds were scudding. The tide was unusually high and completely burying the reefs, covered the entire beach on the lee side of Little Golding Cay... The next morning, Sunday, was clear, but a strong wind was blowing from the northeast... Captain Nelson decided we were in for a northeast gale and determined to ride it out. We already had two anchors with heavy chain cables out forward... About three in the afternoon the launch arrived with Commissioner Elgin Forsyth aboard.

He at once hurried to the captain's cabin and after a short conference, the latter appeared and informed us that a West Indian hurricane was sweeping toward us and was due to arrive at any moment. Mr. Forsyth had received the information from a native fishing boat, which had been sent over from Nassau for that purpose, as we had no telegraphic or wireless communication. Since our anchorage was practically in the storm's path, it would be impossible for us to hold on where we were. The Commissioner advised us to get up our anchors at once, and he would endeavor to pilot us to a place where we would be reasonably safe if the storm did not strike too far inshore. We immediately set about this and at the same time sent a launch over to little Golding Cay to get the younger Mr. Phipps and several others of the party who had landed there earlier in the afternoon. By this time the angry sea was high above the outer reef, which thus offered no protection, and huge waves were rushing upon us in swift succession. The wind was blowing a gale, and the vessel was tugging and straining at the single rope hawser which was now left. Meanwhile, we found she had been dragging in a direct line toward the rocks of Goat Cay; a half mile to leeward... The storm continued to increase all night and was at its worst about four in the morning. At daybreak we looked back toward our old anchorage and saw continuous processions of black cloud masses flecked with white, marching swiftly up the Tongue of the Ocean in the direction of Nassau. All about us the tossing water of the Bight was as white as milk, due to the soft, calcareous mud which had drifted through from the sponge banks on the western shore of Andros. During the night the wind had shifted counter-clockwise from the northeast and was now blowing from the south and southeast. We were forced to remain in our sheltered position for three days, when the storm had abated sufficiently to permit us to make our way out to the bight entrance, near Gibson Cay. That morning an American Coast Guard Cutter came down the Tongue of the Ocean looking for us. She had been sent from Miami at the request of Mr. John S. Phipps, who had been greatly concerned about us. We now learned that the wireless towers of Nassau were down, leaving her with no communication with the world, and that considerable damage had been done at Palm Beach. This was the first of the series of hurricanes that have so devastated the West Indian region during the past few months, and was totally unexpected, as they are seldom known to occur before August or September. We sent telegrams back by the cutter to inform the Museum and our families of our safety, and she started back to Miami. We had come through with no casualties except that our largest launch, the "Barbara," had been driven ashore, her keel torn off and her propeller bent. During the next few days, however, she was overhauled by the captain and crew, and put into as good repair as possible. Now that the hurricane was over, we returned to our work on the reefs. We found that the white mud or marl, from the west shore of Andros had been driven completely through the bight to the lagoon at the eastern entrance, and had so clouded the water that diving was out of the question, and even the fish would not bite.

When our section of the party reached New Providence, we were amazed at the change that had been wrought by the hurricane. The whole island appeared to have been swept by a blight. Nearly every tree had been either stripped bare of foliage or the leaves were dry and withered, due to the suction of the terrific winds. Scores of trees were uprooted, or stood grotesquely maimed, with torn stumps where leafy branches had been. In Nassau, masonry churches were completely demolished or unroofed, many of the frame dwellings reduced to kindling wood, steel telephone poles bent double as if made of tin, and every tree on the Parade laid prostrate. Many of them were centuries old, and had withstood countless storms. The waterfront was strewn with wrecked vessels, while at least forty others, including many of the sponge fleet from the outer islands, were blown out to sea through the harbor entrance and were never heard from again. Fortunately there was no loss of life on land, but many crews of the vessels must have drowned. Four bodies drifted ashore within the harbor. The wharves and buildings along the waterfront suffered severely. One large storehouse for liquors, built of concrete blocks and elaborately ornamented with columns of masonry, was completely demolished by the force of the wind, scarcely one block left standing on another. Many houses escaped miraculously, while others immediately adjoining were destroyed or at least unroofed. The damage had been largely confined to the path of the storm and the more substantial buildings everywhere remained comparatively unscathed. The beautiful flowering vines and shrubs and blooming gardens that so attracted our attention a few weeks previously, were masses of tangled wreckage, while royal palms had lost their graceful tops and now stood with one or two bedraggled plumes, like roosters after a cockfight.

The people of Nassau, however, were calm and cheerful and went about the business of repair with undaunted spirit. They were as cordial and hospitable as ever and related their experiences and narrow escapes with evident thankfulness that the event was no worse, though it was everywhere agreed that it was the most terrific hurricane since that which laid waste the island in 1866. We spent ten days photographing scenes of damage, and on august 15 sailed for New York with all the objects of our trip accomplished and our minds filled with memories of storm and sunshine in tropic seas that we shall not soon forget.

(Courtesy of The American Museum of Natural History, November-December, 1926, Volume XXVI, Number 6, obtained from the private collection of Patricia Beardsley Roker with permission)

Here is another compelling account of *The Nassau Hurricane of 1926* taken from The Nassau Guardian Newspaper on July 28, 1926. Not since a long time has there been written such a vivid account by an eye witness of a Caribbean hurricane than printed below. It gives the scope and magnitude of this great storm.

The hurricane which the Bahamas has just experienced is more fearful and devastating than any most can remember. Nassau is ravaged; from every district come stories of ruin and havoc, and the tale is not yet fully told, for there are the reports from the out islands still to come.

The radio messages on Friday and Saturday morning found most people optimistic. Saturday afternoon brought more serious news. The indication was that the storm was headed straight for these islands; still people talked of the sudden curves to the Gulf. There seemed nothing abnormal in the weather, only fresh breezes, and the glass was steady. On Sunday morning came worse news, a direct warning of the hurricane's approach. The wind rose higher. People looked to see that their shutters were in good order, and nailed and battened down windows. Still the glass was steady; ships of all sizes began to make for a safer anchor in the waterfront near Potter's Cay and at the Eastern Creek. All the time the wind rose; the sky was heavy with clouds, and the sea began to lash angrily. As evening came on all the storm signs grew more intense. The barometer made a sudden drop, and weather-wise people shook their heads. As the sparse congregations came out of the churches after evening service it was plain that the storm was near. The wind rushed along Bay Street, swirling leaves and scraps of paper and stray sponges into doorways. The shopkeepers had almost without exception taken the precaution to board up their windows and Bay Street looked ready for a barricade, as indeed it needed to be. The sea came dashing up

Rawson Square, throwing spray far over, and the harbor at this part was strangely dark and deserted. Here and there electric lights began to fuse, and street after street was plunged into darkness. Hardly anyone was to be seen, save unfamiliar policeman in long dark coats and storm helmets. People were all at home trying to make their houses additionally secure.

The wind was now blowing a heavy gale, dashing through the trees, and shaking the houses, growing steadily more terrible. Everything that could be shaken loose it began tearing down-shutters, signboards, gates. There was little sleep that night for anyone on the island, just listening to this merciless crashing and tearing and roaring, and wondering what would be the outcome. The gale brought storms of rain, not ordinary rain, but sweeping storms of water like spray, traveling too swiftly to fall downward. Soon roofs of houses began to tear away, and water was swept in. some roofs were torn off entirely, and people had to leave everything, stumbling pitifully through the wreckage for shelter elsewhere. Few trees could withstand this tremendous force, and down they came. Worst of all was the turmoil in the harbor. No anchorage was safe for ships on such a night. Bigger vessels kept on full speed ahead, and perilously rode out the storm; others dragged their anchors and were seen drifting down the harbor and away to sea; some, it could be discerned, with people on board gesticulating in terror, but few could attempt to aid them. A true estimate can not yet be made, but it is said that over 40 vessels went helplessly adrift in this way. Men swam ashore in a desperate attempt when they felt their ships giving way. The sea boiled and raged, the harbour was no refuge. The tide swept over Bay Street, carrying boats with it, and plowing up everything in its way. When light came the storm was raging at its height and though everyone welcomed the end of that fearful night, it was seen that the worst was not yet over. The coming of dawn revealed a town lashed unceasingly by a pitless wind intent on demolishing everything in its track, and driving rain as fine as smoke. The hurricane was now approaching its height, and large trees of every description which had withstood the battering of a night went down like ninepins before the awful crescendo which raged during the early morning. The water logged branches of many trees were their ruin, the shallow roots of palms proved a cause of their speedy destruction; but then, what could be expected to stand when concrete telegraph poles with iron cores were bent and broken off by the dozen?

Trees, telegraph wires, corrugated iron, shutters, and debris of every description lay sprinkled in the roadway; in fact, much of the debris was moving about on the ground' for the gale did not design to leave alone what it had so scornfully torn down. For a quarter of a mile East Bay Street below Murphy's warehouse was a foot deep in water lashed by the hurricane into the waves larger than those normally seen in the harbor itself. At the Eastern Parade, Bay Street was totally blocked by trees, and the field was a vast lake. Shirley Street was as impassable as if the bush had been given a hundred years to sprout through the asphalt, while the harbor was a milk-white inferno of turbulent water, running westward with the speed of a millrace. Roofs were being stripped of their shingles as one peels the skin from an orange; the shuttered houses streaming with water gave no sign of the anxious life within, and save for a few hardy wayfarers Nassau seemed a town of the dead.

Yesterday came a calm and sunny day, and everyone was out early to see what damage had been done. Nowhere was the force of the storm better illustrated than at Fort Montagu. What had been trim lawns and shrubberies and neat paths is now as ravaged as if it had been the scene of modern warfare, with tanks in action. The ground is all torn up; trees are uprooted; there are ruts and sand drifts and the scene is desolate. The Fort Montagu Hotel stands in a lake. A little further east it is even worse with the road itself torn up, littered with trees, and boats cast ashore. The western end of the island is the same. Fox Hill suffered terribly, many of the small dwellings having fallen like playing cards. In Grant's Town there is great distress. The scene has entirely changed; there are so many houses down and trees thrown across the roads, while to add to the hardships there are floods in the streets. A great many people are homeless. Other of the poor people are mourning the loss of their boats, their sole means of livelihood, while others are in fear for safety of their relatives out in sponging vessels or at sea on trips to the Out Islands. All over the island there is distress and loss, beside which the destruction of many of our beautiful vistas is a small matter. Some of the finest trees in the city have been lost and among them, sad to say, the two tall Caicos palms in the Deanery garden which 50 years ago were reputed to be the oldest palms in the island. The Firebird had her engines giving full speed ahead for four hours, and lost two shackles while the hurricane was at its height. One of her officers who has seen typhoons in China Sea and has also had experience in West Indian hurricanes, said he has seen nothing to equal this. A conglomeration of 65 boats, mostly pleasure craft, is to be seen on the beach near Matthew Avenue. Of 49 boats in the back channel, 42 are said to have been blown out of the harbour. We have heard of many courageous acts performed during the storm, but one of the most outstanding was that of Captain Richardson, of the dredger Lucayan. He, it is said, saved over a dozen lives. People who were swept past on sloops clung to the forestructure of the dredger, and the captain rushed to save them as they came, unheedful of the peril to himself. A great many automobiles were damaged, the covers being shred to ribbons and the enamel "burnt" off by the velocity of the wind; exposed paint work generally seemed to have undergone the fire of blow lamps. It is generally agreed that the best roofing to resist hurricane onslaughts is that of cypress and cedar shingles, though few houses remained entirely dry throughout the storm. In some houses umbrellas were used when going from one room to another.

This account of the *Nassau Hurricane of 1926* was taken from the Tribune Newspaper on Wednesday, August 11, 1926. It also gives the scope and magnitude of this great storm.

At 2pm a hurricane of great velocity accompanied by much rain, was on us meeting every one quite unprepared for this storm. Fruit trees yielded their fruits to its fury and were uprooted; houses swayed to and fro, people ran here and there assisting the needy ones in nailing up and securing property. At last nightfall came and it did blow and it did blow and rain. The hurricane lasted about 48 hours and persons who were here in the "66" gale say "This was much heavier." All through the settlement trees are uprooted, some thrown across the roads; a few homes, toilets and kitchens have been moved from their base and damaged. Boats can sail through the settlement as the water in some roads and yards is about 4 ½ feet deep. The pear crop is gone, it is estimated that about one hundred thousand pears, sixty thousand dillies, mangoes, etc, are lying on the ground. The crops in the farms are under water and faces complete destruction....

Here is another compelling account of the *Nassau Hurricane of 1926* taken from the Tribune Newspaper on August 14, 1926. It gives the scope and magnitude of this great storm on the island of Exuma as reported by Exuma resident Mr. T. Gibson. Eleuthera native Mr. Timothy Gibson in 1926 was the public school teacher at Georgetown, Exuma who in his later years went onto write and compose the Bahamas

National Anthem *"March on Bahamaland"* wrote a compelling narrative about this storm:

"When we awoke on Sunday morning we found that the high wind of Saturday night had considerably increased in strength; the waves lashed the shore. Nature wrinkled her face and donned a dusky garment as if for battle; and she certainly give battle, the desolation of which is so evident to the sight at every step.

The wind grew stronger and stronger, and at 9am it had increased to 40 miles per hour. The rain came, and it was evident to everyone, even to the most incredulous that something out of common was about to happen. The wise of us put bars to our windows and doors and prepared for the event.

We did not have to wait long; the mad tempest plunged upon us with all the strength it could gather and only the strong face it. The drops of rain that shot horizontally like missiles stung the face like so many pellets; the wind blew with terrific force in the neighbourhood of 100 miles per hour. In this crisis the sight could penetrate no more than a few yards ahead and neighbours who had neglected to securely fasten their windows and doors, soon saw their folly and set to work(it availed but little) to makeup for it; but in most cases they were too late and the wind had its ruthless way.

Latrines forsook Mother earth and took to the sky; kitchens gave up the ghost and yielded up the pots; barns that were empty threw open their doors as if for the corn to rush in and take shelter, but no corn rushed into them and they fell disappointed. Stone walls cracked and were rent in twain; corn fields were destroyed in the flower of their beauty and the trees presented a sight representable of the dreadful event.

In summing up losses it is enough to make one shudder: 800 houses, barns, kitchens and latrines were totally destroyed 90% of the remainder being more or less damaged; 8 persons were found drowned; 10 vessels sunk and partly damaged, to say nothing of the total corn crop for the season."

Mr. Andrew McKinney

During the *Nassau Hurricane of 1926*, there was a man by the name of Mr. P.C. Cavill who was a former long distance swimmer in competitive meets around the world. He held the world record for a short time for swimming the English Channel. On his first attempt, he unofficially broke the record but sadly when he got to the coast of

England, the weather was so bad and the seas were so rough that he had to be taken out of the water just a few feet away from the shore without ever touching land-a requirement that was needed to have the record to be made official. Mr. Cavill lived in Australia with his family before moving to the Bahamas. In Australia, his family had a swimming pool and the boys would often make good use of the pool by having competitive swimming with each other. Somehow, P.C. Cavill would always out swim the other boys and his family kept wondering how was it that he was able to swim much faster than the others getting from one end of the pool to the next end. Then they closely watched his movement in the water and noticed that when he swam he would always swim with his legs going up and down and rather that from side to side as it was common to do in those days. They patented this style of swimming that he discovered and initially it was known as *the Australian Crawl* which they named after their birth country but today it is now referred to as *the American or Australian Crawl* and this method is used in international swimming competition all around the world. During the hurricane Mr. Cavill lived on an inlet cay near the Southern Bight in Andros. During the *Nassau Hurricane of 1926*, this cay became inundated with rising flood waters from the storm, so he was forced to swim across the creek to get to safety on the Andros mainland. When he got to the mainland he discovered that it was completely flooded so he was forced to stay up into a pine tree for three days until the flood waters subsided and only coming down briefly to drink water. Sadly, 9 other persons drowned in this storm trying the same fete of trying to swim across that creek to get to the mainland as Mr. Cavill successfully did.

Mr. Alvin Adderley

I was very young at the time and lived with my mom and dad along with 6 boys and 2 girls just on the south side of Oddle Corner. I was so young at the time but yet I can still vividly remember this storm as if it had occurred yesterday. This was because during the storm, I became very afraid and would become one of the most frightening experiences of my life because of the loud noises associated with the powerful winds and rainfall of the storm. Inaddition, the house was creaking so loudly and rocking from side to side that it was impossible to hear one another speak. There wasn't anywhere in the house to sleep out the storm because the rainwater kept coming through the ceiling and doors, hindering any attempt for any of us to lay down comfortably and fall sleep. I can vividly recall during the storm, peeping through the window of our house looking at the neighbours' homes. Initially, I saw several of the houses rocking from side to side like trees blowing in the wind and eventually these houses gave way to the storm and were blown away forcing the occupants to seek shelter elsewhere during the height of the storm. All during the storm, I could hear my mom and dad and a few of my older brothers and sisters with a frightened look on their faces praying very loudly to God and asking for His divine protection during the storm. After the storm was over there was widespread devastation everywhere on Oddle Corner because the majority of the homes were blown away and many more badly damaged or destroyed. Many of the families in the area were forced to live with other family members, friends and relatives for many months after the storm had passed until they were able to rebuild their own homes. After the storm, it took a lot time, effort and money to rebuild and there was little help from the government because there were so many persons throughout the Bahamas who suffered tremendously and required much more immediate assistance than us.

Mr. Jerry Gibson

During the Nassau Hurricane of 1926, I was living with my father and mother, Benjamin and Blooming Gibson in the settlement of the Bluff, South Andros. Just before the onset of the hurricane, I saw many persons in the community going about preparing for this storm in a very hurried manner. So I became very afraid and asked my mother what was happening and she told me that a powerful storm was travelling. During this time, we had very little warning that a major storm was approaching the island until the weather started to deteriorate. Many persons throughout the community then rushed to their houses to batten them down with the small window of opportunity they had left. I recalled that many of these persons were actually moving at a 45 degree angle against the force of the wind and some even fell down. I became very curious about this, so I asked my mother why the wind was blowing them like that because I as a young boy had never seen the winds that strong before nor had I seen it have that effect on people like it did. She said the wind was blowing them like that because a powerful hurricane with very strong winds was travelling and making them walk like that. That explanation did not satisfy me, so with my curiosity aroused, I sneaked out of the house and ran into the wind and a strong gust of wind caught me and picked me up and blew me across the street into a Buttonwood Tree which was located on the sea rock. I immediately held onto that Buttonwood Tree for my dear life or else I would have been blown off the rocks and into the water and would have surely died. Fortunately, I was not hurt but was very stunned and surprised by the strength of the wind. I tried to get up but that was impossible because the winds were so strong that I actually had to creep on the ground like a dog to get back across the street. When I got back into the house and I immediately told my mother what had happened.

We stayed in the house until 10pm that night when we started to feel the brunt of the storm. During the storm, the house was shaking so much that my father went out into the storm and braced the house with some pieces of lumber to reduce the violent shaking which helped for a while but eventually they also gave way. At this time the winds blew the roof of the house off and water started pouring into the house and then the walls of the house started to crack and it eventually gave way. At this point in time, I became very afraid and started screaming and I said "Mama the roof is leaking." She then replied and said "Don't be afraid my son because that is simply God's power in action and there is nothing we can do about it." Then my mother told my father to get the children out of the house because it was not safe to stay there anymore. My father then took each of the children one by one in the midst of the raging storm and into the neighbour's Richard Solomon's house to ride out the rest of the storm.

When morning finally arrived and the storm abated, I was curious to see what damage the house had suffered but when I got to the location, I was amazed to find out that the house was not there anymore. I asked my mother who was nearby if my father had moved the house and she then came over and told me no and tried to comfort me by telling me not to worry because my father will rebuild another house. Fortunately, we were able to live with my uncle Ernest for quite a few weeks after the storm, until my father was able to rebuild the house. Many other persons in this settlement also had to live with other family members and friends because many of their houses were also destroyed in the storm. Before we entered the newly built home, it was customary to say a special prayer to bless the house, so my father asked Pastor Simeon Davis(who's son Joshua died in the 1929 Hurricane) to come and pray for the house so that it would not get destroyed by another hurricane. Then my mother asked me to say a special prayer as well, so I then asked the Lord to Bless the house and then I sung the popular church hymn at the time '*A charge to keep I have, a God to glorify, a never dying soul to save, and fitted for the sky.*' After the storm, we were amazed to find out that so many houses in this settlement were destroyed in this storm. I recalled that the neighbours, Ellen Rolle and Dings Thompson houses were blown away and many other houses in the settlements of the Bluff and High Rock were also blown away. The majority of the farm produce were destroyed, including all of the corn, peas, sweet potato and cassava crops. After the storm, things were so tough that we had to ration the remaining food that was left untouched by the storm. My father further supported us by selling sponges and cutting sisal to sell to the dealers in Nassau.

Mr. Rupert Roberts Jr.

Mr. Roberts, the President of Super Value Food Stores recalled that his Father Mr. Rupert Roberts Sr. and his mother Mrs. Miriam Roberts often spoke very highly about these terrible and powerful storms in 1926, while he growing up as a boy in the settlement of Marsh Harbour, Abaco. In 1926 my father lived on the coast in Marsh Harbour in a house with rolling pins. During the Hurricane of 1926, as my father was making preparations for the storm, he placed my young aunt Winifred on the bed and in his excitement in preparing for this storm; he took a suitcase filled with clothes and threw it on top of my Aunt Winifred by accident while she was lying on the bed. Fortunately, she was not injured but had quite a story to tell to her friends and family members for years to follow after the storm had passed.

When the storm was over, my father tried to open the door but to his amazement, it was stuck and was not able to get out, so he tried to open one of the windows in the house but to his amazement it was also stuck and was not able to open it either. To get out of the house he had to break down the back door. His initial assessment after observing pine trees everywhere was that the Pine Barrens had come out to them in the settlement. However, to his surprise the entire house had moved and travelled all the way into the Pine Barrens quite a distance from where they were initially located in Marsh Harbour. The noise from the storm was so loud that none of them in the house realized that the house had moved of its rolling pins quite some distance from where they were located. Infact, my Aunt Winifred distinctly remembered that when my dad took them to the back steps of the house to get out, the water from the storm was so deep that it was up to his neck. After the storm, a search party was assembled and went looking for them, fearing the worse for them, but fortunately, they were all ok. Coming out of the Pine Barrens, they saw that many of the pine trees were broken off by the house during its movement into the Pine Barrens. He recalled that in the settlement of Marsh Harbour, August Van Ryn's baby girl Pearl Eleanor Van Ryn died when she was washed out of his arms by the storm surge.

Sir Clifford Darling

The former Governor General of the Bahamas Sir Clifford Darling was 4 years old at the time the Hurricane of 1926 hit the Bahamas and remembers this storm very well. I was living in the settlement of Chester's on the island of Acklins. At the time there were no weather reports to warn us or anybody about an approaching storm. The Family Island Commissioner of Acklins had a barometer and whenever he saw the pressure starting to drop significantly, he would go about informing the residents throughout the settlements to take the necessary precautions for an approaching storm. This was a difficult task because sometimes it was difficult to distinguish the pressure drop between a severe weather event such as a thunderstorm and a hurricane passing over the island. Fortunately, in Nassau some of the residents knew when a hurricane was approaching the island from a man by the name of Mr. Cambridge, who would go and put a hurricane flag on top of the hill on Fort Fincastle to warn the residents of this approaching storm.

When the Hurricane of 1926 hit the island of Acklins, my uncles were busy working on the island of San Salvador in the wreckage and salvaging industry and my father on *'the Contract.'* In Acklins, several ships were wrecked with various supplies during the storm with quite a number of usable goods such as, candy, ropes, flour, rice, lumber, sugar and the locals made good use of these shipwrecked goods in their homes and gave others away to persons in other settlements. When the residents of my settlement in Chester's Acklins found out that this 1926 hurricane was approaching Acklins, we started making our way from our various homes to get to the higher grounds of the hills but unfortunately, the hurricane arrived before we were able to reach our destination so we were forced to ride out the storm in the open wilderness. I was so afraid as a little boy by the heavy rainfall and the loud and powerful winds of the storm and my brother noticed this and so he took me and placed me in a canvas bag with just my head hanging out of the bag as we made our way to the hills. My other brother took my little sister and placed her in a similar bag and placed her on his back also with only her head hanging out as well. After the storm subsided a bit we went to my cousin's house which was the only one left standing where we rode out the remainder of the storm.

When we got back home after the hurricane had passed, we found out that the hurricane blew the roof off our house. My brother turned the roof right side up and then cut a hole in the roof. We were forced to live in that roof for about 2 to 3 weeks until my father was able to come home from working on 'the Contract' to build them a new house. Unfortunately, four of my uncles drowned in this storm when they left San Salvador to come to Acklins in a sailing boat but they were caught in the storm. After this hurricane, Acklins became a hurricane ravaged wasteland because there was total devastation everywhere as far as the eyes could see. The hurricane demolished almost all of the homes on the island and sunk every ship at sea and the death toll was unbearably high. There were quite a number of sloops that were caught travelling from Acklins to Nassau but were forced to stop in Long Island or the Exuma Cays to seek shelter from the storm. The journey from Acklins to Nassau by boat often took quite a long time and sometimes as much as a month by sailboat depending on the prevailing weather conditions.

Mrs. Nora Melinda Hanna-Knowles

Mrs. Knowles was 5 years old at the time when the Hurricane of 1926 hit the island of Acklins and recalled it being a very fierce and powerful storm. Most people in Acklins at the time had no idea that a storm was travelling. My father was one of the fortunate ones and was the only one in the settlement of Spring Point, Acklins who actually had a barometer. The barometer in 1926 was today's version of the radio, television or the computer to warn Bahamians of any impending hurricane in the vicinity of the Bahamas. My father was a blessed man because he was a man of many trades, a businessman, a marriage officer, a boat builder, a sponge merchant and he also sold sisal and bark. During those days, whenever a resident in Spring Point suspected a storm was travelling, they would immediately come to look at my father's barometer for confirmation. When the hurricane of 1926 was approaching Acklins, my father noticed that the barometer was rapidly falling and so he made immediate preparations for this storm because this was a sure sign that a storm of great magnitude was in the vicinity of Acklins. After gathering a few important items from the house, my family proceeded to make our way to a higher shelter on a hilltop because our house was near the water and situated on a very flat land and my father said it would not be a safe place to be during a hurricane.

At this time the weather had started to deteriorate at a very rapid pace and the night had already started to set in, which made it very difficult to move in the dark because some of us stumbled in a few potholes and even hurt ourselves. When we got to the top of the hill we covered ourselves in a canvas exposed to the elements of the weather and it was the most terrifying experience of my life. We stayed under this canvas until the storm was over and during the storm I recalled looking at the water and seeing several huge tidal waves on the water front and the storm surge rose well over five feet in our house. Everyone in Acklins was affected by this storm and the death toll was so high that in every family there was a death of a family member. I can recall 5 brothers who drowned when they went to secure their boat on the other end of the island and the water came in and engulfed them. Inaddition, there were many more persons who lost their lives trying to get to higher ground during the storm and infact quite a few persons from the settlement of Salina Point drowned when they tried to get to higher ground.

When we got from under the canvas after the storm, I could not believe my eyes because every single house in our settlement was blown down and totally destroyed. When we got back to our home I started to cry when I saw the condition it was in because the storm devastated our home. We found the piano and organ totally destroyed and the water destroyed everything in my father's store including all the flour, rice and sugar which he had for sale. After this storm, many of the residents of Acklins got together and made a decision to build a strong and sturdy 'Gale or Hurricane House' as they called it on top of the hill to shelter the residents from future storms so that what happened to residents in the 1926 storm will never ever happen again to any other future Acklins residents. This house was specially made with the roof facing to the east and it extended all the way to the ground and the building was built extra strong and sturdy to withstand future hurricane force winds. This building to this day is still there and has withstood many hurricanes.

Mr. Conrad Knowles

Mr. Knowles, the former chairman of the Bahamas Licensing Authority Board, encountered the Nassau Hurricane of 1926 living in the settlement of Braddox's, Long Island, which is a small settlement located between McKann's and Thompson's Bay. My father's home was situated near the sea, only about 300 yards from the water's edge. My father was Timothy Knowles and my mother was Rebecca Knowles. My father at the time was a sea captain who took farm products, sponges and fresh fish from Long Island to be sold in Nassau. Farm animals such as cows, chickens, goats and sheep would be bought in Nassau and taken back to Long Island on his boat for these residents. Inaddition, he would also transport building supplies, grocery and other manufactured goods back to the island from Nassau. This storm had a very traumatic experience on my life. In 1926, we had no information that a storm was approaching other than a few basic signs such as, looking at the clouds, the birds or watching the sudden rise of the seas. My father and many other persons within the community of Long Island underestimated this powerful storm and as a result, many Long

Islanders lost their lives at sea and on land. We were very fortunate because, whenever a hurricane was approaching Long Island, my father and others had a 'six sense' for knowing the arrival of a storm. They watched the waters, birds and looked at the clouds movement and speed which would gradually become overcast and they would move much faster than the normal speed.

During this storm, we were in our house situated near the waters and to our surprise the waters came rushing into our yard. Suddenly, the waters started to rush into our house. Sensing danger, my father immediately took me up and placed me on the partition while he and my mother gathered some much needed clothing and foodstuff to evacuate the house. When the first wave of high water from the storm crashed against the house and rushed inside, my father immediately with a frightened look on his face said it was time to leave. My father quickly grabbed me and placed me on his shoulders and I put my hands around his neck and held on tightly because I too was afraid. At this time the house became engulfed with water so my father gathered my mother, my two sisters Chalotilda and Ida and my brother George together and immediately left that home. While leaving, I looked back at the house a few seconds later, I saw the roof starting to blow off and the waters started to break the walls apart and the house immediately began to collapse. We went on the top of a hill in the bushes to shelter from the storm. During the storm, we stayed exposed to the torrents of the heavy rainfall and strong winds all evening and into the night until the next morning.

The next morning my father took us to the public school house in McKann's where the families of that particular settlement had gathered. That school house became our home for about three months after the storm because our house was totally destroyed by the storm. Eventually, my father with the help of a few neighbours built a new house in the settlement of McKann's and never ever went back to the house in Braddox's because of the bad memories associated with that storm there. To this day, this newly built home is still standing in that settlement even though it has weathered many storms. After the storm, we found out that a number of persons were not as fortunate as us because quite a number of people had drowned in various settlements throughout the island. Inaddition, many persons were left starving because the storm destroyed all of the field crops on the island. The majority of the homes were totally destroyed and many persons were rendered homeless for many months after the storm. The death toll was also great and I can vividly remember a lady by the name of Mrs. Bowe from the settlement of Thompson's Bay. She was swept away by the storm and her house was totally destroyed. She was actually found dead the next day with her hair wrapped around the trunk of a tree.

One of the most unusual events of this storm was the fact that during the storm, the water went out of the bay and many fish were caught by surprise on dry land. We gathered up quite a few of them and survived of them for quite a while after the storm. Quite a number of animals like sheep, chickens and goats were killed in this storm and many other persons survived by eating them. The majority of Long Islanders were farmers, fishermen or sponger men and many of them became unemployed for quite some time after the storm. This was because the hurricane destroyed everything that was associated with their trade and in most cases they had to start from scratch. Interestingly, Sir Albert Miller, former Chairman of the Bahamas Port Authority and I are two sisters children and my aunt had reason to come to Nassau to seek medical attention and she took young Albert with her on the trip. They were caught in the same hurricane at sea and had to seek refuge on one of the cays in the Exumas for several days and miraculously they all survived on this cay exposed to the weather elements during this very intense hurricane. I owe my father and mother a great debt of gratitude and thanks to their quick actions in this storm of 1926-I am alive today. I admonished that people should not take hurricane warnings lightly because in my days growing up on Long Island, we didn't have that luxury of the technological advancements of today so Bahamians should learn to appreciate and take advantage of these early warnings to prepare for these storms.

Mr. Lawrence Knowles

Mr. Lawrence Knowles recalled experiencing the Nassau Hurricane of 1926 living on the island of Long Island in the Central Bahamas. My father was Herbert Knowles and was a sea captain and whenever he travelled out to sea he would always take his trustworthy barometer (like most sailors did at the time) to determine if there was a hurricane approaching Long Island. Actually, I still have this keepsake barometer that he used in the 1926 hurricanes as a reminder of the good ole days of living on Long Island as a child. On that Sunday, just a few hours before the hurricane struck, my father noticed that the barometer was falling rapidly and concluded that a very intense hurricane was approaching the island. So he made a decision to go and harvest as much of his crops out of our field so as to prevent them from being destroyed in the storm and he took me along to help him. He then proceeded to batten down the windows and doors of his house.

During the storm, I was stunned to see that our house was shaking violently and the shingles of our roof and the entire roof of the neighbour's house were being blown off. This frightened me because I had not witnessed anything like this before. During the lull of the storm I was happy because I thought that the storm was over and wanted to go outside to play but my father held me back and told me that the storm was not over but was simply catching its breath and will return with a greater force from the opposite direction a short while later. That helpful bit of advice more than likely saved my life because within a few minutes, the storm came rushing back from the opposite direction. Fortunately, our house was one of the few homes on Long Island which were not destroyed in this hurricane. My father had a schooner and a 10 feet dinghy boat but sadly, they were destroyed in the storm. In fact, the dinghy boat was blown many miles inland and it was eventually discovered many days later totally destroyed. This hurricane devastated Long Island and many persons were in deep grief for months after these storms, because quite a number of persons in various settlements had died during the storm. Inaddition, there were many persons from Long Island who were unaware that a storm was approaching and was travelling from Nassau to Long Island by boat and perished when the storm caught them out at sea.

Rev. Henry Pratt

Rev. Pratt who is descended from the settlement of Bain's Town in Cat Island said that the *Nassau Hurricane of 1926* was devastating because many persons from Cat Island lost their lives in this storm both at sea and on land. One of the lucky ones was Napoleon Rolle from the settlement of Devil's Point who was on the mail boat *The Mountain*

King travelling from Nassau to Cat Island. I recalled that *The Mountain King* belonged to a man by the name of James E. Smith, who like many other boats were hired to take freight and passengers to and from Cat Island to Nassau. The journey often took as much as eight days to complete by boat. When *The Mountain King* began its journey; none of them knew a storm was travelling until they encountered the storm near Cat Island, because *The Mountain King* did not have a barometer onboard which would have been a valuable instrument to give them some kind of fore-warning of the approaching storm. The reason why *The Mountain King* went down in the storm was because two stubborn boat captains could not agree to take the boat into a safe harbour and wait out the storm on dry land.

Many persons died on this boat and the majority of the bodies were never found because the boat sunk in the middle of the ocean. Napoleon Rolle who I recalled performing the burial rites at his funeral many years ago, was the sole survivor on this boat. Napoleon like many of the passengers on this boat jumped off the boat with the intentions of swimming into the land. When Napoleon started swimming in the rough seas, he briefly looked back at the boat and saw it rocking violently from side to side with quite a few passengers still onboard and when he looked back a second time he saw that the boat had completely disappeared with no sign of the remaining passengers. When he got near to the land on a cay called Bird Cay, the storm surge pushed him well over fifty feet into the bushes on dry land and for a brief while he kept on swimming not realizing that he was now safe on dry land. He remained on that cay for quite sometime without food or water. He was finally rescued when he placed the shirt of his back on a tall stick and beckoned the passing ship *Hero* to his rescue and it would only be much later that he would learn the fate of the other passengers.

Mrs. Viola Collie

Mrs. Viola Collie who was 10 years old at the time recalled experiencing the Hurricane of 1926 living near the sea in the Settlement of Mason's Bay, Acklins. We had no knowledge that a hurricane was travelling other than when the weather showed up and destroyed our home. We had no radios, televisions or barometers to warn us about this approaching storm. When we first started to feel the effects of the storm, my grandfather Moses Kemp-a preacher by profession and my aunt came over into our home from their respective homes to ride out the storm. They felt they stood a better chance of surviving the storm in our house rather than theirs because our house was only recently built so it was relatively new. That would prove to be an unwise decision because, during the storm the roof of our house blew off and landed well over 300 feet away from its original location. During this time the wind and the waters came rushing inside of the house. At this moment our house started to collapse and one of my sisters, Wilda had some large boulders fells on top of her and trapped her feet for quite a while before my grandfather was able to free her feet. At this time, the surge of the storm was at least 20 feet high and we had to swim to get out of the way of the flood waters. Unfortunately, two of my sisters were not so lucky because they drowned in the water. My two sisters, Melvern who was 3 years old and Julia who was 3 months old at the time were in the house and were engulfed by the flood waters and drowned. It was a double blow for our family because Julia was suppose to be christened on that day of the storm and was already in her new christening clothes and was washed away out of my aunt's hands. My grandfather later found her body drifting in the floodwaters and took the baby and covered her up with a dress until morning when the storm was over. The baby was later buried in the same christening clothes because all of the other clothes we had were all washed away by the storm.

After the storm, we went to look at the damage throughout the settlement and I cried because there was widespread devastation everywhere and all of the houses lay flat on the ground totally destroyed, especially those in the low lying areas and the areas that were situated near to the sea. There were so many dead bodies lying around that they had to bury them in mass graves rather than one by one. The storm the surge took quite a number of bodies out to sea and they were never found. My neighbour Mr. Ferguson, who had only recently return to Acklins a day before the storm from Florida working on 'The Contract', lost both his wife and his son in this storm. I recalled he had just bought a new roll of cloth from Florida to make some dresses and a few pants for his wife and son and the hurricane rolled out the entire roll and scattered it all over their yard. He was so smitten with grief over their loss that for months and years after the storm he would often go by their graves and put fresh flowers on the headstones and cry for hours in the front of their graves. After the storm, my family and I were forced to live in a neighbour's house for months after the storm until our house was rebuilt. After the storm, my daddy who was busy in Florida at the time working on *'the Contract'* came home and built us a new house on the same location where the previous one was destroyed. The ruins of that house are still there to this day. To ensure that the memory of this storm will never ever be forgotten, I passed on the stories of these storms onto my children, who I hope in turn will tell their children about the devastation of this 1926 Hurricane.

Mr. Chester Thompson**

At the time of the hurricane, my mother, Lena was seven months pregnant and patiently awaiting my birth. My parents lived in a one storey cottage in the up-a-long area of Hope Town, Abaco, on a gentle hill overlooking other houses to the north. My father Maurice, a sea captain, had just returned from a voyage to Cuba. Three older brothers of six, four and two, Hartis, Leonard and Roscoe, always underfoot and hungry, kept my mother quite busy. They were housebound by intermittent showers from low scudding clouds, driven by increasing winds from the northeast. Earlier, my father had spotted two frigate birds (or often called the *'hurricane bird'* by many of the Family Island residents) flying near the ground-a sure sign that there was an approaching hurricane he said. He reminded my mother of ancient mariners portent *"Frigate birds fly low it's going to blow."* The barometer was falling and he was thankful that his ship, the *Alma R.*, had been secured into the harbour and was safely at a hurricane mooring. Muffled sounds of hammering were heard as the neighbours battened down their houses.

My mother sat awkwardly in a rocking chair, cradling her swollen stomach, frightened by increasing gusts of winds. Darkness came quickly. Kerosene lanterns were lit and the boys tucked themselves into makeshift beds, on the floor. "I don't feel right" moaned my mother "I believe the baby's coming." My father was worried. Aunt Louisa, the midwife, lived at the far end of the village, its narrow streets now made dangerous by wind-driven coconuts, tree branches and other debris. The house creaked in every joint as blasts of wind, like the judgment of the Lord, battered the house. The room was dimly lit by a single lantern. My father crouched near my mother whispering encouragement but aware that their lives were in danger. The boys, who lay just beside them, whimpered and clung to each other. Suddenly there was an almighty crash from the attic. A wind blown object had shattered the dormer window and wind came shrieking down the stairs. My parents fell to the floor, their bodies protecting the boys. Flurries of rain and salt spray swept in from the ocean and water poured down from the attic, drenching the floor. "The roof will go soon," shouted my father, "I'll take you to Ben Russell's house." "No, no," screamed my mother. "Take the boys first." My father crept and hugged the ground for the fear of being blown away, wriggled under some sea grape branches, with my brothers held onto him-clinging onto him like terrified monkeys. Occasional gusts pinned them to the ground. Sheets of salty rain, driven horizontally, drenched them to the skin. Aided by frequent lightning flashes, my father made his way to the lee side of Ben Russell's house. Banging on the door he thrust the boys into Ben Russell's arms and shouted "I'm going for Lena, the baby's coming."

When I was eighteen my mother told me what happened back then. The edges of her memory were blurred by time and she was hesitant to relate the physical details of birth to a teenage son. With the boys on the way to safety she felt a great relief, which turned to terror as the house moved on its foundations and a portion of the roof blew away. Her labour pains were increasing in frequency. She remembered my father's wet body and his strength as they tried to reach Ben Russell's house. Halfway there they sheltered under the low spreading branches of a giant seagrape tree where they found Ben Russell on his way to help. In the midst of the storm and under that seagrape tree I was born. The two men carried my mother and baby to Ben Russell's house. There Ceva Russell and her sister took charge. Faced with the ageless drama of birth they forgot their fear of the hurricane. Calmly and competently, they made my mother comfortable and brought the baby to her. Overcome with emotion, my mother burst into tears. She told me years later: "You were a scrawny, tiny thing and I thought you wouldn't live. But you were whimpering and waving your matchstick arms and leg around. Mr. Russell weighed you on his fish scale and you were only three pounds."

As the eye of the hurricane passed directly over Elbow Cay its savagery gave way to an unearthly calm. There was feverish activity in both assessing the damage and reinforcing doors and windows on what had been the lee side. It was known that, when the eye passed through, the wind would blow from the opposite direction. In about an hour the wind increased, with violent squalls and driving rain. As dawn came reluctantly, the hurricane was raging at its former force. Squalls came sweeping over at shorter intervals. The wind's eerie shrieking was punctuated by the crashing of wind blown debris. The women became hysterical and prayed to God for help. Mr. Russell's father started singing *'We shall meet in the sweet bye and bye'* but was told to be quiet. There was a splintering crash from the roof as if the sky and the earth had come together. Water poured in torrents into the living room sending everyone scurrying to the bedroom. When there was a lull, Mr. Russell, clinging to the ground, made his way to the adjoining house. He returned to say that the roof was undamaged and we would be welcomed there. My father wrapped me in flannel, pushed me feet first into a quart measure and ran crouching through the storm, dodging around piles of wreckage. My mother followed, assisted by Mr. Russell. A dry place was found for her to lie down with her baby. "You were hungry" she told me "and you've never lost your appetite." During the morning the wind moderated to a strong gale and by afternoon the danger had passed. Like animals hesitantly leaving their lairs, people emerged dazed and disoriented from their damaged houses. The devastation was so widespread that women cried and men were speechless. Litters of smashed timbers and uprooted trees covered the village street. Many houses had disappeared. My father told me years later "It was a miracle of cooperation. Families without homes were given temporary housing by the more fortunate. Everyone, even children, helped in re-building." We returned to our house where an old sail was used to make a temporary cover for the hole in the roof. To my mother's relief the kitchen building was undamaged and the daily routine of cooking for four boys could continue. With the help of his crew all repairs were completed before my father left on the next voyage.

Mr. August Van Ryn*

There were a number of severe hurricanes in 1926. The first one was in July which greatly affected the city of Nassau, and surrounding places. It also struck some of the vessels engaged in sponging and fishing. Some of the men saved earlier that year were lost in that July storm. The next violent storm struck the United States, especially between Miami and West Palm Beach and it did a lot of damage. And the third one, that affected us so, hit the island of Abaco, where we lived; especially the town of Marsh Harbour, accompanied by a fearful tidal wave which did nearly all the damage. We must tell you a little of our experience in connection with the storm.

We had had beautiful weather in October, as usual in those islands. The night before everything broke loose it was a lovely, balmy evening. We had some friends staying with us and as we looked at the beautiful full moon and felt the gentle ocean breeze we said to each other, "There will certainly be no hurricane tonight." For the report had come somehow that a hurricane was on its way to us. So we went to bed, but were awakened around midnight by the roaring of the wind, when the violence began to smash the town. The velocity of the wind increased till it blew close to 200 miles an hour, as we learned later. Our house stood firm (I had built it myself and knew it was solid and well founded as were nearly all the houses in the town). Those folks were accustomed to hurricanes and as the gale increased that night it drove the heavy rain through the roof and it soaked through the upstairs floor and into the rooms downstairs, and I spent part of the night trying to dry things out a little. But the house stood.

Then, about 7 O' Clock in the morning there fell a complete calm. It was a really eerie sensation-this perfect calm seconds after the raging winds. So I said to my father-in-law, who had lived in the islands all his life, "What does this sudden calm mean?" And he said, "It means that we are in the exact center-the eye of the hurricane. The storm is moving ahead at the rate of 15 miles per hour or so, and in a short time the winds will come again and they will come from the opposite direction." Then I said to him, "Well, if the gale comes again it will come from the ocean this time (for until then it had been blowing from the land side); won't it bring the sea along with it?" "Oh no," he replied, "We have never seen a tidal wave, but he (and we too that day) saw and felt one that morning. Our house stood very close to the water-not to the ocean itself, but to inland waters with direct access to the ocean in the distance some five miles away. It is from there-from the Atlantic-that the storm surge came and drove its furious course in till it reached our town. There was about half an hour of this curious calm and then the sea drove in-at first a solid wall of water about six feet high. It smashed against our house; drove in the front door and windows and broke away an addition to my house I had recently built. Now the water stood about two or three feet high in our living room. It was too deep for us with our small children to remain there; so we stood together on the stairs that led to the second floor. There we were with our four little children, not knowing what to do; but we could and did pray. Our oldest girl was then seven years old, the next one, a boy, about four and one half, then a little girl two and a half, and the baby, about five months old. I had grabbed the baby out of the arms of a young lady who was staying with us at the time, while the other three children stood between us. And then, in a few minutes more the storm surge rolled in. We could hear its fearful roar before we could see it; it was a solid wall of water rising about twenty feet high. When my wife and I saw it bearing down on us and on our home, we kissed each other and I said to her, "Goodbye darling, we'll see each other in the glory." That's all we expected at the moment; it did not seem possible that anyone of us could escape death. The storm surge struck the house and smashed it to smithereens. I myself apparently went through the glass window on the stairway by which we stood, for my left leg had great big cuts on it. The next thing I knew I came to my senses lying on a piece of wreckage. I had been knocked unconscious and had lost our dear baby. When I came to, I saw my wife in the raging waters further inland, with the three small children clinging to her and she to them. My wife held onto the wreckage of houses and boats that had floated all around. Praise God; they were all still alive and apparently unhurt. So I dropped off the side of a house. I was lying on and let the sea, driven by the violent winds, carry me down her way till after awhile we managed to be together.

Then, between us we sheltered the children as best as we could. It is amazing how easy children take things in their stride. So long as we were with them, they did not panic in the least. It later on struck me as quite a lesson of how we should trust in our heavenly Father. I prayed aloud, while we were banged around, that it might please God to spare us and we thanked Him for the wonderful way He kept us till then. I prayed it might be His will to bring us safely through this ordeal. I had hardly done so, when a roof of a house washed by us. The rafters of the second floor were bare and visible so I hoisted the children one by one and made them lie flat on those rafters, keeping them more or less out of the way of the junk flying about. Since there was less danger of drowning now, we all felt a little safer. And so our oldest girl, our seven year old, Lorraine, spoke up and said, "Daddy, pray again, the Lord heard us that time." A little while after Elliot, the almost five year old one, while we were still in real danger, said, "Daddy, where are you going to put the house next time?" Kids don't get discouraged very quickly.

When we got under the roof of this broken up house, I noticed how badly my upper left leg was cut; it was bleeding profusely; it was likely due to the heavy bleeding that I had lost consciousness at first. So my wife tore off her underskirt and tied it as tightly as possible above the wound to try and stop the loss of blood, later on it took 38 stitches to close the cuts. After awhile the strong gale drove the wreckage we clung under on to some higher land further back and the roof settled down at a steep angle against the hillside and against other wreckage.

While we were caught and jammed underneath this wreckage, unable to get out, the tidal wave kept rising and we had to move from the lower end of the roof all the way to the higher end to keep our heads and the children's above the water. Eventually, the water rose so high that we had to lift the heads of the youngsters right against the roof of the place and it began to look as if the water would drown us right there. And then, at the extreme moment, there was a terrific crash and the upstairs of my father-in-law's house crashed on to the roof we were under, with my wife's mother in it. This broke our roof and enabled us to crawl on the top of it. Then we could see why the water had risen and had made us move to the upper end. Had we remained at the lower end where we first sat, we would have been crushed to death-all of us-for the house above us crumbled the roof we were under. With amazement and joy we realized that very morning our God had twice saved us from death-first from the sea, and now on the land. Oh! How we praised His glorious Name-then and ever afterwards.

There was not even a bruise on the bodies of our dear children, but my wife and I were covered with them from head to toe. We had kept the children between us to save them from harm. We are not saying this in pride, but in humble gratitude to God. After awhile, as is well known, those storm surges go back where they came from in a strong undertow, and so did this one. It carried every bit of our property with it; we never saw the smallest piece of it again. I built the house, spent many weeks remodeling it and enlarging it and the whole thing went in fifteen seconds.

A good deal of the town was destroyed in the storm and storm surge. The houses close to the shore were all smashed and those further back were damaged or some drifted away, carried by the sea. There were not many lives lost; just two or three, I believe. The reason for this was that many felt that their homes might not stand the force of the winds, so they had left them and had gone further back into the hills; others found shelter in the strongly built schoolhouse which stood some distance in from the shore. So we were thankful for not much loss of life, but there was a great deal of property loss.

We later on learned to our great joy that, while there were quite a number of sailing vessels broken up, as well as a very large three-masted sailing vessel which was driven high up on the rocks by the waves, our boat-'*The Evangel*' was the only vessel which came through it all without any damage; most of the others were injured or driven on the rocks. The anchors of our yacht held it secure which was truly another great mercy from our God; we could also use it immediately to get needed help, food, supplies, etc.

As I said before, the Lord gave us four dear children prior to the hurricane; we lost our little baby-Pearl Eleanor in the storm-who has gone ahead of us and we believe we shall see her again in the glory bye and bye. That left us three children and then, about a year later God gave us another boy, Carroll, in place of the one who had left us for brighter scenes. So now we again have four children-two boys and two girls. We built another house with the material which the government provided to those who had been hit hard by the storm.

*This account was given to me by Mr. Rupert Roberts Jr. about Mr. August Van Ryn and his family's dramatic experience with Hurricane #10 of 1926 living on the island of Abaco.

**This account was given to me by Mr. Chester Thompson taken from his book *'The Fledgling-A Bahamian Boyhood'*

CHAPTER TWELVE

HURRICANE PREPAREDNESS

BE PREPARED BEFORE THE HURRICANE SEASON

- Know the storm surge history and elevation of your area.

- Learn safe routes inland and try not to wait until the last minute to begin your evacuation.

- Learn locations of official Hurricane Shelters.

- Review needs and working conditions of emergency equipment such as flashlights, battery-powered radios and cell phones (ensured that before the hurricane the battery is charged to 100% capacity).

- Ensure that non-perishable foods, can goods and water supplies are on hand and are sufficient to last for at least two weeks.

- Obtain and secure materials necessary to secure your home properly, such as plywood and plastic.

- Know the hurricane terms *Hurricane Alert, Hurricane Warning* and *Hurricane Watch* well in advance of an approaching storm and develop a clear and concise evacuation plans for your home, school, office or business in the event a hurricane threatens your area.

- Check your home for loose and clogged rain gutters and downspouts.

- Keep trees and shrubbery trimmed. Cut weak branches and trees that could fall or bump against the house and damage it in a hurricane. When trimming, try to create a channel through the foliage to the center of the tree to allow for airflow.

- Determine where to move your boat in an emergency.

- Obtain and store material, such as plywood, which are necessary to properly secure your windows and doors.

- Review your insurance policy to ensure that it provides adequate coverage and try not to wait until the hurricane season to take out or renew your policy because some insurance companies will not cover your home or business if the policy is taken out just before a storm and in most cases it takes some time for the policy to become in effect but this varies from company to company so check with your individual company about this aspect of the policy.

- Take pictures of your home, inside and out to bolster insurance claims.

- Individuals with special needs should contact the local office of Emergency Management.

- For information and assistance with any of these items, contact your local Meteorological Office, Office of Emergency Management, or the Red Cross Society.

WHEN A HURRICANE WATCH IS ISSUED

- Be prepared to take quick action

- Monitor radio, television, and hurricane hotline numbers frequently for official bulletins of the storm's progress.

- Fuel and service family and business vehicles.

- Inspect and secure all business and homes.

- Prepare to cover all window and door openings with shutters or other shielding materials.

- Secure unanchored garbage cans, building materials, garden-tools and patio furniture immediately.

- Take down television, radio, and satellite antennae.

CHECK FOOD AND WATER SUPPLIES

- Have clean, airtight containers on hand to store at least a two-week supply of drinking water (about 14 gallons per person).

- Stock up on canned provisions.

- Get a camping stove with fuel.

- Keep a small cooler with frozen gel packs handy for packing refrigerated items.

- Check prescription medicines; obtain at least ten days to two weeks' supply.

- Stock up on extra batteries for radios, flashlights, and lanterns.

- Prepare to store and secure outdoor lawn furniture and other loose, lightweight objects, such as garbage cans, garden tools, and potted plants, which can be used as projectiles and missiles during the storm.

- Check and replenish first aid supplies.

- Have an extra supply of cash on hand.

WHEN A HURRICANE WARNING IS ISSUED

- Closely monitor radio, TV, or hurricane hotline telephone numbers for official bulletins.

- Follow instructions issued by local officials and leave immediately if ordered to do so.

- Complete preparation activities, such as putting up storm shutters and securing loose objects.

- Evacuate areas that might be affected by storm surge flooding such as coastal and low lying areas.

- If and when evacuating, leave early (if possible, in daylight).

- Notify neighbours and family members outside the warned area of your evacuation plans.

EVACUATION

Plan to evacuate if you:

- Live in a mobile or small wooden house. Do not stay in a mobile or wooden home under any circumstances. They are unsafe in high winds and/or hurricane conditions, no matter how well fastened they are to the ground.

- Live on a coastline, on an island or in an area prone to flooding.

- Live in a high rise such as a hotel or office building. Hurricane winds are stronger at higher elevations. Glass doors and windows may be blown out of their casings and weaken the structure.

When you leave:

- Stay with friends or relatives or at low-rise inland hotels or motels outside the flood zones.

- Leave early to avoid heavy traffic, road blocked by early floodwaters, and bridges impassable due to high winds.

- Put food and water out for your pets if you cannot take them with you or take them to the local humane society for safekeeping. Public shelters do not allow pets, and nor do most motels/hotels.

- Go to a hurricane shelter if you have no other place to go. Shelters may be crowded and uncomfortable, with no privacy and no electricity. Do not leave your home for a shelter until government officials announce on radio or television that a particular shelter is open. If you must leave your home for a shelter or to a family or friends, remember turn off the main electricity switch and cut off your gas supply, as these can become fire hazards during the storm.

What to bring to a shelter:

- First aid kit, medicine, baby food and diapers, playing cards, games and books for entertainment purposes, toiletries, battery-powered radio, flashlights (one per person), extra batteries, blankets or sleeping bags, identification, valuable papers (insurance and passport), and cash.

IF STAYING AT HOME:

- Reminder: Only stay in a home if you have not been ordered to leave. If you are told to leave, do so immediately!

- Store water. Fill sterilized jugs and bottles with water for a two-week supply of drinking water. Fill bathtub and large containers with water for sanitary purposes.

- Turn refrigerator to maximum cold, and open it only when necessary.

- Turn off utilities if told to do so by authorities. Turn off propane tanks.

- Unplug small appliances

- Stay inside a well-constructed building. Examine the building and plan in advance what you will do if winds become strong. Strong winds can produce deadly missiles and structural failure.

If winds grow strong:

- Stay away from windows and doors, even if they are covered. Take refuge in a small interior room, closet, or hallway. Take a battery-powered radio and flashlight with you to your place of refuge.

- Close all interior doors. Secure and brace external doors, particularly double inward-opening doors and garage doors.

- If you are in a two-story house, go to the basement, an interior first floor room such as a bathroom or closet, or under the stairs.

- If you are in a multi-story building and away from the water, go to the first or second floor and take refuge in a hall or interior room, away from windows. Interior stairwells and the areas around elevator shafts are generally the strongest part of a building.

- Lie on the floor under a table or another sturdy object.

- Be alert for tornadoes, which often are spawned by hurricanes.

- If the 'Eye' of the hurricane should pass over your area, be aware that the improved weather conditions are only temporary. The storm conditions will return with winds coming from the opposite direction, sometimes within just a few minutes and usually within an hour so it is important that you stay indoors until the weather officials give the 'All-Clear.'

AFTER THE STORM PASSES

- Stay in your protected area until announcements are made on the radio or television that the dangerous winds have passed.

- If you have evacuated, do not return home until officials announce that your area is ready. Remember, proof of residency may be required in order to re-enter evacuated zones.

- If your home or building has structural damage, do not enter until officials check it.

- Avoid using candles and other open flames indoors.

- Beware of outdoor hazards

- Avoid downed power lines and any water in which they may be lying. Be alert for weakened bridges and washed-out roads. Watch for weakened limbs on trees and/or damaged overhanging structures.

- Do not use the telephone unless absolutely necessary. The system usually is jammed with emergency calls during and after a hurricane.

- Guard against spoiled food. Use dry or canned food. Do not drink or prepare food with tap water until you are certain it is not contaminated.

- When cutting up fallen trees, use caution, especially if you use a chain saw. Serious injuries can occur when these powerful machines snap back or when the chain breaks.

CONCLUSION

Nature is often said to be tamed, but natural disasters such as hurricanes kills several thousand people around the world every decade, and leave millions more homeless. There is nothing tamed or tamable about hurricanes. Hurricanes are known as the "Greatest Storms on Earth," and rightly so because these storms can cause widespread destruction and a significant death toll over a wide area and can affect millions of lives during their brief life here on Earth. Drawing on energy from the sun, oceans or the Earth's residual heat, these titanic forces called hurricanes landscape the planet according to their random design. There is no refuge or protection against them except to get out of their way. Hurricanes develop out at sea and are today tracked by weather satellites and radars. Forecasts of their tracks and ferocity have enough credibility that people all over the world take their evacuation orders seriously. Every year between June 1 and November 30, hurricanes threaten the Eastern and Gulf Coasts States of the United States, Mexico, Central America and the Caribbean. The inhabitants of Southeast Asia name them *"Typhoons."* In Australia, they are called *"Willy-Willies,"* and in the Indian Ocean, they are simply known as *"Cyclones."* No matter what name they may go by, these storms are a nightmare for everyone who lives in a tropical region because these storms can strike fear into the hearts of the bravest of souls, and those foolish enough to challenge these storms can lose everything, including their lives.

Extreme rainfall, unbelievably high waves, winds of incredible ferocity-nothing can compare to the destructive power of hurricanes. Hurricanes wreak havoc when they make landfall, and they can kill thousands of people and cause billions of dollars in property damage when they hit heavily populated areas. Hurricanes are severe tropical cyclones, which, though not nearly so frequent as mid-latitude cyclones, receive a great deal of attention from lay people and scientists alike, mainly because of their awesome intensity, strength and their great destructive powers. Abundant, even torrential rainfall and winds of great speeds (from 74 to 150 mph or more) characterize hurricanes. Though these storms develop over the warm oceanic waters and often can spend their entire lives there but at times their tracks do take them over islands and coastal lands. The results can be devastating by causing the destruction of property worth millions of dollars and sometimes even death. It is not just the rainfall and raging winds that can produce such tremendous damages to people and their surroundings, for accompanying the hurricane are unusually high seas, called storm surges, which can flood entire coastal communities.

As I grew up in a small settlement in the Bluff, South Andros, here in the Bahamas, with its sporadic hurricanes from time to time, I quickly learned that weather for better or for worse is an integral part of everybody's life because weather is one of the most common denominators of our lives. It helps shape our culture, character, conduct, and health. It frequents the pages of our history and can even change our course in life. It colours our conversations, folklore, and literature; it rains on our parades, awes us with its destructive power and beauty, frightens us, and sometimes it even kills. The long term weather patterns of a given area are used to categorize its prevailing climate. These patterns include the seasonal, monthly, and daily variations, as well as any weather extremes experienced such as hurricanes, droughts, or thunderstorms. Trying to figure out what the weather is going to do has been a matter of great importance ever since mankind first evolved. We do not know much about what our earliest ancestors did in this respect, but from recorded times onward weather forecasting has played a central part in many societies. The fortunes of humanity have been linked to the vagaries of the weather since time immemorial. Knowing whether it is going to be hot or cold, wet or dry, is just as important today as it was for our ancestors. Extreme conditions-such as hurricanes can lead to starvation, sickness, and death, and still do in many parts of the world. As evidence of climate change becomes more compelling, never before has good knowledge of climate and weather conditions been so significant to the peoples of the world.

Hurricanes have been an integral part of the Caribbean, the Bahamas and the history of the United States, since Christopher Columbus first arrived here in the New World. The experience of Columbus with hurricanes on his early voyages to the New World is well documented. The greatest loss of life in North Atlantic was caused by the Great Hurricane of 1780 that resulted in over 22,000 deaths in Barbados, St. Lucia, St. Eustatius, and Martinique. In the United States, the unpredicted hurricane that struck the Galveston, Texas coast in 1900 resulted in over 8,000 deaths. Closer to the Bahamas, the Great Lake Okeechobee Hurricane in 1928 moved through South Florida resulted in over 2,500 deaths, many of them Bahamian migrant workers. Then in 1715, well over 1,000 persons died from a massive hurricane that struck the Bahamas. Not many Bahamians are aware of these great loss of lives from these historic hurricanes, so often times they let their guards down by simply not preparing for them.

The hurricane challenge facing Bahamians in the twenty first century involves several components, knowledge, preparation and planning for these storms. Although we cannot control hurricanes, we can encourage better preparation and planning here in the Bahamas and in this region as a whole, so that similar tragedies can be avoided in the future. New concerns have also emerged in the Bahamas as coastal population growth and property development has exploded exponentially to help accommodate the ever-increasing tourism and new homes industries. Infact, currently the Bahamas population increases are significantly largest in coastal communities. As a result, property damage costs due to hurricanes have skyrocketed in the last twenty years; placing the insurance industry on the brink of financial chaos should a major hurricane like the ones in 1926 ever strike again. Infact, many coastal residents are now finding it difficult to obtain insurance now. As a meteorologist, it is my hope and desire that this book will allow you to recognize and understand that the possibility exists that we may be faced with a major hurricane at some point in the future. It is also my objective that this book will encourage you to seek out additional preparedness information, not only for hurricanes, but for all types of disasters. It is the responsibility of both the government and the individual to be prepared for hurricane disasters, and to plan for a worst case scenario. As to what's going to happen in the near future, well that's anybody's guess, but the need to be prepared for all hurricane hazards should be a priority for every community, every family, and every individual.

SOURCES:

❖ *"HURRICANE!"*A Familiarization Booklet by NOAA, April, 1993

❖ *The Bahamas Journal of Science Vol. 6 No.1 Historic Weather at Nassau-*Ronald V. Shaklee, Media Publishing Ltd.

❖ *The Bahamas Journal of Science Vol. 5 No.1 Historical Hurricane Impacts on the Bahamas, Part I: 1500-1749* Ronald V. Shaklee, Media Publishing Ltd.

❖ *The Bahamas Journal of Science Vol. 5 No.2 Historical Hurricane Impacts on the Bahamas, Part II: 1750-1799* Ronald V. Shaklee, Media Publishing Ltd.

❖ *The Bahamas Journal of Science Vol. 8 No.1 Historical Hurricane Impacts on the Bahamas: Floyd on San Salvador & Early Nineteenth Century Hurricanes 1800-1850* Ronald V. Shaklee, Media Publishing Ltd.

❖ *Reports from the House of Assembly of the Bahamas* commencing, 01st September 1926 to 30th March, 1927.

❖ *Reports from the House Of Assembly of the Bahamas* commencing, 18th March, 1930 to 7th July, 1930

❖ *Reports from the House of Assembly of the Bahamas Special Session* commencing 16th October 1929 to 24th October 1929.

❖ *Harper's Weekly-A Journal of Civilization Vol. X-No 516,* Saturday, 17th 1866 *Hurricane in the Bahamas.'*

❖ *The Journal of the American Museum of Natural History Vol. XXVI Nov.-Dec, 1926-The Bahamas in Sunshine and Storm* Roy Waldo Miner

❖ *The Colonial Office Records (CO 23) Reports on the Three Hurricanes of 1926 from 01st July to 25th November, 1926* Department of Archives-Nassau.

❖ *The Sponging Industry Booklet* 18th February, 1974, Public Records Office-Department of Archives, Nassau, Bahamas.

❖ *The Tribune,* Saturday, July 31st 1926 pgs 1,2 & 3 *'Out Islands Devastated'*

❖ *The Tribune,* Wednesday, August 04th 1926 pgs 1 & 2 *'Hurricane Relief Movements'*

❖ *The Tribune,* Wednesday, August 11th August, 1926 pgs 1,2 & 3 *'Hurricane Damage'*

❖ *The Tribune,* Saturday, August 14th 1926 pg 1 *'Relief'*

❖ *The Tribune,* Wednesday, September 19th 1928 pgs 1 & 2 *'Extraordinary Hurricane Hits Bahamas.'*

❖ *The Tribune,* Wednesday, February 18th 2009 pg 7 *'Lessons from Bahamas and Florida sponge fishery.'*

❖ *The Nassau Guardian,* June 30th 2005 *'The Sponging Industry'* Dr. Gail Saunders

❖ *The Nassau Guardian,* July 28th 1926 pgs 1,2 & 3 *'Hurricane Havoc-Terrible Storm hits The Bahamas-Loss and Ruin Everywhere.'*

❖ *The Nassau Guardian, July 31ˢᵗ 1926* pgs 1 & 4 '*The Aftermath*' *& Casualties at Sea.*'

❖ *The Nassau Guardian, August 04ᵗʰ 1926* pgs 1 & 4 '*The Out Islands.*'

❖ *The Nassau Guardian, August 07ᵗʰ 1926* pg 4 '*The Out Islands.*'

❖ *The Nassau Guardian, August 11ᵗʰ 1926* pg 4 '*Counting the Cost-Some of the damage done by the Storm.*' *& '*The Governor's visit to the Out Island.*'

❖ *The Nassau Guardian, August 14ᵗʰ 1926* pgs 3 & 4 '*Out Island Notes.*' *& '*Relief taken to the Out Islands-Governor's Return.*'

❖ *The Nassau Guardian, September 21ˢᵗ 1926* pg 4 '*The Out Islands.*'

❖ *The Nassau Guardian, October 06ᵗʰ 1926* pg 4 '*The Sponge Industry*' *& '*The Out Islands.*'

❖ *The Nassau Guardian, October 28ᵗʰ 1926* pg 4 '*The Hurricane at the Out Islands.*'

❖ *The Nassau Guardian, October 30ᵗʰ 1926* pgs 1 & 4 '*The Out Islands,*' '*Disastrous Hurricane at Governor's Harbour,*' *& '*Hurricane at the Out Island.*'

❖ *The Nassau Guardian, November 03ʳᵈ 1926* pg 4 '*The Hurricane at Abaco.*'

❖ *Florida Historical Society: The Florida Historical Quarterly Volume 65 issue 3*

❖ *Weathering the Storms: Hurricanes and Risk in the British Greater Caribbean.* Business History Review, Vol. 78, No. 4, Winter 2004.

❖ Ahrens, D. (2000) *Meteorology Today, An Introduction to Weather, Climate, and The Environment,* USA, Brooks/Cole Publishing.

❖ Buckley, B., Hopkins, E., Whitaker R. (2004) *Weather-A Visual Guide*, Sidney, Australia, Firefly Books

❖ Burroughs, Crowder, Robertson, et al. (1996) *The Nature Company Guides to Weather*, Singapore, Time-Life Publishing Inc.

❖ Burton, H., Burton, S. (2000) *The Impact of Tropical Cyclones*, Barbados, CIMH.

❖ Butler, E. (1980) *Natural Disasters*, Australia, Heinemann Educational Books Ltd.

❖ Calderon, M.E. *The Tainos of Puerto Rico: Rediscovering Borinquen*, USA, Yale University.

❖ Challoner, J. (2000) *Hurricane and Tornado*, Great Britain, Dorling Kindersley

❖ Clarke, P., Smith, A. (2001) *Usborne Spotter's Guide To Weather*, England, Usborne Publishing Ltd.

❖ Craton, M.(2001) *A History of the Bahamas (3ʳᵈ Ed)* Canada, San Salvador Press

❖ Davis, K.(2005) *Don't Know Much About World Myths*, HarperCollins Publishers.

❖ Day, F., Downs, R. et al,(2005) *National Geographic Almanac of Geography*, National Geographic, Washington, D.C.

❖ Douglas.S.M. (1958), *Hurricane,* USA, Rinehart and Company Inc.

❖ Duedall, I., Williams, J. (2002) *Florida Hurricanes and Tropical Storms 1871-2001*, USA, University Press Of Florida.

❖ Durschmied, E. (2001) *The Weather Factor-How Nature has changed History*, New York, Arcade Publishing, Inc.

❖ Emanuel, K. (2005) *Divine Wind-The History and Science of Hurricanes*, New York, Oxford University Press.

❖ Fitzpatrick, J.P. (1999), *Natural Disasters-Hurricanes*, USA, ABC-CLIO, Inc.

❖ Gore, A.,(2006), *An Inconvenient Truth*, New York, USA, Rodale Books

❖ J.D. Jarrell, Max Mayfield, Edward Rappaport, & Chris Landsea *NOAA Technical Memorandum NWS TPC-1 The Deadliest, Costliest, and Most Intense United States Hurricanes from 1900 to 2000(And Other Frequently Requested Hurricane Facts)*

❖ Jones W. (2005) *Hurricane-A Force of Nature*, Bahamas, Jones Communications Intl Ltd. Publication.

❖ Hook, P. (2006) *Weather Watching*, London, HarperCollins Publishers Ltd.

❖ Kahl, J. (1998) *National Audubon Society First Field Guide To Weather,* Hong Kong, Scholastic Inc.

❖ Kindersley, D., (2002) *Eyewitness Weather,* London, Dorling Kindersley Ltd.

❖ Lauber, P. (1996) *Hurricanes: Earth's Mightiest Storms*, Singapore, Scholastic Press

❖ Ludlum, D. M., 1989. *Early American Hurricanes 1492-1870*. Boston, MA: American Meteorological Society

❖ Lyons, A.W.' (1997) *The Handy Science Weather Answer Book,* Detroit, Visible Ink Press.

❖ MacPherson, J. (1967) *Caribbean Lands-A Geography of the West Indies, 2nd Edition*, London, Longmans, Green and Co Ltd.

❖ Millas C.J. (1968) *Hurricanes of The Caribbean and Adjacent Regions 1492-1800*, Edward Brothers Inc/Academy of the Arts and Sciences of the Americas Miami, Florida.

❖ Pearce, A.E., Smith G.C. (1998) *The Hutchinson World Weather Guide,* Great Britain, Helicon Publishing Ltd.

❖ Redfield; W.C., (1846), *On Three Several Hurricanes of the Atlantic and their Relations To the Northers of Mexico and Central America,* New Haven

❖ Reynolds, R., (2000) *Philip's Guide To Weather*, London, Octopus Publishing Group Ltd.

❖ Saunders, A. (2006) *History of Bimini Volume 2*, Bahamas, New World Press.

❖ Saunders, G, and Craton, M. (1998*) Islanders in the Stream: A History of the Bahamian People Volume 2,* USA, University of Georgia Press.

❖ Sharer, C. (1955) *The Population Growth of the Bahamas Islands*, USA, University of Michigan Press.

❖ Sheets, B., Williams, J.(2001) *Hurricane Watch-Forecasting the Deadliest Storms on Earth,* USA, Vintage Books.

❖ Tannehill, I.(1950) *Hurricanes-Their Nature and History-Particularly those of the West Indies and the Southern Coasts of the United States*, USA, Princeton University Press.

❖ Treaster, J.(2007) *Hurricane Force-In the Path of America's Deadliest Storms,* USA, Kingfisher.

❖ Triana, P.(1987) *San Salvador-The Forgotten Island*, Spain, Ediciones Beramar.

❖ Viele, J.(2001) *The Florida Keys Volume 3-The Wreckers*, USA, Pineapple Press Inc.

❖ Williams, J. (1997) *The Weather Book*, USA, Vintage Books Ltd.

❖ www.enchantedlearning.com

❖ www.aoml.noaa.gov

❖ www.noaa.gov

❖ www.nasa.gov

❖ www.nhc.noaa.gov

❖ www.wmo.ch

❖ www.hurricanecity.com

❖ www.weather.unisys.com

❖ www.sun-sentinel.com

❖ www.weathernotebook.org

❖ www.hurricaneville.com

❖ www.deadlystorms.com

❖ www.bom.gov.au

❖ www.stormcarib.com

❖ www.bbc.co.uk

❖ www.answers.com

❖ www.weather.com

❖ www.wxresearch.org

❖ www.heldref.org

❖ www.history.com

❖ www.bermuda-online.org

❖ www.weathernotebook.org

❖ www.wunderground.com

❖ www.usatoday.com

❖ www.keyshistory.org

Wayne Neely

- ❖ www.palmbeachpost.com
- ❖ www.wikipedia.org
- ❖ www.colorado.edu
- ❖ www.iri.columbia.edu
- ❖ www.nationalgeographic.com
- ❖ www.weathersavvy.com
- ❖ www.usaid.gov
- ❖ www.caribbeannetnews.com

Acknowledgements

The writing and development of this book has been a highly satisfying project, made so by the subject itself but also by the people who have helped and assisted me in some way or the other. To these vast array of individuals-scientists, corporations, researchers, authors, readers, meteorologists, friends, and moral supporters-I owe a great debt of appreciation. To list them all would fill another book, but I especially wish to express my sincere thanks and gratitude to several outstanding people below in no particular order below:-

Mr. Lofton and Francita Neely
Mr. Andrew McKinney
Mr. William Holowesko
The Hon. Glenny's Hanna-Martin
Mr. Murrio Ducille
Mr. Charles Carter
Mr. Bryan Norcross
Mrs. Patricia Beardsley Roker
Mr. Herbert Saffir
Mr. Peter Graham
Mr. Dwight Hart
Rev. Theo and Blooming Neely and family
Mr. Coleman and Diana Andrews and family
Mr. Joshua and Darlene Taylor and family
Dr. Myles Munroe

Dr. Timothy Barrett
Mr. Charles Whelbell
Mr. Rupert Roberts Jr.
Mrs. Lindsey Peterson
Mrs. Suzette Hall-Moss
Mrs. Macushla Hazelwood
Mr. Keith Culmer
Mr. Neil Williams
Mr. Ray Duncombe
Ms. Stephanie Hanna
Mr. Leroy Lowe
Mrs. Leanora Archer
Mr. Rodger Demeritte
Mrs. Shyvonne Moxey-Bonaby
Mr. Orson Nixon
Mr. Omar Theolophis
Mr. Michael and Philip Stubbs
Mr. Neil Sealey
Mrs. Carole Balla
Ms. Elisa Montalvo
Ms. Sherrine Thompson
Staff and Management of Fine Image Photography
Staff and Management of the Nassau Guardian Newspaper
Staff and Management of Media Enterprises
Staff and Management of Graham Thompson and Co.
Staff and Management of the Tribune Newspaper
Staff and Management of IslandFM Radio Station
Staff and Management of the Exuma Breeze Radio Station and Newspaper
Staff of the Broadcasting Corporation of the Bahamas (ZNS)
Staff of the Department of Archives
Staff of the Department of Meteorology
Staff of the Caribbean Meteorological Institute
Staff of NOAA and National Hurricane Center in Miami
Mr. Jim Williams and staff of Hurricane City
Mr. Jack and Karen Andrews
Ms. Pleasant Russell

Mrs. Margaret Jeffers
Ms. Kathy-Ann Caesar
Mr. Horace & Selvin Burton
Mr. Nigel Atherly

For Booking and Speaking Arrangements here is my Contact Information: -

Mr. Wayne Neely
P.O. Box EE-16637
Nassau, Bahamas

E-Mail: wayneneely@hotmail.com
Or wayneneely@yahoo.com

I would like to sincerely thank each one of these sponsors both individual and corporate below who assisted me financially and in other ways in making this book project a reality and without them this book would have not been possible, so from the bottom of my heart I thank each and every one you:

Mr. Andrew McKinney
Mr. William Holowesko
Mr. Charles Carter
Mrs. Patricia Beardsley Roker
Mrs. Macushla Hazelwood
Mr. Raymond E. Duncombe
Mr. Neil Williams
Mr. Jim Williams
Mr. Christopher Landsea
Mrs. Susan Larson
Mrs. Stephanie Hanna
Mr. Dwight Hart
Mr. Rupert Roberts Jr.
Mr. Jeremy MacVean
Mr. Leroy Lowe

J.S. JOHNSON
PEACE OF MIND
INSURANCE AGENTS & BROKERS

34 Collins Ave.
P.O. Box N-8337
Nassau, Bahamas
Phone: 242-322-2341
E-Mail: info@jsjohnson.com
www.jsjohnson.com

 Bobcat Bahamas

Crawford St. Oakes Field
P.O. Box N-8170
Nassau, Bahamas
Phone: 242-323-5171
E-Mail: rduncombe@cavalierbahamas.com
www.bobcatbahamas.com

dive paradise with

East Bay Street
P.O. Box SS-5004
Nassau, Bahamas
Phone: 242-393-6054
Reservations: U.S. Toll Free (800) 398-DIVE
E-Mail: bahdiver@coralwave.com
www.bahamadivers.com

98.3 the breeZe fm
coolin' down the islands

The Exuma
BreeZe
Radio Station and Newspaper

Ocean Addition
Exuma, Bahamas
Phone: 242-358-7201
Fax: 242-358-7203
E-Mail: hartdwight@yahoo.com
www.thebreezefmexuma.com

Comfort Suites Paradise Island
Paradise Island Dr, Paradise Island, Bahamas.
Phone: (242) 363-3680   Fax: (242) 363-2588

JOHNBULL AND ITS GROUP OF COMPANIES
284 Bay Street
P.O. Box N-3737
Nassau, Bahamas
Phone: 242-322-4253
Email: info@johnbull.bs
www.JohnBull.com

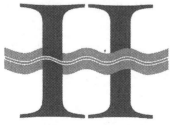

HIGHBOURNE CAY
EXUMA • BAHAMAS

P.O. Box SS-6342
Nassau, Bahamas
Phone: 242-355-1008
Fax: 242-355-1003
E-Mail: highborne@earthlink.net

Insurance Company of The Bahamas Ltd.

33 Collins Avenue
P. O. Box N-8320, Nassau

TEL: 322-2341 OR 322-2344   FAX: 323-3720

Security & General
I N S U R A N C E

Atlantic House
2nd Terrace & Collins Ave.
P.O. Box N-3540
Nassau, Bahamas
Phone: 242-326-7100
Fax: 242-325-0948
E-Mail: nwilliam@atlantichouse.com.bs

WEATHER DEFINITIONS:

Air

This is considered the mixture of gases that make up the earth's atmosphere. The principal gases that compose dry air are Nitrogen at 78.09%, Oxygen at 20.95%, Argon at 0.93, and Carbon Dioxide at 0.033%. One of the most important constituents of air and most important gases in meteorology is water vapour.

All Clear

All Clear simply means that the hurricane has left the affected area and all the warnings, and watches are lifted but the residents in that area should exercise extreme caution for downed power lines, debris fallen trees, flooding etc.

Anemograph

An instrument used to measure the wind speed and direction.

Atmosphere

The envelope of gases that surround a planet and are held to it by the planet's gravitational attraction. The earth's atmosphere is mainly nitrogen and oxygen.

Atmospheric Pressure

The pressure exerted by the atmosphere at a given point. It measurements can be expressed in several ways. One is Millibars, another is Hector Pascal's and another is in inches or millimeters of Mercury.

Barometer

A weather instrument used for measuring the pressure of the atmosphere. The two principle types are aneroid and mercurial.

Bermuda High

A semi-permanent, subtropical area of high pressure in the North Atlantic Ocean that migrates east and west with varying central pressure. Depending on the season, it has different names. When it is displaced westward, during the Northern Hemispheric summer and fall, the center is located in western North Atlantic, near Bermuda. In the winter and early spring, it is primarily centered near the Azores Islands.

Best Track

A subjectively-smoothed representation of a tropical cyclone's location and intensity over its lifetime. The best track contains the cyclone's latitude, longitude, maximum sustained surface winds, and minimum sea-level pressure at 6-hourly intervals. Best track positions and intensities, which are based on a post-storm assessment of all available data, may differ from values contained in storm advisories. They also generally will not reflect the erratic motion implied by connecting individual center fix positions.

Calm

Atmospheric conditions devoid of wind or any other air in motion and where smoke rises vertically. In oceanic terms, it is the apparent absence of the water surface when there is no wind.

Cape Verde Islands

A group of volcanic islands in the eastern Atlantic Ocean off the coast of West Africa. A Cape Verde hurricane originates near here.

Cape Verde Type Hurricane

A hurricane system that originated near the Cape Verde Islands just west of the west coast of Africa.

Center

Generally speaking, the vertical axis of a tropical cyclone, usually defined by the location of the minimum wind or minimum pressure. The cyclone center position can vary with altitude.

Central Pressure

The central Pressure is sometimes referred to as the Minimum Central Pressure is the atmospheric pressure at the center of a high or low. It is the highest pressure in a high and lowest pressure in a low, referring to the sea level pressure of the system on a surface chart.

Climate

The historical record and description of average daily and in seasonal weather events that help describe a region. Statistics are generally drawn over several decades. The word is derived from the Greek klima, meaning inclination, and reflects the importance early scholars attributed to the sun's influence.

Cold Front

The boundary created when a cold air mass collides with a warm air mass.

Convergence

Wind movement that results in a horizontal net inflow of air into a particular region. Convergent winds at lower levels are associated with upward motion.

Coriolis Force

This is an apparent force observed on any free-moving objects in a rotating system. On the earth, this deflective force results from the earth's rotation and causes moving particles (including the wind) to be deflected to the right in the Northern Hemisphere and to the left in the Southern Hemisphere. It was first described in 1835 by French scientist Gustave-Gaspard Coriolis.

Cyclone

An area of low atmospheric pressure, which has a closed circulation, that is cyclonic (counterclockwise in northern hemisphere and clockwise in southern hemisphere). It is a particularly severe type of tropical storm with very low atmospheric pressure at the centre and strong winds blowing around it. Violent winds and heavy rain may affect an area of some hundreds of miles. The name applies to such storms in the Indian Ocean. 'Typhoons' and 'hurricanes' are other names applied to the same phenomena in the Pacific and Atlantic Oceans respectively.

Depression

It is a region where the surface atmospheric pressure is low. A distinctive feature on a weather map and the opposite of an anticyclone.

Usually associated with clouds and rain and sometimes-strong winds. A less severe weather disturbance than a tropical cyclone.

Disturbance

This has several applications. It can apply to a low or cyclone that is small in size and influence. It can also apply to an area that is exhibiting signs of cyclonic development. It may also apply to a stage of tropical cyclone development and is known as a tropical disturbance to distinguish it from other synoptic features.

Doppler radar

An advanced kind of radar that measures wind speed and locates areas of precipitation. It is like conventional radar in that it can detect areas of precipitation and measure rainfall intensity. But a Doppler radar can do more-it can actually measure the speed at which precipitation is moving horizontally toward or away from the radar antenna. Because precipitation particles are carried by the wind, Doppler radar can peer into a severe storm and reveal its winds.

El Niño

A Spanish term given to a warm ocean current, and to the unusually warm and rainy weather associated with it, which sometimes occurs for a few weeks off the coast of Peru (which is otherwise an extremely dry and cool region of the tropics). Several years may pass without this current appearing.

Equator

The ideal or conceptual circle at 0 degrees latitude around the Earth that divides the planet into the northern and southern hemispheres.

Evacuate

To leave an area, usually to escape some impending danger.

Extratropical

A term used in advisories and tropical summaries to indicate that a cyclone has lost its "tropical" characteristics. The term implies both pole ward displacement of the cyclone and the conversion of the cyclone's primary energy source from the release of latent heat of condensation to baroclinic (the temperature contrast between warm and cold air masses) processes. It is important to note that cyclones can become extratropical and still retain winds of hurricane or tropical storm force.

Eye

A region in the center of a hurricane (tropical storm) where the winds are light and skies are clear to partly cloudy.

Eyewall

This is a wall of dense thunderstorms that surrounds the eye of a hurricane.

Feeder Bands

These are the lines or bands of thunderstorms that spiral into and around the center of a tropical system. Also known as outer convective bands or spiral Rainbands, a typical hurricane may have several of these bands surrounding it. They occur in advance of the main rain shield and are usually 40 to 80 miles apart. In thunderstorm development, they are the lines or bands of low level clouds that move or feed into the updraft region of a thunderstorm.

Flash Flood

A localized flood caused by heavy rain falling in a short period of time.

Flood

Overflowing by water of the normal confines of a stream or other body of water, or accumulation of water by drainage over areas that are not normally submerged.

Front

The transition or boundary between two air masses of different densities, which usually means different temperatures. The several types of fronts bring distinct weather patterns.

Funnel Cloud

A violent, rotating column of air visibly extending from the base of a towering cumulus of cumulonimbus toward the ground, but not in contact with it.

Gust

A sudden brief increase in the speed of the wind, followed by a lull or slackening.

Hemisphere

The top and bottom halves of the earth are called the Northern and Southern Hemisphere.

High

The center of an area of high atmospheric pressure, usually accompanied by anticyclonic and outward wind flow. This is an area where the atmospheric pressure is high in contrast to the areas surrounding it forming a distinctive pattern on a weather map. The weather is usually calm and settled at or near the centre of the high. Also known as an anticyclone.

Hurricane

This the term used in the North Atlantic Ocean, Caribbean Sea, Gulf of Mexico, and in the eastern North Pacific Ocean to describe a severe tropical cyclone having winds in excess of 64 knots (74mph) and capable of producing widespread wind damage and heavy flooding; Beaufort scale numbers 12 through 17. The same tropical cyclone is known as a typhoon in the western Pacific and cyclone in the Indian Ocean.

Hurricane Alert

A hurricane alert indicates that a hurricane poses a threat to an area (often within 60 hours) and residents of the area should start to make any necessary preparations.

Hurricane Season

The part of the year having a relatively high incidence of hurricanes. The hurricane season in the Atlantic, Caribbean and Gulf of Mexico runs from June 1 to November 30.

Hurricane Warning

A formal advisory issued by hurricane forecasters when they have determined that hurricane conditions are expected in a coastal area or group of islands within a 24 hour period. A warning is used to inform the public and marine interests of the storm's location, intensity, and movement. At this point residents should have completed the necessary preparations for the storm.

Hurricane Watch

A formal advisory issued by forecasters when they have determined that hurricane conditions are a potential threat to a coastal area or group of islands within 24 to 36 hour period. A watch is used to inform the public and marine interest of the storm's location, intensity, and movement and residents of the area should be prepared.

Knot

The unit of speed in the nautical system; one nautical mile per hour. It is equal to 1.1508 statute miles per hour or 0.5144 meters per second.

Landfall

The intersection of the surface center of a tropical cyclone with a coastline. Because the strongest winds in a tropical cyclone are not located precisely at the center. It is possible for a cyclone's strongest winds to be experienced over land even if landfall does not occur. Similarly, it is possible for a tropical cyclone to make landfall and have its strongest winds remain over the water.

Latent Heat

The energy released or absorbed during a change of state or quite simply, the energy stored when water evaporates into vapor or ice melts into liquid. It is released as heat when water vapor condenses or water freezes.

Lightning

A sudden and visible discharge of electricity produced in response to the build up of electrical potential between cloud and ground, between clouds, within a single cloud, or between a cloud and surrounding air within a cumulo-nimbus cloud.

Low

An area of low barometric pressure, with its attendant system of winds. Also called a depression or cyclone.

Meteorologist

A scientist who studies and predicts the weather by looking at what is happening in the atmosphere.

Meteorology

The study of the atmosphere and the atmospheric phenomena as well as the atmosphere's interaction with the earth's surface, oceans, and life in general.

Millibar

A unit of pressure, which directly expresses the force exerted by the atmosphere. Equal to 1000 dynes/cm^2 or 100Pascals.

National Hurricane Center

The National Weather Service office in Coral Gables, Florida, that tracks and forecasts hurricanes and other weather in the Atlantic, Gulf of Mexico, Caribbean Sea, and parts of the Pacific.

National Weather Service

The federal agency that observes and forecasts weather. Formerly the U.S. Weather Bureau, it is part of the National Oceanic and Atmospheric Administration, which is part of the Department of Commerce.

NOAA

National Oceanic and Atmospheric Administration.

Precipitation

Any and all forms of water particles, liquid or solid, that falls from the atmosphere and reach the ground.

Radar

Acronym for **RA**dio **D**etection **A**nd **R**anging. An electronic instrument used to detect objects (such as falling precipitation) by their ability to reflect and scatter microwaves back to a receiver.

Radiosonde balloon

A balloon-borne instrument for the simultaneous measurement and transmission of meteorological data. An upper air observation that evaluates the winds, temperature, relative humidity, and pressure aloft by means of a balloon-attached radiosonde that is tracked by a radar or radio direction-finder. It is a radiosonde observation combined with a winds-aloft observation, called a rawin.

Rain

This is the amount of precipitation of any type, primarily liquid. It is usually the amount that is measured by a rain gauge. Precipitation composed of liquid water drops of more than 0.5 mm in diameter, falling in relatively straight, but not necessarily vertical, paths.

Rain gauge

Instrument for measuring the depth of water from precipitation that is assumed to be distributed over a horizontal, impervious surface and not subject to evaporation and measured during a given time interval. Measurement is done in hundredths of inches(0.01").

Reconnaissance Aircraft

This is an aircraft, which flies directly into the eye of a hurricane to make a preliminary survey to gain information about a hurricane using advanced meteorological instruments.

Saffir-Simpson Damage-Potential Scale

A scale relating a hurricane's central pressure and winds to the possible damage it is capable of inflicting and it was first introduced in 1971 by Herbert Saffir and Robert Simpson.

Satellite

Any object that orbits a celestial body, such as a moon. However, the term is often used in reference to the manufactured objects that orbit the earth, either in geostationary or a polar manner. Some information that is gathered by weather satellites, such as GOES9, includes upper air, temperatures and humidity, recording the temperatures of cloud tops, land, and ocean, monitoring the movement of clouds top determines upper level wind speeds, tracing the movement of water vapour, monitoring the sun and solar activity, and relaying data from weather instruments around the world.

Satellite Images

Images taken by weather satellite that reveal information, such as the flow of water vapour, the movement of frontal systems, and the development of a tropical system.

Shower

Precipitation from a cumuliform cloud. Characterized by the suddenness of beginning and ending, by the rapid change in intensity, and usually by a rapid change in the condition of the sky. The solid or liquid water particles are usually bigger than the corresponding elements in other types of precipitation and usually lasts less than an hour in duration.

Storm

An individual low pressure disturbance, complete with winds, clouds, and precipitation. Wind with a speed between 56 and 63 knots (64 and 72 mph); Beaufort scale number 11.

Storm Surge

This is the mound or rise in ocean water drawn up by the low pressure below a hurricane; it causes enormous waves and widespread damage if the hurricane reaches land.

Storm tide

The actual level of sea water resulting from the astronomic tide combined with the storm surge.

Swells

Ocean waves that have travelled out of their generating area. Swells characteristically exhibits a more regular and longer period and has a flatter wave crests than waves within their fetch.

Temperature

In thermodynamics, the integrating factor of the differential equation referred to as the first law of thermodynamics, in statistical mechanics, a measure of translational molecular kinetic energy (with three degrees of freedom). In general, the degree of hotness or coldness of a body as measured on some definite temperature scale by means of any of various types of thermometers.

Thunderstorm

A local storm produced by cumulonimbus clouds and always accompanied by lightning and thunder.

Tornado

The name given to a very strong and damaging whirlwind with a clearly visible dark, snake-like funnel extending from a cumulonimbus cloud to the ground. The track of a tornado at the ground level is rarely very wide, but buildings, trees, and crops may be totally devastated.

Tropics

The region of the earth located between the tropic of Cancer, at 23.5 degrees North Latitude, and the Tropic of Capricorn, at 23.5 degrees South latitude. It encompasses the equatorial region, an area of high temperatures and considerable precipitation during part of the year.

Tropical depression

A mass of thunderstorms and clouds generally with a cyclonic wind circulation between 20 and 34 knots.

Tropical disturbance

An organized mass of thunderstorms with a slight cyclonic wind circulation of less than 20 knots. It is a moving area of thunderstorms, which maintains its identity for 24 hours or more.

Tropical storm

A storm that forms over warm waters, with spinning winds between 40 and 73 miles per hour.

Tropical Wave

An inverted, migratory wave-like disturbance or trough in the tropical region that moves from east to west, generally creating only a shift in winds and rain. The low level convergence and associated convective weather occur on the eastern side of the wave axis. Normally it moves slower than the atmospheric current in which it is embedded and is considered a weak trough of low pressure. Tropical waves occasionally intensify into tropical cyclones. They are also called Easterly Waves.

Tropical Storm Watch

A tropical Storm Watch is issued when tropical storm conditions, including winds from 39 to 73 mph (35 to 64 knots) pose a possible threat to a specified coastal area within 36 hours.

Tropical Storm Warning

A tropical storm warning is issued when tropical storm conditions, including winds from 39 to 73 mph (35 to 64 knots) are expected in a specified coastal area within 24 hours or less.

Typhoon

The name given in the Western Pacific and particularly in the China Sea to violent tropical storms or cyclones with maximum sustained winds of 74 miles per hour or higher. This same tropical cyclone is known as a hurricane in the eastern North Pacific and North Atlantic Ocean, and as a cyclone in the Indian Ocean.

Weather

The state of the atmosphere, mainly with respect to its effects upon life and human activities. As distinguished from climate, weather consists of the short-term (minutes to months) variations of the atmosphere.

Willy Willies

A colloquial Australian term for a violent tropical storm or cyclone affecting the coast of northern Australia.

Wind

Air in motion relative to the surface of the earth. Almost exclusively used to denote the horizontal component.

Wind direction

The direction from which the wind is blowing, measured in points of the compass or in azimuth degrees.

Wind Shear

The rate of the wind speed or direction change with distance. Vertical wind shear is the rate of change of the wind with respect to altitude. Horizontal wind shear is the rate of change on a horizontal plane. Directional shear is a frequent change in direction within a short distance, which can also occur vertically or horizontally.

World Meteorological Organization (WMO)

This is the governing sub-body for meteorology within The United Nations made up of 185 member states and territories. It succeeded the International Meteorological Organization, which was founded in 1873. It is the United Nations system's authoritative voice on the state and behaviour of the Earth's atmosphere, its interaction with the oceans, the climate it produces and the resulting distribution of water resources.

ABOUT THE BOOK

Every year, hurricanes seem to be increasingly severe and unpredictable, ensuring that they remain one of the most frequent topics of conversation in our everyday lives. This *Great Bahamian Hurricanes of 1926 book* provides you with the perfect introduction to the complexities and dynamics of hurricanes, focusing on how they develop, what causes them to be so powerful, the history behind them and how hurricanes affect us all, and much more. Whether you're interested in learning a few little-known facts about hurricanes in general to impress your family, friends or co-workers or simply in the process of becoming an amateur meteorologist, this book has all you need to know to understand the 'hows' and 'whys' of hurricanes and of these three powerful hurricanes impact on the Bahamian Society in 1926. Wayne Neely tells the story of three of the worst natural catastrophes in the history of the Bahamas. But this book is a story not only of three big storms, but of the many Bahamians who had to endure them. These storms struck as the men, women, and children of the Bahamas were in the midst of the sponging era. In telling individual stories of heroism and cowardice, tragedy and redemption, Wayne brings these storms vividly to life. The awesome power of these three hurricanes changed the lives of many thousands of people here in the Bahamas because of the great damages they inflicted on our Bahamian Community. Each hurricane season brings with it a remainder that our tenure on this earth is subject to many factors over which we have no control, and powerful hurricanes like these ones are a great remainder of this fact. This book provides a rare glimpse of three significant meteorological events that affected every part the Bahamian Society in 1926. Through vivid and unique historical photographs of actual damages from these three storms, this book shows the widespread devastation that these three storms inflicted on our country of the Bahamas. Drawing on his unique database of many newspaper accounts, ships and Family Island Commissioners reports from throughout the Bahamas, and captivating personal recorded recollections from all aspects of the Bahamian Society, Wayne provides a fascinating glimpse of these hurricanes as they devastated the Bahamas. But he also explains with childlike clarity the scope and character of hurricanes and what makes them work.

ABOUT THE AUTHOR

Wayne Neely is an international speaker, best-selling author, lecturer on hurricanes, Educator, and Meteorologist. Travelling extensively throughout the region and the world, Wayne addresses critical issues affecting all aspects of hurricanes, especially Bahamian Hurricanes which is one of his central areas of expertise. Inaddition, in most of his books he also includes controversial topics such as, Global Warming, El Niño and man's overall impact on the weather and climate of the region and the rest of the world, but if you were to ask him he would tell you his area of familiarity and love is for Bahamian hurricanes. The central themes of his books are always on hurricanes in general and the impact of hurricanes on all aspects of mankind's ever expanding society. He has a great passion for writing and does it in his spare time when he is not working at his main job as a Weather Forecaster at the Department of Meteorology. Wayne Neely is a certified Meteorologist working at the Department of Meteorology in Nassau, Bahamas for the last 19 years as a Weather Forecaster-prior to that he majored in Geography and History at the College of The Bahamas in Nassau. He then attended the Caribbean Meteorological Institute in Barbados where he majored and specialized in weather forecasting. His love for hurricanes and the weather came about while growing up on the island of Andros where he listened quite regularly to his parents, grand parents and other older residents within the community talking about a major hurricane which occurred in 1929 and devastated the Bahamas. That piqued his interest in hurricanes and got him started on writing his first book called '*The Great Bahamas Hurricane of 1929.*' He then went onto write his second book called '*The Major Hurricanes to Affect the Bahamas*' followed by his third book '*Rediscovering Hurricanes' (Foreword by Herbert Saffir)* and now this is his fourth book on hurricanes and the rest is history. Over the years, Wayne has written several articles on hurricanes and other severe weather events for some of the major local and international newspapers and magazines. He speaks quite regularly to schools, colleges, universities and frequently does radio and television station interviews both locally and abroad about the history and impact of Bahamian and Caribbean hurricanes and hurricanes in general.